Prentice Hall
LITERATURE
Timeless Voices, Timeless Themes

Selection Support:
Skills Development Workbook

Teacher's Edition

BRONZE

Prentice
Hall

Upper Saddle River, New Jersey
Glenview, Illinois
Needham, Massachusetts

ISBN 0-13-058352-9

1 2 3 4 5 6 7 8 9 10   05 04 03 02 01

CONTENTS

UNIT 1: INDENPENDENCE AND IDENTITY

UNIT 2: COMMON THREADS

UNIT 3: WHAT MATTERS

UNIT 4: RESOLVING CONFLICTS

UNIT 5: JUST FOR FUN

UNIT 6: SHORT STORIES

UNIT 7: NONFICTION

UNIT 8: DRAMA

UNIT 9: POETRY

Name _____ Date _____

"The Cat Who Thought She Was a Dog and the Dog Who Thought He Was a Cat"
by Isaac Bashevis Singer

Build Vocabulary

Using the Prefix *pro-*

In "The Cat Who Thought She Was a Dog and the Dog Who Thought He Was a Cat," a character has teeth that *protruded*. The word *protruded* is formed by adding the prefix *pro-*, which means "forward," "before," or "in front of," to the word part *trude*, which means "jut out." Therefore, *protruded* means "jutted out in front of."

A. DIRECTIONS: Read the definition of each word. Then, write a sentence using the word.

1. progress: move forward

_____

2. prognosis: prediction of the future course of an illness

_____

3. propel: drive or push forward or ahead

_____

4. proceed: advance; move ahead

_____

Using the Word Bank

protruded	enthralled	anguish
console	afflicted	vanity

B. DIRECTIONS: Use a word from the Word Bank to complete each of the following sentences.

1. Someone with _____ cares too much about his or her appearance.

2. A mirror _____ from the peddler's sack.

3. After purchasing the mirror, the family acted strangely, as if _____ by an odd kind of disease.

4. When they first sighted the mirror among the peddler's items for sale, the family was

_____ by it.

5. After purchasing the mirror, the Skiba family felt _____ rather than joy.

6. To _____ his suffering wife and daughters, Jan returned the mirror.

C. DIRECTIONS: Circle the letter of the word that is closest in meaning to the word in CAPITAL LETTERS.

1. COVER:
   a. project
   b. promise
   c. protect
   d. profit

2. DRIVE:
   a. proclaim
   b. propel
   c. profess
   d. program

"The Cat Who Thought She Was a Dog and the Dog Who Thought He Was a Cat"
by Isaac Bashevis Singer

Build Spelling Skills: The *gw* Sound Spelled *-gu-*

Spelling Strategy   In Isaac Bashevis Singer's folk tale, the Skiba family members were in an-guish after seeing their reflections. Notice that the *gw* sound you hear in *anguish* is spelled *gu*.
  • The *gw* sound is often spelled *gu*: lan<u>gu</u>age. This sound often appears after *n*, as in lan<u>gu</u>age or an<u>gu</u>ish.

A. Practice: Complete each of the defined words by adding *gu* in the blank. Then, use the words to complete the sentences that follow. Write each word on the line.

_____**acamole**, a dip made with mashed avocado

lin_____**ist**, one who studies languages

lin_____**ine**, pasta noodles in narrow, flat strips

La_____**ardia**, last name of a former mayor of New York City

lan_____**ish**, to lose health; to become weak

_____**ava**, a small, yellowish tropical fruit

Uru_____**ay**, a South American country south of Brazil

1. The small child seemed to _____ from the flu.

2. The _____ speaks eight languages.

3. _____ Airport was named after a mayor of New York City.

4. I prefer _____ to spaghetti.

5. The _____ dip tastes great with corn chips.

6. Jodi visited _____ last summer.

7. _____ juice is sweet and refreshing.

B. Practice: Use the following word parts to complete each unfinished word in the sentences below. Word parts may be used more than once. The first sentence is done for you.

   -tinguished   -lingual   -uana   -guished

1. Isaac Bashevis Singer grew up bi<u>lingual</u>, speaking Yiddish and Polish.

2. Learning English made him tri _____.

3. A dis_____ writer, Singer won a Nobel prize.

4. In Singer's story, the cat, never having seen her reflection, would not have known if she had been an ig _____ .

5. So discouraged were the women by their reflections in the mirror that they lan _____ and stopped doing chores.

6. The Skiba's happiness vanished from their home like a flame ex _____ by water.

Name _____ Date _____

"The Cat Who Thought She Was a Dog and the Dog Who Thought He Was a Cat"
by Isaac Bashevis Singer

Build Grammar Skills: Nouns

Nouns are words that name people, animals, places, things, feelings, and ideas. "The Cat Who Thought She Was a Dog and the Dog Who Thought He Was a Cat" includes many different kinds of nouns.

> **Examples of nouns:** In their *anguish,* both the *dog* and *cat* stopped eating.
> **Noun naming feelings:** anguish
> **Nouns naming animals:** dog, cat

A. Practice: On the lines provided, write *all* of the nouns in each of the following sentences and indicate whether each noun names a person, animal, place, thing, idea, or feeling. Be careful not to include pronouns, such as *he, she, him, her, they.* The first one has been done for you.

1. They asked the peddler his price and he said a half gulden, which was a lot of money.

   peddler (person), price (idea), gulden (thing), money (thing)

2. The dog chased rabbits and the cat hunted mice.

   _____

3. From his sack the peddler drew yellow beads, false pearls, tin earrings, brooches, rings, colored kerchiefs, and other trinkets.

   _____

4. A mirror set in a wooden frame enthralled the women of the house most.

   _____

5. Once there was a poor peasant, Jan Skiba by name.

   _____

6. One daughter discovered that her nose was too short and too broad.

   _____

7. The young women were afflicted with the vanity of girls who live in the city.

   _____

B. Writing Application: Write a sentence using each of the following nouns from "The Cat Who Thought She Was a Dog and the Dog Who Thought He Was a Cat."

1. rage _____

2. week _____

3. space _____

4. danger _____

"The Cat Who Thought She Was a Dog and the Dog Who Thought He Was a Cat"
by Isaac Bashevis Singer

Reading Strategy: Clarifying Word Meanings

As you read, you will sometimes come across words or phrases that are unfamiliar or that may have more than one meaning. To enhance comprehension, it is best to **clarify**—get a clearer understanding of—word meanings. You can do this by checking the surrounding text for details. You may find a restatement or an explanation of the unfamiliar word. You may also find related examples that can offer a clue to its meaning.

DIRECTIONS: Complete the following chart to help you clarify some words from the story. Check the text for restatement or explanation, and cite the useful details you find. Then summarize your clarification of the word.

Unfamiliar Word	Restatement or Explanation	Clarification
The cat lurked after mice.		
. . . bedazzled by all the pretty doodads.		
. . . he said a half gulden		
. . . that they would find suitors . . .		
. . . she became terribly perplexed.		
When the peddler came for his monthly installment		
. . . bought kerchiefs and slippers for the women.		

"The Cat Who Thought She Was a Dog and the Dog Who Thought He Was a Cat"
by Isaac Bashevis Singer

Literary Analysis: The Moral of a Story

Some folk tales, especially fables, end with a **moral,** or lesson in living. Fables with morals may have originated with Aesop, a slave in ancient Greece. According to legend, Aesop told his famous fables to convey messages and advice to his master. Because it was not a slave's place to advise his master directly, Aesop's message or lesson was implied by what happened to the characters in the fable. At the end of his tale, Singer states the moral through the words of the local priest, who is the final authority on morals in the village.

A. DIRECTIONS: Below is a list of morals followed by summaries of three stories. On the lines provided, match each of the morals to one of the summaries. Note that there is one extra moral.

Morals
Don't judge worth solely by appearance.
There is no honor among thieves.
Don't put off until tomorrow what you can do today.
Treat others as you would have them treat you.

1. The manager of a business pays his assistant poorly and treats him badly. In time, the assistant in-herits a large sum of money and buys the business. He then treats the manager as he was treated.

Moral _____

2. Two neighbors visit the same horse breeder to buy horses. One neighbor buys a stunning white stallion. The other buys an unattractive, dirt-colored mare who is very spirited. The two neighbors enter their horses in a race. The dirt-colored mare wins the race and a large cash prize.

Moral _____

3. A cocker spaniel and a boxer see a collie bury some bones. That night, the cocker spaniel and the boxer dig up the collie's bones. They carry them into the woods and bury them where no one will find them. The next night, the cocker spaniel sneaks to the hiding place to take all the bones for himself. The bones are all gone.

Moral _____

B. DIRECTIONS: On the lines below, write a moral for the following story.

Ian was thinking about a job interview scheduled the next day with the manager of a local supermarket. The thought of supermarket work didn't appeal to Ian, but he wanted a part-time job to earn spending money. Suddenly, he heard his neighbor, Mr. Watson, call out: "Ian, would you do me a big favor and finish weeding my flower beds? I think I've sprained my wrist." Ian didn't feel like working just then, but he decided to help his neighbor. A little later, as Ian pulled out the last stubborn weed, he realized that he really had enjoyed working out-doors, which made the prospect of working at the supermarket seem especially grim. Then, Mr. Watson walked up. "Ian," he said, "you did a great job. How would you like to take care of my yard over the summer, doing things like weeding, trimming bushes, and mowing the lawn? I'll pay you by the hour." Ian replied, "Great! I'd love to!" and his job search was over.

_____

_____

"Two Kinds" by Amy Tan

Build Vocabulary

Using the Suffix -ness

The suffix -ness means "the quality or condition of." It changes an adjective into a noun. For example, the word *nervousness* is formed by adding the suffix -ness to the adjective *nervous*.

A. DIRECTIONS: Change the italicized word in each sentence into a noun by adding the suffix -ness. Then write a related sentence using the new word. The first one has been done for you.

1. Jing-mei did not understand why her mother was so *eager* to make her a prodigy.

   _____Jing-mei found her mother's eagerness to make her a prodigy annoying._____

2. Jing-mei's mother did not dwell on her *sad* losses in China.

   _____

3. Jing-mei's mother admired the *clever* prodigies on television.

   _____

4. After her failed performance, Jing-mei was frightened because her mother seemed *hopeless*.

   _____

5. In a *kind* gesture, Jing-mei's mother gave her daughter the piano.

   _____

6. As *frank* as ever, she told Jing-mei, "You just not trying."

   _____

Using the Word Bank

prodigy	reproach	mesmerizing	sauciness
conspired	debut	devastated	fiasco

B. DIRECTIONS: Match each word in the left column with its definition in the right column. Write the letter of the definition on the line next to the word it defines.

____	1. prodigy	a. hypnotizing
____	2. reproach	b. planned together secretly
____	3. mesmerizing	c. a child of unusually high talent
____	4. sauciness	d. first performance in public
____	5. conspired	e. a complete failure
____	6. debut	f. disgrace; blame
____	7. devastated	g. boldness; spirit
____	8. fiasco	h. destroyed; completely upset

"Two Kinds" by Amy Tan

Build Spelling Skills: Adding Suffixes to Words Ending in y

Spelling Strategy   The word *sauciness* in the Word Bank is formed by adding the suffix *-ness* to the base word *saucy*. Notice that the letter *y* in saucy is changed to *i* in *sauciness*.

- Whenever you add a suffix to words ending in *y* preceded by a consonant, change the *y* to *i*. Do not change the *y* to *i* if the suffix begins with an *i*.

  saucy + -ness = sauciness
  identify + -ing = identifying

- Whenever you add a suffix to words ending in *y* preceded by a vowel, do not change the *y* to *i*.

  enjoy + -ment = enjoyment

A. Practice: Add the indicated suffix to each word. Write the new word on the line.

1. lazy + -ness _____
2. pry + -ing _____
3. mercy + -ful _____
4. steady + -ing _____
5. annoy + -ance _____

6. supply + -ing _____
7. soggy + -est _____
8. handy + -er _____
9. party + -ed _____
10. employ + -able _____

B. Practice: Complete the following paragraph by adding the indicated suffix to each given word and writing the new word in the blank.

The mother (try + -ed) _____ to force her daughter to be a prodigy in various fields, from the (petty + -ness) _____ of memorizing state capitals to the (lofty + -ness) _____ of (play + -ing) _____ the piano. After being (notify + -ed) _____ that she would be (study + -ing) _____ piano, the young daughter met her piano teacher. The elderly instructor wasn't the (spry + -est) _____ of individuals. He was deaf, and the daughter's (testy + -ness) _____ over having to submit to piano lessons led her to play carelessly and with (sloppy + -ness) _____, making errors her teacher couldn't hear.

Challenge: Using at least six of the following words, write a paragraph of three or four sentences on a topic of your choice. Be sure to add the indicated suffix to each word before using it in your paragraph.

funny + -er	enjoy + -able	fly + -ing	hurry + ed	supply + -ing
try + -ed	handy + -est	heavy + -er	likely + -est	dry + -ed

_____
_____
_____
_____
_____

"Two Kinds" by Amy Tan

Build Grammar Skills: Common and Proper Nouns

Because "Two Kinds" includes a variety of characters and places, it contains many proper nouns. **Proper nouns** name specific people, places, things, and ideas. "Two Kinds" also contains many **common nouns,** or general names for people, places, things, and ideas. Proper nouns are capitalized, and common nouns are not.

A. Practice: In the following sentences from "Two Kinds," the author uses both proper nouns and common nouns to refer to the same persons or things. Each of the sentences contains a person or thing that is named by *both* a common noun and a proper noun. The common nouns are underlined. On the lines provided, write the common nouns and proper nouns that name the same person or thing. The first one is done for you.

1. Auntie Lindo's <u>daughter</u>, Waverly, who was about my age, was standing farther down the wall about five feet away.

    Common noun: _____ daughter _____ **Proper noun:** _____ Waverly _____

2. Mr. Chong was a retired piano <u>teacher</u> and my mother had traded housecleaning services for weekly lessons and a piano for me to practice on every day, two hours a day, from four until six.

    Common noun: _____ **Proper noun:** _____

3. And then one day I heard my mother and her <u>friend</u> Lindo Jong both talking in a loud bragging tone of voice so others could hear.

    Common noun: _____ **Proper noun:** _____

4. She would present new tests, taking her examples from stories of amazing children she had read in *Ripley's Believe It or Not,* or *Good Housekeeping, Reader's Digest,* and a dozen other <u>magazines</u> she kept in a pile in our bathroom.

    Common noun: _____ **Proper noun:** _____

5. I opened the Schumann book to the dark little <u>piece</u> I had played at the recital. It was on the left-hand side of the page, "Pleading Child."

    Common noun: _____ **Proper noun:** _____

6. And for the first time, or so it seemed, I noticed the <u>piece</u> on the right-hand side. It was called "Perfectly Contented."

    Common noun: _____ **Proper noun:** _____

B. Writing Application: Rewrite the following sentences, replacing the common nouns with proper nouns to give more specific information. You may need to make other changes.

1. The girl lived in the city.

    _____

2. The piano teacher told the girl to practice.

    _____

3. Her aunt and uncle enjoyed listening to the girl perform.

    _____

"Two Kinds" by Amy Tan

Reading Strategy: Applying Word Identification Strategies

When you encounter unfamiliar words, use **word identification strategies**, such as breaking words into syllables and familiar word parts, to help you determine their meanings. Suppose the word *unspeakable,* for example, proves difficult for you. By looking inside the word, you can find the familiar one-syllable word *speak,* combined with the prefix *un-* and the suffix *-able.* You can figure out that the word *unspeakable* means "not able to be spoken or discussed."

DIRECTIONS: Use the chart below to show how word identification strategies can help a reader make sense of unfamiliar words from the story. In the left column, you will find a word from the story. In the second column, write the shortest word you find within the word to the left. In the third column, write the other word parts, such as prefixes and suffixes, that you find. Then, figure out the meaning of the entire word, write the meaning in the fourth column, and verify the meaning in the dictionary. The first row is completed for you.

Word	Shorter Word	Other Word Parts	Meaning
1. envisioned	vision	en-, -ed	pictured in the mind
2. impatient			
3. ungrateful			
4. invisible			
5. unreachable			
6. disproved			
7. review			
8. nervousness			
9. humorous			
10. forgiveness			

"Two Kinds" by Amy Tan

Literary Analysis: Characters' Motives

Characters' motives, or the emotions and goals that drive characters to act, often create the conflict in a story. Two or more characters may have conflicting goals, or conflicting ways of approaching a shared goal. In many stories, the plot and events are created by the actions characters are motivated to take. Sometimes characters are motivated by emotions that may set them at cross purposes with their true goals.

DIRECTIONS: Each of the following excerpts from the story states or hints at motives for one of the actions shown in the chart below. Complete the chart by writing the number of the excerpt that states or suggests a motive for the character's action. The first one is done for you.

Motives

1. And I could sense her anger rising to its breaking point. I wanted to see it spill over.

2. I was filled with a sense that I would soon become *perfect*. My mother and father would adore me. I would be beyond reproach.

3. And after seeing my mother's disappointed face once again, something inside of me began to die.

4. I saw the offer as a sign of forgiveness, a tremendous burden removed.

5. I won't let her change me, I promised myself. I won't be what I'm not.

6. Only ask you be your best. For you sake.

Action	Character Who Took the Action	Character's Motive
1. Tries to be a prodigy	Jing-mei	2
2. Pushes her daughter to be a prodigy	Jing-mei 's mother	
3. Stops trying to be a prodigy	Jing-mei	
4. Deliberately does not try to achieve and resists her mother's efforts to drill her.	Jing-mei	
5. Wishes herself dead and mentions the dead twins	Jing-mei's mother	
6. Offers daughter the piano	Jing-mei's mother	

from *Song of Myself* by Walt Whitman
"I'm Nobody" by Emily Dickinson
"Me" by Walter de la Mare

Build Vocabulary

Related Words: Forms of *equal*

Song of Myself includes the word *equal*, which means "the same" or "having the same measure or value." Related forms of *equal* include the following:

equalize—"to make the same in number, measure, or value"
equally— "in the same way, or to the same measure or extent"

A. DIRECTIONS: Choose the form of *equal* that best completes each sentence.

equally   equalize   equality

1. In a nation in which all citizens enjoy true _____, poets are allowed to express themselves freely about important issues.

2. Poetry can be enjoyed _____ by young and old alike.

3. To _____ everyone's access to great poetry, librarians must continue to add books to their poetry collections.

Using the Word Bank

B. DIRECTIONS: Match each word in the left column with its definition in the right column. Write the letter of the definition on the line next to the word it defines.

assume	loaf	content	equal
banish	bog	forlorn	

____ 1. assume   a. of the same amount

____ 2. loaf   b. alone and miserable

____ 3. content   c. believe to be a fact

____ 4. equal   d. small marsh or swamp

____ 5. banish   e. spend time idly

____ 6. bog   f. happy enough

____ 7. forlorn   g. send away; exile

C. DIRECTIONS: On the lines, write the word that best completes each sentence.

1. Rather than be constantly productive, Whitman is happy to _____.

   a. bog   b. forlorn   c. assume   d. loaf

2. Emily Dickinson is perfectly _____ to be Nobody.

   a. forlorn   b. content   c. equal   d. banish

3. You can _____ that being himself is just fine with Walter de la Mare.

   a. loaf   b. banish   c. assume   d. content

Name _____ Date _____

from Song of Myself by Walt Whitman
"I'm Nobody" by Emily Dickinson
"Me" by Walter de la Mare

Build Spelling Skills: The *kw* Sound Spelled *qu*

Spelling Strategy   The *kw* sound, which you hear in *equal*, is almost always spelled *qu*. One of the exceptions is the word *cuisine*, meaning "the food or manner of preparing food in a given culture."

A. Practice: On each line, complete the word that contains the *kw* sound spelled *qu* and fits the definition. In the first three items, part of the word is given. For the last three items, you must supply the whole word.

1. _____iver   to shake or tremble

2. _____tet   a group of four musicians

3. _____easy   nauseated or sick to the stomach

4. _____   the sound made by a duck

5. _____   one fourth of a gallon

6. _____   a shaking of the crust of the earth

B. Practice: Complete each sentence with a word from the following list that matches the definition in parenthesis.

quarrel   quarter   qualities   quizzes   quoted

1. Walt Whitman's famous lines are often (repeated) _____ by speakers and other writers.

2. For his poems, he invented a self with some (traits) _____ that were different from his own.

3. During her lifetime, Emily Dickinson published fewer than a (fourth) _____ of the poems she wrote.

4. You and your classmates may have answered questions about her poems on short tests called _____.

5. Whether it is better to be a famous person or a nobody could be the topic of a long (argument or dispute) _____.

Challenge: Many words that begin with *qu* are formed from the Latin root *quadr*, meaning "four." Divide each of the following words into parts. If the parts are familiar, use them to try to determine the meaning of the word. Look up unfamiliar words in a dictionary. Then, for each word, write a sentence that shows an understanding of the word's meaning.

1. quadruple _____

2. quadriceps _____

3. quadruped _____

from *Song of Myself* by Walt Whitman
"I'm Nobody" by Emily Dickinson
"Me" by Walter de la Mare

Build Grammar Skills: General and Specific Nouns

General nouns name a broad category of items. **Specific nouns** name a narrower category. The following excerpt from "Me" includes an example of both kinds of noun.

Like a flower, / For its hour / A primrose . . .

General noun: *flower*
Specific noun: *primrose*

It is important to note that some general nouns are more general than others, and some specific nouns are more specific than others. For example, the noun *plant* is more general than *flower*, and the noun *Chinese primrose* is more specific than *primrose*.

A. Practice: In the following sentences, identify the noun that is more general and the noun that is more specific. Write the nouns in the spaces provided. The first one has been done for you.

1. Many poems qualify as great literature.

   More general: _____ literature _____ More specific: _____ poems _____

2. They often express feelings such as love.

   More general: _____ More specific: _____

3. They may describe qualities such as beauty.

   More general: _____ More specific: _____

4. They may narrate events such as battles.

   More general: _____ More specific: _____

5. These three poets were all great writers.

   More general: _____ More specific: _____

B. Writing Application: Rewrite each of the following sentences, replacing the nouns in parentheses with more specific nouns. You may need to change a few other words. For help, use the information under "Meet the Authors" on page 28 of your textbook.

1. Poets create images with words as (artists) create (pictures) with brushes.

   _____

   _____

2. During the Civil War, Walt Whitman nursed wounded (people), including his (relative).

   _____

   _____

Name _____ Date _____

from *Song of Myself* by Walt Whitman
"I'm Nobody" by Emily Dickinson
"Me" by Walter de la Mare

Reading Strategy: Identifying Analogies, Similes, and Metaphors

Poets often express an image or idea through a comparison that is not meant to be taken literally. Three types of comparisons used in prose and poetry are analogies, similes, and metaphors. Each of these comparisons illustrates a point by showing similarities between situations or things that are mostly not alike.

- An **analogy** is a comparison that shows a similarity between two ideas or situations that are unlike each other: Her personality lights up a room as the sun brightens a summer day.
- A **simile** is a comparison using *like* or *as*: Her personality is like a sunny summer day.
- A **metaphor** is a comparison that uses one thing to name another: Her personality is sunshine.

DIRECTIONS: Each of the following lines is taken from one of the poems in this group. Complete the chart to explain and analyze the comparison the poet uses. Describe the objects or ideas being compared. Then, tell how you would interpret the line.

Comparison	Things Being Compared	Interpretation
1. Analogy: How dreary—to be—Somebody! How public—like a Frog— *from "I'm Nobody"*		
2. Simile: I shall always be My Self—and no other, Just me. Like a tree. *from "Me"*		
3. Metaphor: One world is aware, and by far the largest to me, and that is myself. *from "Song of Myself"*		

Name _____ Date _____

from _Song of Myself_ by Walt Whitman
"I'm Nobody" by Emily Dickinson
"Me" by Walter de la Mare

Literary Analysis: The Speaker in Poetry

Every poem has a distinct **speaker** who expresses the poem's thoughts and feelings. Even poems that deal with similar ideas will have different speakers. In reading "Song of Myself," "I'm Nobody," and "Me" you encounter speakers who deal with the similar subject of self and identity. The speakers, however, are very different from one other. What are your impressions of each speaker's attitudes, personality, likes, and dislikes?

A. DIRECTIONS: Complete the following chart to help you identify some characteristics of these speakers. You may not find every characteristic for each speaker.

	Speaker in "Song of Myself"	Speaker in "I'm Nobody"	Speaker in "Me"
Likes:			
Dislikes:			
Mood(s):			

B. DIRECTIONS: Below is a list of speaker traits. Identify those that _probably_ describe each speaker and those that might _possibly_ describe each speaker. Write the letter of the trait in the appropriate place on the chart. You may use each letter more than once, and you may assign more than one trait to each speaker.

   A. bold, confident
   B. happy
   C. satisfied with who speaker is
   D. reserved, private
   E. unhappy

Poem	Probably	Possibly
1. "Song of Myself" by Walt Whitman		
2. "I'm Nobody" by Emily Dickinson		
3. "Me" by Walter de la Mare		

Name _____ Date _____

Build Vocabulary

Using the Prefix *un-*

Adding the prefix *un-* to a word creates an antonym, or word that is opposite in meaning.

Example: attractive   unattractive

A. DIRECTIONS: Rewrite the following sentences, adding *un-* to the words in italics.

1. Alex Haley wondered whether the *written* stories of his grandmother could be proved authentic.

   _____

2. Haley was astonished because the results of his research had been *expected.*

   _____

3. The writer made progress on his book because he was *interrupted* for long periods of time.

   _____

Using the Word Bank

intrigue	uncanny	cherished
queried	eminent	destination

B. DIRECTIONS: Use a word from the Word Bank to complete each of the following sentences.

1. The book that made Alex Haley _____ as a writer is *Roots: The Saga of an American Family.*

2. Haley's investigations in the National Archives gave him a sense of _____.

3. To Haley, it was _____ seeing in print the names of people mentioned by his grandmother.

4. Haley _____ the stories of his family history.

5. The African linguistic scholar _____ Haley about the handing down of the story through many generations.

6. Haley's travel _____ was the Gambia River in Africa.

C. DIRECTIONS: Circle the letter of the word that is the best antonym for the underlined word in each of the following sentences.

1. The girls were <u>uncertain</u> about what time the television miniseries would start.

   a. worried   b. sure   c. ignorant   d. particular

2. <u>Unfortunately</u>, they would not be home in time to see the first episode in its entirety.

   a. probably   b. rarely   c. luckily   d. cleverly

"My Furthest-Back Person" by Alex Haley

Build Spelling Skills: Adding Prefixes

Spelling Strategy The word *uncanny* is formed by adding the prefix *un-* to the word *canny*. Notice that the addition of the prefix *un-* does not change the spelling of the original word *canny*.

• Whenever you add a prefix to a word, don't change the spelling of the base word. Notice the following examples:

un- + afraid = unafraid   re- + invent = reinvent.

A. Practice: Add the prefix to each word. Write the new word on the line.

1. re- + arrange _____

2. mis- + spell _____

3. un- + interested _____

4. re- + educate _____

5. team- + mate _____

6. un- + believable _____

7. re- + build _____

8. un- + necessary _____

B. Practice: Complete each sentence by adding the prefix to the word in parentheses and writing each new word on the line.

1. One day an (un- + fortunate) _____ boy of the Kinte clan went to chop wood.

2. His relatives were (un- + able) _____ to find him after that.

3. Some (un- + kind) _____ traders had captured him and sold him into slavery.

4. His masters tried to (re- + name) _____ him.

5. At one point Kinte escaped but was (re- + captured) _____ .

6. Alex Haley (re- + traced) _____ Kinte's steps from Africa to America.

Challenge: Some words, such as the word *uncanny*, are formed by adding prefixes to words that may be unfamiliar. For each item below, add the prefix re- to the given word. Then, write a sentence using the new word. Look up the word in a dictionary if you don't know its meaning.

1. re- + cite _____

2. re- + cycle _____

3. re- + kindle _____

4. re- + sketch _____

5. re- + submit _____

Name _____ Date _____

Build Grammar Skills: Collective Nouns

A **collective noun** is a noun that in its singular form names a group of individual persons, animals, or things. For example, in "My Furthest-Back Person," Alex Haley talks with an African language scholar who says the following:

"These sounds your *family* has kept sound very probably of the tongue called 'Mandinka.'"

The singular noun *family* is a collective noun because it names a group of individual persons, namely relatives.

A. Practice: Each of the following sentences contains a collective noun. Identify the collective nouns. Write the collective nouns, and the type of person, animal, or thing they include in the context of the sentence. The first item has been completed for you.

1. The class of history students began to study *Roots* by Alex Haley.

    Collective noun: _____class_____ Type of person, animal, or object: _____students_____

2. Haley did not know the tribe to which his ancestors belonged or where in Africa they lived.

    Collective noun: _____ Type of person, animal, or object: _____

3. He spoke to a number of African language scholars about the words and sounds he had heard.

    Collective noun: _____ Type of person, animal, or object: _____

4. A couple of scholars recognized the sounds.

    Collective noun: _____ Type of person, animal, or object: _____

5. Dr. Jan Vansina told Haley the name of his ancestors was the name of a very old clan in Gambia.

    Collective noun: _____ Type of person, animal, or object: _____

6. In Gambia, Haley met with a group of officials.

    Collective noun: _____ Type of person, animal, or object: _____

7. A trio of interpreters accompanied him.

    Collective noun: _____ Type of person, animal, or object: _____

8. He was greeted by the villagers and a herd of goats.

    Collective noun: _____ Type of person, animal, or object: _____

9. They listened quietly to the history of the clan.

    Collective noun: _____ Type of person, animal, or object: _____

10. After Haley told the story of his ancestor Kinte, he was welcomed by a throng of villagers.

    Collective noun: _____ Type of person, animal, or object: _____

B. Writing Application: Write a sentence for each of the following collective nouns. In your sentences, be sure to identify the individuals that make up the groups.

1. team _____

2. bunch _____

3. flock _____

4. crew _____

"My Furthest-Back Person" by Alex Haley

Reading Strategy: Breaking Down Long Sentences

Sometimes it is difficult to understand the meaning of a long sentence. However, a sentence that seems unmanageable can become easier if you break it into smaller parts. One way to break down a long sentence is to identify the subject of the sentence and then find what the sentence is saying about the subject. The sentence may have words and phrases that describe the subject or tell what the subject did. They may also tell where, when, and how the subject did it.

A. DIRECTIONS: When you identify the subject of a long sentence, rethink the sentence with the subject as the first word. Use the chart below to find out what meaning is contained in each numbered sentence. Next to the number of the sentence, write the subject in the left column. In the other columns, write what the sentence tells you about the subject. You will not fill every column for every sentence. The first item is done for you.

1. During the next several months I was back in Washington whenever possible, in the Archives, the Library of Congress, the Daughters of the American Revolution Library.

2. Walking on, I kept wishing that Grandma could hear how her stories had led me to the "*Kamby Bolong.*"

3. So Kunta Kinte was down in some ship probably sailing later that summer from the Gambia River to Annapolis.

	Subject	What Subject Did	Where	When
1	I	was	back in Washington, in the Archives, the Library of Congress, the Daughters of the American Revolution Library	during the next several months
2				
3				

B. DIRECTIONS: Sometimes writers use semicolons (;) to combine two or more sentences into one long sentence. Break the sentence below into three separate sentences. Write the sentences on the lines.

Now flat broke, I went to some editors I knew, describing the Gambian miracle, and my desire to pursue the research; Doubleday contracted to publish, and *Reader's Digest* to condense the projected book; then I had advances to travel further.

1. _____

2. _____

3. _____

Name _____ Date _____

"My Furthest-Back Person" by Alex Haley

Literary Analysis: Personal Essay

An **essay** is a short composition on a single topic. A **personal essay**, unlike other types of essays or nonfiction accounts, contains intimate and detailed descriptions of the writer's feelings and experiences. It also explains the meaning of the experiences for the writer. In reading a personal essay, the reader receives a personal portrait of the writer, often including the writer's innermost thoughts.

DIRECTIONS: Eight of the excerpts below share the personal experience that characterizes a personal essay. The others could appear in any first-person nonfiction account. Write the word yes next to each excerpt that relates personal experience typical of a personal essay. Write no next to the others.

_____ 1. And when a main reading room desk attendant asked if he could help me, I wouldn't have dreamed of admitting to him some curiosity hanging on from boyhood about my slave forebears.

_____ 2. After about a dozen microfilmed rolls, I was beginning to tire, when in utter astonishment I looked upon the names of Grandma's parents: Tom Murray, Irene Murray . . . older sisters of Grandma's as well—every one of them a name that I'd heard countless times on her front porch.

_____ 3. Dr. Vansina telephoned an eminent Africanist colleague, Dr. Philip Curtin. He said that the phonetic "Kin-tay" was correctly spelled "Kinte," a very old clan that had originated in Old Mali.

_____ 4. The Kinte men traditionally were blacksmiths, and the women were potters and weavers.

_____ 5. The first native Gambian I could locate in the U.S. was named Ebou Manga, then a junior attending Hamilton College in upstate Clinton, N.Y.

_____ 6. He and I flew to Dakar, Senegal, then took a smaller plane to Yundum Airport, and rode in a van to Gambia's capital, Bathurst.

_____ 7. Ebou and his father assembled eight Gambia government officials.

_____ 8. Walking on, I kept wishing that Grandma could hear how her stories had led me to the "Kamby Bolong."

_____ 9. Goose-pimples the size of lemons seemed to pop all over me.

_____ 10. They were all—little naked ones to wizened elders—waving, beaming; amid a cacophony of crying out; and then my ears identified their words: "Meester Kinte! Meester Kinte!"

_____ 11. But I remember the sob surging up from my feet, flinging up my hands before my face and bawling as I had not done since I was a baby.

_____ 12. Back home, I knew that what I must write, really, was our black saga, where any individual's past is the essence of the millions'.

_____ 13. Now flat broke, I went to some editors I knew, describing the Gambian miracle, and my desire to pursue the research.

_____ 14. Doubleday contracted to publish, and Reader's Digest to condense the projected book; then I had advances to travel further.

Name _____   Date _____

"The Third Level" by Jack Finney

Build Vocabulary

Using the Suffix *-ist*

The suffix *-ist* means "someone who performs a particular action." In "The Third Level," Sam is a person who performs an action. He is a psychiatrist, or one who practices psychiatry—the treatment of illnesses of the mind.

A. DIRECTIONS: Complete the definition of each term listed below. You may need to consult a dictionary to check word meaning or spelling.

1. One who creates cartoons is a _____

2. One who plays the guitar is a _____

3. One who studies ecology is an _____

4. One who writes a column is a _____

5. One who sings solos is a _____

6. One who excels in conversation is a _____

Using the Word Bank

psychiatrist	arched	currency	premium

B. DIRECTIONS: Use all the words from the Word Bank in a one-paragraph anecdote, or brief story, about a person traveling in a foreign country.

_____

_____

_____

_____

Analogies

C. DIRECTIONS: Each of the following items consists of a pair of related words in CAPITAL LETTERS, followed by four lettered pairs of words. Choose the lettered pair that best expresses a relationship similar to that expressed in the pair in capital letters. Write the letter of your choice on the line.

____ 1. PSYCHIATRY: PSYCHIATRIST ::
    a. geologist: physicist
    b. astronomy: astronomer
    c. science: scientific
    d. history: historical

____ 2. CURRENCY: DOLLAR ::
    a. refuge: shelter
    b. arched: square
    c. premium: pay
    d. airplane: jetliner

"**The Third Level**" by Jack Finney

Build Spelling Skills: Adding the Suffix -ist to Words

Spelling Strategy   The suffix -ist means "someone who performs a particular action." The word *psychiatrist* in the Word Bank is formed by adding the suffix -ist to the word *psychiatry*. Notice that the final *y* in *psychiatry* is dropped when adding -ist to the word. Follow these rules when adding -ist to a word.

- When the word ends in a silent *e* preceded by a consonant, drop the *e*:

  flute + -ist = *flutist*   *style* + -ist = *stylist*

- When the word ends in *y*, drop the *y* when the *y* sounds like long *e*:

  geology + -ist = *geologist*   *biology* + -ist = *biologist*

- Occasionally, you will find an exception: *canoe* + -ist = *canoeist*

A. Practice: Add -ist to each of the following words, and write the new word on the line. Use a dictionary to find the meaning of unfamiliar words.

1. cycle _____

4. geology _____

2. dental hygiene _____

5. conservation _____

3. machine _____

6. separate _____

B. Practice: Complete the paragraph by adding -ist to each word in parentheses and writing each new word on the line.

Charley was ordinary. He was not an (extreme) _____ of any kind. Sam was a (therapy) _____ who specialized in treating mental illness. When Charley told Sam about the third level, Sam thought Charley was an (escape) _____ . Sam was a (real) _____ at first, but he changed as he listened to Charley. Like Charley, Sam had a preference for the past. When he did travel into the past, he needed to change his profession. A (psychiatry) _____ would not have had much business in the Galesburg of 1894.

Challenge: The word *psychiatrist* refers to a doctor who treats mental disorders. The suffix -ist is also used in referring to those who work in other branches of medicine. Fill in the blanks below with the word that fits each definition. Use a dictionary for help with unfamiliar words.

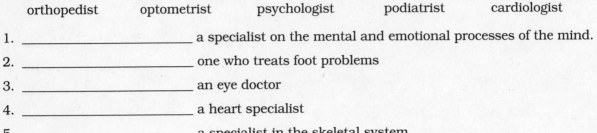

orthopedist   optometrist   psychologist   podiatrist   cardiologist

1. _____ a specialist on the mental and emotional processes of the mind.

2. _____ one who treats foot problems

3. _____ an eye doctor

4. _____ a heart specialist

5. _____ a specialist in the skeletal system

Name _____ Date _____

"The Third Level" by Jack Finney

Build Grammar Skills: Concrete and Abstract Nouns

"The Third Level" contains **concrete nouns**, which name physical items that you can see, hear, taste, smell, or touch. For example, *Charley* takes a *subway*, works at an *office*, and finds a new *tunnel*. The words *Charley, subway, office,* and *tunnel* are concrete nouns.

The story also contains **abstract nouns**, which name ideas, qualities, and feelings that cannot be experienced through the five senses. For example, Sam says Charley dreamed about the third level as the *fulfillment* of a *wish*. The words *fulfillment* and *wish* are abstract nouns.

A. Practice: The following sentences use both concrete and abstract nouns. Identify the concrete and abstract nouns, and write them in the spaces provided.

1. Charley found a tunnel to what seemed a fantasy.

   Concrete noun(s): _____ Abstract noun: _____

2. It turned out to be a doorway to the past.

   Concrete noun(s): _____ Abstract noun: _____

3. He tried to buy a ticket to a town where he could enjoy old-fashioned values and peace.

   Concrete noun(s): _____ Abstract noun: _____

4. The clerk did not know the new bills were the currency of the future.

   Concrete noun(s): _____ Abstract noun: _____

5. In fact, he suspected his strange customer of dishonesty.

   Concrete noun(s): _____ Abstract noun: _____

6. His attitude convinced Charley he should leave.

   Concrete noun(s): _____ Abstract noun: _____

7. To carry out his plan, he drew his savings from the bank.

   Concrete noun(s): _____ Abstract noun: _____

8. He bought old money, which lost its value in the exchange.

   Concrete noun(s): _____ Abstract noun: _____

B. Writing Application: Complete each sentence with an abstract noun.

1. Charley's psychiatrist told him the third level existed only in his _____.

2. Charley insisted that he took a very real _____ to the third level.

3. All of Charley's _____ to find the third level again failed.

4. Imagine Charley's _____ when he discovered Sam had made it to Galesburg first!

Name _____ Date _____

"**The Third Level**" by Jack Finney

Reading Strategy: Using Context to Unlock Meaning

You may be able to learn the meaning of an unfamiliar word in a selection by using the clues found in the **context**—the words, phrases, and sentences surrounding the unfamiliar word. Context clues also may be used to determine which meaning of a multiple-meaning word is intended. The clues may appear either in the same sentence as the unfamiliar word or in the sentences before and after. The following are examples of types of context clues:

1. definition or restatement
2. synonym or comparison
3. antonym or contrast
4. example
5. description
6. information that suggests meaning

For example, the following excerpt from "The Third Level" contains context clues to the meaning of the word *premium.*

> You can buy old money at almost any coin dealer's, but you have to pay a *premium.* My three hundred dollars bought less than two hundred in old-style bills . . .

You might not know the meaning of *premium.* However, the next sentence tells you that three hundred dollars bought only two hundred in old currency. This suggests that premium means "additional charge."

DIRECTIONS: Read the following passages from "The Third Level." Practice using context clues to unlock the meaning of each italicized word, even if you already know the meaning of the word. In the left column, circle the words, phrases, or sentences that give clues to the meaning. In the middle column, write the meaning based on the context alone; use a dictionary to verify the meaning. In the right column, write the number or numbers of the types of clues provided. Choose from the above list of six types.

Word and Context	Meaning From Context	Type of Clue
1. The *corridor* I was in began angling left and slanting downward . . .		
2. The clerk figured the *fare*—he glanced at my fancy hatband, but he figured the *fare*—and I had enough for two coach tickets, one way. But when I counted out the money and looked up, the clerk was staring at me.		
3. "I . . . bought old-style *currency* . . . You can buy old money at almost any coin dealer's but you have to pay a premium."		
4. When a new stamp is issued, stamp collectors buy some and use them to mail envelopes to themselves on the very first day of sale; and the postmark proves the date. The envelope is called a first-day *cover.* They're never opened; you just put blank paper in the envelope.		

Name _____ Date _____

"The Third Level" by Jack Finney

Literary Analysis: Time in a Setting

Time and place make up a story's **setting.** "The Third Level" is set in what was the present when Finney wrote the story. However, some of the events in the story take place in 1894. Because it shifts between the (then) present and the past, time is an important element of the setting of "The Third Level."

DIRECTIONS: Order the story events that took place in 1894 on the left side of the timeline, under the heading "1894." Order the story events that take place in the present time on the right side of the timeline, under the heading "Present Time." Even though you cannot write exact dates, you can place the events in order. Identify each event by number.

1. Sam writes Charley a letter.

2. Charley tells Sam about the third level.

3. Charley withdraws his savings from the bank.

4. Charley finds a new corridor in Grand Central Station.

5. Sam buys a ticket to Galesburg.

6. Charley decides to take the subway.

7. Sam tells Charley he is imagining the level.

8. Charley tries to buy two coach tickets to Galesburg, Illinois.

9. Louisa joins the search for the Third Level.

10. Charley glances at a stack of newspapers.

11. Charley finds Sam's letter.

12. Charley walks into Grand Central Station.

13. Sam starts a hay, feed, and grain business in Galesburg.

14. Charley buys old currency.

1894	The Present

"A Day's Wait" by Ernest Hemingway

Build Vocabulary

Using the Root -vid-

A. DIRECTIONS: Each word below on the left contains the root -*vid*-, meaning "to see." Match each word with its definition. Write the letter of the definition on the line next to the word it defines.

____ 1. video   a. easy to see; clear; obvious

____ 2. videotape   b. another name for a movie rental

____ 3. evident   c. something you can see that proves or makes clear

____ 4. evidence   d. a tape that records and plays things you see

Now write an original sentence using each word with the -*vid*- root.

5. video _____

6. videotape _____

7. evident _____

8. evidence _____

Using the Word Bank

epidemic	evidently

B. DIRECTIONS: Write the Word Bank word that can replace the italicized group of words in each sentence.

1. The food seller *it seems* did not cook the hamburger patties long enough before selling them to customers. _____

2. As a result, the *widespread disease* of food poisoning affected nearly everyone who ate the undercooked meat. _____

C. DIRECTIONS: For each pair of related words in CAPITAL LETTERS, choose the lettered pair that best expresses a *similar* relationship. Circle the letter of your choice.

1. EPIDEMIC : DOCTORS ::
   a. hospital : nurses
   b. riot : police
   c. sick : well
   d. medicine : science

2. EVIDENTLY : SEEMINGLY ::
   a. evidence : trial
   b. slowly : quickly
   c. suddenly : sudden
   d. certainly : surely

"A Day's Wait" by Ernest Hemingway

Build Spelling Skills: Changing the Adjective Ending *-ent* to the Noun Ending *-ence*

Spelling Strategy The Word Bank word *evidently* comes from the word *evident*. The adjective *evident* can be turned into the noun *evidence* by changing its ending from *-ent* to *-ence*.

• To change an adjective that ends in *-ent* to a noun that ends in *-ence*, drop the final *-ent* and add *-ence*.

Examples:

evident – ent + -ence = evidence

independent – ent + -ence = independence

A. Practice: Change each adjective in the left column into a noun by adding *-ence*. Write your new word on the line.

Adjective	Noun
1. competent	_____
2. diligent	_____
3. excellent	_____
4. existent	_____
5. different	_____
6. persistent	_____
7. permanent	_____

B. Practice: Complete each sentence below by changing the adjective in parentheses to a noun that ends in *-ence*. Write your new word on the line.

1. Schatz's father worried because his son's behavior seemed to lack (coherent)

_____ .

2. Schatz took on a strange (silent) _____ that his father could not figure out.

3. No one could visit Schatz because of his (insistent) _____ that everyone stay away.

4. Schatz made a mistake that any child of normal (intelligent) _____ might have made.

Challenge: The Word Bank word *evidently* may be pronounced two different ways. Say the word aloud. Which syllable did you stress the most? Now try to guess the other pronunciation of *evidently* that is acceptable. Look in a dictionary to see if you are correct.

"A Day's Wait" by Ernest Hemingway

Build Grammar Skills: Pronouns

A **pronoun** is a word that takes the place of a noun or a group of words acting as a noun.

noun   pronoun

Example: When the *doctor* came, *he* took the boy's temperature.

These are some of the most common pronouns:

I	she	we	it
me	her	us	itself
mine	hers	ours	who/whom
myself	herself	ourselves	which
you	he	they	that
your	him	them	this
yours	his	theirs	these
yourself	himself	themselves	those

A. Practice: Underline the pronoun or pronouns in each sentence.

1. Schatz had a fever, and it worried him quite a bit.

2. Schatz shut the windows when he saw they were open.

3. The doctor left three different medicines and instructions for giving them.

4. His father felt Schatz wanted to be by himself.

5. Schatz's misunderstanding was a mistake that we ourselves might have made as young children.

B. Writing Application: Imagine that Schatz kept a diary in which he described his thoughts and feelings about being sick. Write sentences that Schatz might have written. Use the nouns and pronouns below. Add at least one more pronoun to each sentence.

1. father, he

   _____

2. books, them

   _____

3. temperature, it

   _____

4. fear, they

   _____

5. father, me

   _____

"A Day's Wait" by Ernest Hemingway

Reading Strategy: Identifying Word Roots

One way to avoid struggling with words is to learn **word roots**—the basic form of a word after all the added parts are removed. A word root may come at the beginning, middle, or end of the whole word. All roots have a meaning, but not all roots are words. Some must be "bound" or tied to other word parts to make sense. The *mis* in *miserable* is a bound root. Other word roots are "independent" or free. They are words that can stand alone. The word root *loud*, as in *aloud*, is independent.

DIRECTIONS: Complete the chart about some roots used in this story. First tell whether the root is bound or independent. Then give the meaning of the root and the meaning of the entire word in which it appears. You may use a dictionary.

Root	Word With the Root	Bound or Independent?	Meaning of Root	Meaning of Whole Word
struct	instructions			
void	avoided			
var	various			
stead	unsteadily			
pos	position			
meter	kilometers			
therm	thermometer			
port	importance			

"**A Day's Wait**" by Ernest Hemingway

Literary Analysis: Internal Conflict

An **internal conflict** is one that takes place inside a character's mind. In "A Day's Wait," Schatz struggles all day with a personal fear that he is unwilling to share with anyone else, including his father and the doctor. Although you don't discover the exact nature of Schatz's conflict until the end of the story, you find hints of it along the way. For example, early in the story, Schatz's father says that his son "seemed very detached from what was going on." That detail indicates that something else is occupying Schatz's mind.

DIRECTIONS: Write your answers to the following questions.

1. How does Schatz behave when his father reads to him the first time? Why does the boy behave that way?

   _____

   _____

2. How does Schatz respond when his father suggests that he try to go to sleep? Why does the boy respond that way?

   _____

   _____

3. Why doesn't Schatz allow anyone into his room later? What does this indicate about his fear?

   _____

   _____

4. Why isn't Schatz able to fall asleep?

   _____

   _____

5. Why does Schatz think that he is going to die?

   _____

   _____

6. Why do you think Schatz chose not to reveal his fear to his father or to the doctor?

   _____

   _____

Name _____ Date _____

"Was Tarzan a Three-Bandage Man?" by Bill Cosby
"Oranges" by Gary Soto

Build Vocabulary

Using the Suffix -ly

A. DIRECTIONS: In each sentence, replace the italicized phrase with one of the following words ending in -ly, meaning "in a (specific) way": *kiddingly, gently, beautifully, loudly.*

1. The nurse put the baby in the crib (*in a soft, tender way*) _____.

2. The comedian spoke (*in a joking way*) _____ about his childhood.

3. The train rumbled (*in a noisy way*) _____ into the station.

4. The opera star sang (*in an appealing way*) _____ from start to finish.

Write an original sentence using each word below.

5. seriously _____

6. simply_____

7. loosely_____

8. frequently _____

Using the Word Bank

incorporate	rouge	tiered	dejectedly	hissing	tourniquets

B. DIRECTIONS: Write the Word Bank word that best completes each sentence.

1. We were surprised by the sudden _____ of steam from the radiator.

2. The _____ trays of donuts were loaded into the delivery truck.

3. The losing team sat _____ on the bench after the game.

4. The store owner decided to _____ her business.

5. A driver on the highway stopped and ripped his shirt to make _____ for the accident victims.

6. When Aunt Alice was young, she wore cheerful shades of _____ .

C. DIRECTIONS: For each pair of related words in CAPITAL LETTERS, choose the pair in small letters that best expresses a *similar* relationship. Circle the letter of your choice.

1. TOURNIQUETS : BLOOD ::
   a. bandages : doctor
   b. dams : water
   c. books : readers
   d. games : players

2. DEJECTEDLY : HAPPILY ::
   a. quickly : fast
   b. carefully : painfully
   c. seriously : sadly
   d. slowly : quickly

"Was Tarzan a Three-Bandage Man?" by Bill Cosby
"Oranges" by Gary Soto

Build Spelling Skills: *k* Sound Spelled *qu*

Spelling Strategy The Word Bank word *tourniquets* contains the *k* sound spelled *qu*.

• In certain words, mainly those that come from French, the *k* sound is spelled *qu*.

Examples: bouquet   antique

A. Practice: Fill in the missing *qu* in each word. Write the entire word. Then write its meaning. Use a dictionary for help.

1. rac _ _ etball _____

   Meaning: _____

2. uni _ _ e _____

   Meaning: _____

3. cro _ _ et _____

   Meaning: _____

4. _ _ iche _____

   Meaning: _____

B. Practice: In each sentence, find a word with the *k* sound that is spelled incorrectly. Cross out the word and write it correctly.

1. Bill Cosby writes that the toughest guys in his neighborhood wore tournickets around their necks.

2. Cosby picked unicque athletes to look up to and tried to imitate their walk.

3. Cosby admired the techneaks of both Jackie Robinson and Sugar Ray Robinson.

4. Do you think Cosby would have admired a tennis player who had been injured by his rakqit?

Challenge: The Word Bank word *tourniquets* comes from a French word for "swivel" or "a turning instrument." Other words in the English language also begin with the letters *tour*. Use a dictionary to find the meanings of the following words. Write each word in a sentence.

1. tour de force

   _____

2. tourist

   _____

3. tournament

   _____

"Was Tarzan a Three-Bandage Man?" by Bill Cosby
"Oranges" by Gary Soto

Build Grammar Skills: Personal Pronouns

A personal pronoun is a pronoun that identifies (1) a person speaking, (2) a person spoken to, or (3) a person, place, or thing spoken about. Personal pronouns may be singular or plural.

	Singular	Plural
First person (the person speaking)	I, me, my, mine	we, us, our, ours
Second person (the person spoken to)	you, your, yours	you, your, yours
Third person (the person, place, or thing spoken about)	he, his, him she, her, hers it, its	they, them, their, theirs

Example: I told <u>him</u> about <u>our</u> win today. You should have seen <u>his</u> surprise.

A. Practice: Identify the personal pronouns in each sentence. Write whether each pronoun is in *first*, *second*, or *third* person and whether it is singular or plural.

1. We discussed Bill Cosby's article after reading it.

   Pronoun: _____   Person: _____   Singular/Plural: _____

   Pronoun: _____   Person: _____   Singular/Plural: _____

2. My teacher asked the students, "What did you think of Cosby's mother?"

   Pronoun: _____   Person: _____   Singular/Plural: _____

   Pronoun: _____   Person: _____   Singular/Plural: _____

3. The people in Gary Soto's "Oranges" amused me with their charming behavior.

   Pronoun: _____   Person: _____   Singular/Plural: _____

   Pronoun: _____   Person: _____   Singular/Plural: _____

B. Writing Application: In each sentence, replace the underlined word or words with a personal pronoun. Then expand the sentence by adding at least one more personal pronoun.

   Example: Cosby had to take <u>the bandage</u> off.

   Cosby had to take <u>it</u> off after <u>his</u> mother told <u>him</u> to.

1. <u>Athletes</u> now incorporate themselves.

   _____

2. <u>Cosby</u> speaks of childhood years.

   _____

3. The comedian writes about <u>friends</u>.

   _____

"Was Tarzan a Three-Bandage Man?" by Bill Cosby
"Oranges" by Gary Soto

Reading Strategy: Context Clues

As you read, you may come across a word whose meaning you don't know. Sometimes you can figure out the meaning of the unfamiliar word by using **context clues**—words and phrases surrounding the unfamiliar word that offer hints about its meaning.

For example, in the title of Bill Cosby's article, you might not recognize the name *Tarzan*. Two other words in the title offer you hints: *Was* and *Man*. These context clues suggest that *Tarzan* refers to a man who lived in the past. In addition, the phrase *Three-Bandage* suggests that Tarzan was someone who lived a rough or dangerous life.

DIRECTIONS: Find words from Bill Cosby's article or Gary Soto's poem that you do not know. In the chart below, first, write each unfamiliar word. Then, identify context clues in the passage that can help you guess the word's meaning. Write your prediction. Finally, check with a dictionary to see how close you were. One example and several words are provided. Fill in the rest of the chart.

Unfamiliar Word	Context Clues	Predicted Meaning
locomotion	we walked pigeon-toed, a painful form of locomotion	a way of walking or moving
bowlegged		
acne		
dejectedly		

"Was Tarzan a Three-Bandage Man?" by Bill Cosby
"Oranges" by Gary Soto

Literary Analysis: Anecdote

An **anecdote** is a brief story about an interesting, amusing, or strange event. Most anecdotes are personal or autobiographical narratives. The purpose of an anecdote can be

- to entertain
- to teach a lesson
- to make a point

The comedian Bill Cosby is known for his humorous anecdotes—his brief, funny stories. "Was Tarzan a Three-Bandage Man?" both entertains and makes a point about the foolish behavior of young boys trying to impress other people. Gary Soto's poem "Oranges" is an anecdote, too. However, it is told in poetic rather than in narrative form. The poetic anecdote gives a brief account of a young boy's escape from embarrassment through the kindness and understanding of a shopkeeper.

DIRECTIONS: Read each quotation. Identify it as taken from the Cosby narrative or the Soto poem. Decide whether the particular quotation entertains, teaches a lesson, or makes a point. Then describe the tone of the quotation. Tell whether you find it to be funny, serious, poignant, embarrassing, ironic, mean, and so on.

1. "You'd know who they are if you read more books instead of makin' yourself look like an accident."

   _____

   _____

2. "Why can't you try to imitate someone like Booker T. Washington?"

   _____

   _____

3. "I smiled, / Touched her shoulder, and led / Her down the street . . ."

   _____

   _____

4. "And perhaps the toughest guys of all wore tourniquets around their necks."

   _____

   _____

5. "And when she lifted a chocolate / That cost a dime, / I didn't say anything."

   _____

   _____

from *In Search of Our Mothers' Gardens* by Alice Walker

Build Vocabulary

Using the Root *-nym-*

A. DIRECTIONS: The root *-nym-*, meaning "name," is found in many English words. Complete each sentence below with one of these words:

anonymity: state of being unknown or unrecognized
acronym: word formed from the first letters of each word in a name or expression
synonymous: having the same meaning
homonym: two or more words that have the same sound but different meanings

1. *Scuba* is the _____ for "Self-Contained Underwater Breathing Apparatus."

2. A _____ for *there* is *they're* or *their*.

3. The word *large* is _____ with *big*.

4. Blake moved from a small town to a big city because he wanted _____.

Using the Word Bank

mutilated	vibrant	anonymous	profusely
radiant	illuminates	hindered	

B. DIRECTIONS: Match each word in the left column with its definition in the right column.

____ 1. profusely   a. filled with light; shining brightly

____ 2. illuminates   b. freely or plentifully

____ 3. mutilated   c. held back

____ 4. radiant   d. brightens; sheds light on

____ 5. vibrant   e. lively and energetic

____ 6. anonymous   f. with no name known

____ 7. hindered   g. damaged or injured

Analogies

C. DIRECTIONS: Each question below consists of a related pair of words in CAPITAL LETTERS followed by four lettered pairs of words. Circle the letter of the pair that best expresses a relationship similar to that expressed in the pair in capital letters.

1. MUTILATED : DAMAGED ::
   a. built : shattered
   b. charred : burned
   c. broke : repaired
   d. hurt : cried

2. RADIANT : DIM ::
   a. bright : burning
   b. early : dawn
   c. colorful : showy
   d. stormy : calm

from *In Search of Our Mothers' Gardens* by Alice Walker

Build Spelling Skills: The Root *-nym-*

Spelling Strategy   In the root *-nym-*, always spell the short *i* sound with *y*, not *i*.

   Example: ano<u>ny</u>mous

A. Practice: Complete each sentence with a word formed from the word equation in parentheses.

1. (acro + nym) The _____ for "as soon as possible" is ASAP.

2. (syno + nym) Jungle is a _____ for rain forest.

3. (patro + nymic) Your _____ is your surname, or your last name.

B. Practice: Complete each sentence by writing one of the following words on the line: *synonym, antonym, patronymic, pseudonym, homonym.*

1. Alice Walker's _____ suggests "someone who walks."

2. Unlike H. H. Munro, whose _____ was "Saki," Alice Walker writes under her own name.

3. Alice Walker is a feminist, but she calls herself a "womanist," a _____ she made up.

4. When I heard that Alice Walker was committed to animal *rights*, I thought the speaker meant animals' *rites*, but that _____ didn't make any sense.

5. Alice Walker is also committed to vegetarianism. This means that she is opposed to its _____, meat-eating.

Challenge: The Word Bank word *illuminates*, like the words below, comes from the root *-lum-*, which means "light." Look up the definition of each word in a dictionary. Then, on the line, write the letter of the word to which each definition refers. Finally, write a sentence using each word.

   a. luminosity   b. luminous   c. luminary

____   1. Which word refers to a celebrity who lights up the social scene?

____   2. Which word describes something shining and bright?

____   3. Which word refers to brightness?

4. _____

5. _____

6. _____

*from **In Search of Our Mothers' Gardens*** by Alice Walker

Build Grammar Skills: Subject and Object Pronouns

You will recall that a **pronoun** is a word that stands for a noun or for another word that takes the place of a noun. Some pronouns change form depending on their use in a sentence. Two of these forms are the **nominative (or subjective) case** and the **objective case**.

NOMINATIVE Case	Use in Sentence	Example
I, we you he, she, it, they	Subject of a verb Subject complement	I write stories. The gardeners were you and he.
OBJECTIVE Case	**Use in Sentence**	**Example**
me, us you him, her, it, them	Direct object Indirect object Object of a preposition.	Dad drove us to school We gave you a chance. Share it with them.

A. Practice: Circle the pronoun in each sentence. Identify each one as a *subjective* or *objective* case pronoun. Then, tell how it is used in the sentence.

1. It was she who made all the family's clothing. _____

_____

2. During the day, she labored in the fields. _____

_____

3. Mother dug up clumps of bulbs and divided them. _____

_____

4. It is easy to imagine the possibilities. _____

_____

5. People asked us for cuttings from the garden. _____

_____

B. Writing Application: Write original sentences about this excerpt from *In Search of Our Mother's Gardens*. Use the pronoun forms specified in each direction.

1. Use two subject pronouns. _____

_____

2. Use one subject pronoun and one object pronoun. _____

_____

3. Use two object pronouns. _____

_____

from *In Search of Our Mothers' Gardens* by Alice Walker

Reading Strategy: Recognizing Word Roots

Many English words have roots from Latin and Greek. If you can learn some common roots, you will be able to understand the meanings of whole groups of new words. The following example shows how knowing a single Greek root can unlock the meaning of several words.

Greek root: *bio-*   Meaning of root: life   Words containing root: biology, biosphere

You can figure out that *biology* is the science of life, and that a *biosphere* is a sphere, or global area, where life exists.

DIRECTIONS: Complete the chart about some word roots used in this story. You may use a dictionary to help you, if necessary.

Root	Word With This Root	Meaning of Root	Other Words With This Root
-nym-	anonymous		
-typ-	typical		
-lab-	labored		
-turb-	undisturbed		
-rupt-	interruption		
-spir-	inspired		
-volv-	involves		
-tract-	distracted		
-mem-	memories		
-vis-	invisible		

Name _____ Date _____

Literary Analysis: Tribute

A **tribute** is a literary expression of admiration. Its main purpose is to show appreciation for the person. Therefore, a tribute uses anecdotes and descriptions that are flattering and that show the positive qualities of the person.

In this tribute to her mother, Alice Walker recalls many aspects of her mother's personality and creative spirit that helped to shape her own personality and creative spirit. In so doing, she reveals some truths about herself. By showing the reader what she most admires about her mother, she reveals her own experiences and values.

DIRECTIONS: As you read, complete this graphic organizer to show what you learn about both Walker and her mother. An example has been given.

Walker's mother   **Alice Walker**

Told stories of her life   Absorbed and wrote her mother's stories

"Seventh Grade" by Gary Soto
"Melting Pot" by Anna Quindlen

Build Vocabulary

Using the Prefix *inter-*

A. DIRECTIONS: The prefix *inter-* means "among or between." The Word Bank word *interloper* refers to someone who pushes into other people's business, thus coming between them. Apply what you know about the prefix *inter-* to define the following words.

1. interact _____

2. interchangeable _____

3. interconnected _____

4. intersection _____

Using the Word Bank

fluent	bigots	interloper	elective
scowl	ferocity	conviction	sheepishly

B. DIRECTIONS: Complete each of the following sentences to demonstrate your understanding of the Word Bank words.

1. Victor tried to prove he was fluent in French by _____

2. To show his conviction in his own strength, Victor _____

3. Victor looked sheepishly at Mr. Bueller because _____

4. Victor tried to show the ferocity of his soul by _____

5. An elective is different from other classes in that _____

6. Newer residents were seen as interlopers because _____

7. Some people showed they were bigots when they _____

8. The GQ model probably had a scowl on his face because _____

Analogies

C. DIRECTIONS: Each question below consists of a word in CAPITAL LETTERS followed by four lettered words or phrases. Circle the word or phrase that best expresses a relationship similar to that expressed in the pair in capital letters.

1. SHEEPISHLY : BOLDLY ::
   a. happily : sadly
   b. angrily : furiously
   c. quickly : easily
   d. musically : quietly

2. EXPRESSION : SCOWL ::
   a. face : eyes
   b. clock : hour
   c. vehicle : car
   d. news : magazine

Unit 2: Common Threads

"**Seventh Grade**" by Gary Soto
"**Melting Pot**" by Anna Quindlen

Build Spelling Skills: Using *c* for the *k* Sound

Spelling Strategy   For the *k* sound before the vowels *a*, *o*, and *u*, usually use *c*. For the *k* sound before the vowels *e* and *i*, usually use *k*.

A. Practice: Complete each word by adding *c* or *k* in the blank. Then use the words to complete the sentences that follow. Write the word on the line.

__ountry   __oins   __anary   __itchen   tur__ey   mon__ey

1. The immigrants came to this _____ seeking a better life.

2. Our traditional meal on Thanksgiving is _____.

3. Did you see the _____ cage in the zoo?

4. The child got four _____ as change for a dollar.

5. The yellow _____ sang a cheerful song.

6. The aromas coming from the _____ were mouthwatering.

B. Practice: Complete each of the defined words by adding *c* or *k* in each of the blanks. Then write the complete word on the line.

1. __onfide, to tell as a secret _____

2. __ultivate, to prepare and use land for growing crops _____

3. __eel, the chief wooden or steel piece supporting the frame of a boat _____

4. __ilometer, a metric unit of length equal to 1,000 meters (or about five-eighths of a mile)
   _____

5. __asserole, an earthenware or glass baking dish in which food can be cooked and served
   _____

6. __on__urrent, occuring at the same time _____

Challenge: The Word Bank word *fluent* comes from a Latin root that means "to flow." The following words, which also come from the same root, are probably unfamiliar to you. Look up the definition of each word in a dictionary. Then use each word in a sentence that demonstrates its meaning.

1. mellifluous _____

2. affluent _____

3. effluent _____

4. superfluous _____

5. confluence _____

"Seventh Grade" by Gary Soto
"Melting Pot" by Anna Quindlen

Build Grammar Skills: Introduction to Verbs

A **verb** is a word that shows action or being.

Action verbs tell what action is occurring. *Sing, dance, think,* and *study* are examples of action verbs. This sentence from "Melting Pot" has an action verb:

The father *speaks* some English, the mother less than that.

Linking verbs connect the subject of a sentence with a word or expression that describes or renames the subject. This sentence part from "Melting Pot" contains a linking verb:

The two daughters *are* fluent in both their native and their adopted languages.

Notice that the linking verb *are* joins *fluent* to *daughters,* the word that *fluent* describes. All forms of the verb *to be (am, is, are, was were, have/has/had been)* are linking verbs, as are these words: *appear, seem, look, sound,* and *stay.*

A. PRACTICE: Underline the verb in each sentence. On the line, indicate whether it is an action verb or a linking verb.

1. The children were upstairs in the house next door. _____

2. They ate dinner with their Ecuadorian neighbors. _____

3. The old-timers in the neighborhood seemed angry with the newcomers. _____

4. Neighbors stare at the new people through the sheer curtains. _____

5. The old men watched the construction workers. _____

6. One of them later moved to the suburbs. _____

B. Writing Application: Write six sentences based on the story "Seventh Grade." Use each of the following verbs at least once: *waited, was, scowled, seemed, answered, were.* Then underline the verbs and identify them as either action or linking.

1. _____

2. _____

3. _____

4. _____

5. _____

6. _____

"Seventh Grade" by Gary Soto
"Melting Pot" by Anna Quindlen

Reading Strategy: Interpreting Idioms

Does the steady drip of a leaky faucet *drive you up a wall?* The words in italics in the previous sentence are an **idiom**—an expression or figure of speech whose meaning cannot be taken literally. Idioms are unique to a particular language or region. They are lively forms of informal language. The intended meaning of an idiom usually differs from its literal, or exact word-for-word, meaning. In the idiom *drive you up a wall*, the literal meaning is to force you to move vertically up the side of a room or building, but that is not what the idiom actually means. It means to greatly annoy or distract you.

DIRECTIONS: Complete the chart, analyzing some idioms that appear in "Seventh Grade" and "Melting Pot." For each idiom given in italics, give its literal meaning, followed by its figurative meaning.

Idiom	Literal Meaning	Figurative Meaning
had a crush on Teresa		
his *mind was somewhere else*		
I wanted to *throw confetti* the day that a family of rough types . . . moved out		
seem to have *reached a nice mix*		
We *live in a pressure cooker*		

"Seventh Grade" by Gary Soto
"Melting Pot" by Anna Quindlen

Literary Analysis: Tone

The **tone** of a literary work reflects the author's attitude toward the subject and the characters. Tone can often be described in a single word, such as *informal, friendly, intimate, solemn, playful,* or *serious.* Some ways an author establishes and controls the tone are choice of subject, choice of words, descriptive details, and sentence structure.

DIRECTIONS: As you read "Seventh Grade" and "Melting Pot," think about the tone each author is creating. Look for details that help establish the tone. List some of these details, and then explain how each contributes to the tone.

"Seventh Grade"

_____
_____
_____
_____
_____
_____
_____
_____

"Melting Pot"

_____
_____
_____
_____
_____
_____
_____
_____

© Prentice-Hall, Inc.

"Fable" by Ralph Waldo Emerson
"Thumbprint" by Eve Merriam
"If—" by Rudyard Kipling

Build Vocabulary

Using the Prefix *uni-*

The prefix *uni-* means "one," as in the Word Bank word *unique*, meaning "one of a kind."

A. DIRECTIONS: Fill in each blank in the sentences below with one word from this list.

uniform   unicycle   unicorn   univalve

1. The _____ is an imaginary animal that looks similar to a horse with one horn.

2. The snail is a _____, meaning that its shell has one valve or part.

3. The flight attendants for a particular airline all wear the same _____.

4. The clown rode a _____, a vehicle with one wheel.

Using the Word Bank

spry	unique	virtue	impostors	base

B. DIRECTIONS: Complete each of the following sentences to demonstrate your understanding of the Word Bank words.

1. Proof that the squirrel was more spry than the mountain was that _____

   _____

2. The fact that each person's fingerprints are unique is important in police work because ____

   _____

3. I could not be a friend to someone who does not practice the virtue of _____

   because _____

4. If you knew that some people were impostors, you would know that they were _____

   _____

5. The poor peasants lived a base existence in their _____

Analogies

C. DIRECTIONS: Circle the letter of the pair of words that best expresses a relationship similar to that expressed by the pair in capital letters.

____ 1. SPRY : QUICK ::
   a. healthy : sick
   b. ailing : slow
   c. covered : thick
   d. physical : mental

____ 2. UNIQUE : COMMON ::
   a. singular : strange
   b. multiple : many
   c. important : trivial
   d. serious : careful

"Fable" by Ralph Waldo Emerson
"Thumbprint" by Eve Merriam
"If—" by Rudyard Kipling

Build Spelling Skills: *k* Sound Spelled *qu*

Spelling Strategy In Eve Merriam's poem, the word *unique* is used to describe the design of a thumbprint. Notice that the *k* sound at the end of the word is spelled *que*. When using *qu* to spell the *k* sound at the end of a word, add an *e*, as in *unique*.

A. Practice: Complete each of the defined words by adding *que* in the blank. Then write the complete word on the line.

mysti___, an atmosphere of mystery about someone or something _____

techni___, a special method used to accomplish something _____

obli___, not straight up or down or across but slanting _____

statues___, like a statue in dignity or beauty _____

pictures___, interesting enough to be used as the subject of a picture _____

B. Practice: Use the following word parts and *-que* to complete each unfinished word in the sentences below. Use each word once.

statues___   obli___   pictures___   techni___   mysti___

1. The squirrel in the shadow of the mountain is a _____ scene.

2. Kipling's poetic _____ in "If—" includes regular rhymes.

3. The angle formed by the mountain and the ground was _____.

4. Do you think the person described in "If—" would have a certain _____?

5. A tall person is likely to be described as _____.

Challenge: The word *thumb* is unusual in that it has a silent *b*. Here are some other words with a silent *b*. Look each one up in a dictionary, and then write a sentence using it in such a way as to demonstrate its meaning.

1. aplomb _____

2. succumb _____

3. plumb _____

4. doubtful _____

5. redoubt _____

Name _____ Date _____

“**Fable**” by Ralph Waldo Emerson
“**Thumbprint**” by Eve Merriam
“**If—**” by Rudyard Kipling

Build Grammar Skills: Verb Tenses

One meaning of the word tense is “time.” Verbs have tenses, or particular forms, that express the time of the event—the present tense, the past tense, or the future tense. The **infinitive** is the base form of a verb and is usually preceded by to.

> **Infinitive:** If you can bear <u>to hear</u> the truth you’ve spoken
> **Present tense:** On the pad of my thumb / <u>are</u> whorls, whirls, wheels
> **Past tense:** Bun <u>replied</u>, / “You are doubtless very big”
> **Future tense:** Imprint my mark upon the world / whatever I <u>shall become</u>.

A. Practice: Underline the verb in each sentence. On the line, indicate whether it is present, past, or future tense, or an infinitive.

1. Ralph Waldo Emerson wrote about the importance of self-reliance. _____

2. Emerson entered Harvard University at the age of fourteen, the youngest member of his class. _____

3. Emerson’s philosophy will be useful to today’s young people. _____

4. Eve Merriam enjoys the sounds and meanings of words. _____

5. To succeed as a poet was Eve Merriam’s hope. _____

6. Kipling’s poetry demonstrates an extraordinary use of language. _____

B. Writing Application: Write three sentences based either on each of the poet’s lives or work or on your own reaction to the poem. Use the present tense, the past tense, and the future tense in your sentences for each poet.

Emerson:

1. (present)_____

2. (past)_____

3. (future) _____

Merriam:

4. (present)_____

5. (past)_____

6. (future) _____

Kipling:

7. (present)_____

8. (past)_____

9. (future) _____

48 Selection Support   © Prentice-Hall, Inc.

"Fable" by Ralph Waldo Emerson
"Thumbprint" by Eve Merriam
"If—" by Rudyard Kipling

Reading Strategy: Paraphrasing Figurative Language

Often the language of poetry is different from that of everyday speech. Poets frequently use **figurative language**—language not meant to be taken literally—to create a word picture. One way to understand poetry more easily is to **paraphrase** the lines, or restate them in your own words.

DIRECTIONS: As you read these poems, fill out the chart below. Choose lines containing figurative language and paraphrase them. One example has been given.

Poem Title	Original Lines	Paraphrased Lines
1. "Fable"	If I cannot carry forests on my back, Neither can you crack a nut.	Even though you have abilities that I lack, you also lack abilities that I possess.
2. "Thumbprint"		
3. "If—"		

"Fable" by Ralph Waldo Emerson
"Thumbprint" by Eve Merriam
"If—" by Rudyard Kipling

Literary Analysis: Rhyme

Rhyme, a common element of poetry, is the repetition of the ending sounds in two or more words. Rhyme often occurs in what is called a **rhyme scheme,** which is a pattern of rhyming sounds. Once you recognize the rhyme scheme of a poem, you can expect rhymes to appear in particular places. Rhyme is one of the things that give poems a musical quality.

Two kinds of rhyme are exact rhyme and half rhyme. An **exact rhyme** repeats the ending sounds of words exactly, as in *year* and *sphere*. A **half rhyme** comes close to repeating the ending sounds of words, but it misses slightly, as in *quarrel* and *squirrel*.

DIRECTIONS: After you have read these poems, fill out the following chart. List the words that rhyme at the end of the lines in each poem. Draw a circle around any pairs that form half rhymes.

"Fable"	"Thumbprint"	"If—"

"Mother to Son" by Langston Hughes
"The Courage That My Mother Had" by Edna St. Vincent Millay
"The Hummingbird That Lived Through Winter" by William Saroyan

Build Vocabulary

Using the Prefix *trans*-

A. DIRECTIONS: In each sentence, replace the italicized phrase with one of the following words starting with *trans*-, meaning "across," "over," "through," or "beyond":

transatlantic   transplant   transports   transparent

1. The monorail (*carries across*) _____ travelers from the train station to the airport.

2. A trip from New York to Paris is (*across the Atlantic Ocean*) _____.

3. Glass and cellophane are both (*able to let light pass through*) _____.

4. Doctors can (*transfer from one body to another*) _____ a human heart.

Using the Word Bank

B. DIRECTIONS: Write the Word Bank word that best matches each clue.

quarried	brooch	pathetic	transformation

1. It might be seen on a woman's dress. _____

2. It's what water undergoes when it becomes ice. _____

3. It describes what the rock digger did all day. _____

4. It describes the look of a shivering stray dog. _____

C. DIRECTIONS: Choose the word or phrase that is most *similar* in meaning to the word in CAPITAL LETTERS. Fill in the letter of your choice.

1. QUARRIED
   a. sheltered   b. worried   c. connected   d. carved

2. BROOCH
   a. pin   b. pen   c. dress   d. coat

3. PATHETIC
   a. lying   b. happy   c. pitiful   d. careful

4. TRANSFORMATION
   a. a trip   b. a question   c. a change   d. an answer

Unit 2: Common Threads

"Mother to Son" by Langston Hughes
"The Courage That My Mother Had" by Edna St. Vincent Millay
"The Hummingbird That Lived Through Winter" by William Saroyan

Build Spelling Skills: Making the Plural of Words Ending in *ch*

Spelling Strategy To make the plural of a word ending in *ch*, add -*es* to the end of the word.

Example: brooch + es = brooches

A. Practice: Change each of the following singular nouns to a plural by adding -*es*. Write the new word. Then use each word in a sentence.

Singular	Plural
1. match	_____ _____
2. ranch	_____ _____
3. lunch	_____ _____
4. itch	_____ _____
5. hunch	_____ _____
6. inch	_____ _____
7. crutch	_____ _____
8. church	_____ _____

B. Practice: Complete each sentence below by changing the singular noun in parentheses to a plural noun that ends in -*es*. Write your new word on the line.

1. In "Mother to Son," the speaker believes that in life you've got to learn to roll with the (punch) _____.

2. Climbing stairs is like climbing (arch) _____: Each step takes you higher and higher.

3. In "The Courage That My Mother Had," the speaker is left with one of her mother's (rich) _____.

4. The daughter has gone on many (search) _____ in hopes of finding courage.

5. In "The Hummingbird That Lived Through Winter," birds rest on the (branch) _____ of the trees outside Dikran's home.

6. Dikran knows just the right (touch) _____ to apply to the sickly bird.

Challenge: The Word Bank word *brooch* may be pronounced two different ways. Say the word aloud. How did you pronounce the double vowel in the middle of the word? Now try to guess the other acceptable pronunciation of *brooch*. Look in a dictionary to see if you are correct.

"Mother to Son" by Langston Hughes
"The Courage That My Mother Had" by Edna St. Vincent Millay
"The Hummingbird That Lived Through Winter" by William Saroyan

Build Grammar Skills: Principal Parts of Irregular Verbs

Verbs show either action or a state of being. Most verbs are regular, forming the past and past participle by adding *-ed* or *-d*. However, the past and past participle of **irregular verbs** do not follow this pattern. Each tense is formed in a special way.

Present	Present Participle	Past	Past Participle
bring	bringing	brought	(have, had, is, was) brought
go	going	went	(have, had, is, was) gone
begin	beginning	began	(have, had, is, was) begun
come	coming	came	(have, had, is, was) come
do	doing	did	(have, had, is, was) done
give	giving	gave	(have, had, is, was) given
take	taking	took	(have, had, is, was) taken
write	writing	wrote	(have, had, is, was) written
leave	leaving	left	(have, had, is, was) left

A. Practice: Read each sentence. If the form of the verb is incorrect, cross it out and write it correctly. If the verb form is correct, write *C* at the end of the sentence. The first one is done for you.

1. The mother in "Mother to Son" has ~~went~~ ^gone^ through a hard life.

2. It taked a lot for her to tolerate life's hardships.

3. She has given her son a warning to keep on going, no matter what.

4. Millay's mother leaved behind a golden brooch.

5. Her mother has tooken her courage to the grave.

6. Dikran done a lot to make the hummingbird well again.

7. Finally the bird went outside to join the other birds.

B. Writing Application: Complete the sentences that have been started below. In each sentence, include the past or past participle form of an irregular verb.

1. The mother on the stairs _____

2. The daughter with the brooch _____

3. The small hummingbird _____

"Mother to Son" by Langston Hughes
"The Courage That My Mother Had" by Edna St. Vincent Millay
"The Hummingbird That Lived Through Winter" by William Saroyan

Reading Strategy: Using Word Parts

You have more tools that you realize to help you find the meaning of a long or unknown word. One way to unlock the meaning is to look for a word part that you recognize. The familiar part can give you a clue to the meaning of the whole word. For example, in the word *transformation* you can see the familiar word part *form*. Breaking the word into smaller parts reveals a clue that the word might have something to do with the form, or shape, of something.

DIRECTIONS: The chart below contains words that appear in the selections that make up this grouping. In each word, identify a word part that you recognize. List that part in the second column. Then suggest what the whole word might mean. In the last column, write another word that shares the same familiar part with the first word.

Word	Familiar Part	Possible Meaning	Related Word
wintertime			
upward			
behold			
suspended			
heartbreaking			
tablespoonful			
weakening			
guardian			

"**Mother to Son**" by Langston Hughes
"**The Courage That My Mother Had**" by Edna St. Vincent Millay
"**The Hummingbird That Lived Through Winter**" by William Saroyan

Literary Analysis: Symbol

A **symbol** is an object that conveys an idea greater than itself. For example, a ring in a story might be a symbol for the love between two individuals. A budding flower might symbolize a new beginning for a character.

In the three selections you read, there are many examples of symbols. Each one represents an idea greater than itself. For example, in "Mother to Son," the crystal stair is a symbol for a life of ease and privilege.

DIRECTIONS: In the chart below, list items that are symbols in each of the three selections. Then explain the greater idea that each item represents. Some symbols have been provided for you.

Selection	Symbol	Idea That It Represents
"**Mother to Son**"	splinters	
"**The Courage That My Mother Had**"	rock	
"**The Hummingbird That Lived Through Winter**"		

"The Third Wish" by Joan Aiken

Build Vocabulary

Using the Suffix *-ous*

Often, you can use the suffix *-ous* to change a noun into an adjective. For example, to describe a holiday that is filled with *joy*, you could use the adjective *joyous*. The suffix *-ous* means "full of" or "characterized by."

A. DIRECTIONS: In each sentence, replace the italicized phrase with one of the following words ending in *-ous*.

disastrous   famous   hazardous   mischievous   nervous   wondrous

1. No one knew why the neighborhood child was so (*full of mischief*) _____.

2. The voyage of the Titanic turned out to be (*characterized by disaster*) _____.

3. Niagara Falls is a sight that is truly (*full of wonder*) _____ to behold.

4. Do you ever dream of becoming (*characterized by fame*) _____ some day?

5. A firefighter's job is certainly one that is (*full of hazards*) _____.

6. How do you calm down when you feel (*characterized by nerves*) _____?

Using the Word Bank

extricate	composure	presumptuous
rash	remote	malicious

B. DIRECTIONS: Write the Word Bank word that best completes each sentence.

1. The hermit lived all alone in a _____ shack in the woods.

2. It takes a _____ person to commit a hateful crime.

3. It took the rabbit several minutes to _____ itself from the thorny bush.

4. Don't be so _____ as to think that you will definitely win the award.

5. We managed to keep our _____ while facing the scary situation.

6. Don't make a _____ decision, but rather take time to think it over.

Recognizing Antonyms

C. DIRECTIONS: Circle the letter of the word or phrase that is most *opposite* in meaning to the word in CAPITAL LETTERS.

1. EXTRICATE
   a. tangle   b. wash   c. deny   d. listen

2. COMPOSURE
   a. loss of hair   b. loss of sight   c. loss of weight   d. loss of control

3. PRESUMPTUOUS
   a. curious   b. modest   c. missing   d. hungry

"The Third Wish" by Joan Aiken

Build Spelling Skills: Adding the Suffix *-ous*

Spelling Strategy   When adding *-ous* to a word that ends in silent *e*, drop the *e*, and then add *-ous*: fame − e + ous = famous.

Exceptions: • If the word ends in *ce*, drop the *e* and add *-ious*: malice − e + ious = malicious
• If the word ends in *ge*, do not drop the *e*: outrage + ous = outrageous
• When adding *-ous* to a word that ends in a consonant and *y*, change the *y* to *i* and add *-ous*: victory − y + i + ous = victorious

A. Practice: Change each word in the left column to an adjective by adding the *-ous* suffix. The circled letters spell a message that tells you what you've been doing lately.

Word	Adjective
1. space	___ ___ ◯ ___ ___ ___ ___
2. industry	___ ___ ◯ ___ ___ ___ ___ ___ ___
3. adventure	___ ◯ ___ ___ ___ ___ ___ ___ ___
4. melody	___ ___ ___ ___ ◯ ___ ___ ___
5. harmony	___ ___ ___ ___ ◯ ___ ___ ___
6. glory	◯ ___ ___ ___ ___ ___
7. envy	___ ___ ___ ◯ ___ ___
8. courage	___ ___ ◯ ___ ___ ___ ___ ___
9. fury	___ ___ ___ ___ ___ ◯
10. Message:	___ ___ ___ ___ ___ ___ ___ ___ ___ ___

B. Practice: Complete each sentence below by changing the word in parentheses to an adjective with an *-ous* suffix. Write your new word on the line.

1. Mr. Peters meets a (mystery) _____ little man while driving in the forest.

2. The bachelor reveals that he is (desire) _____ of a beautiful wife.

3. Mr. Peters becomes (rapture) _____ upon seeing the beautiful Leita.

4. Soon there are (vary) _____ indications that Leita is unhappy.

5. Leita finds life as a human less (luxury) _____ than life as a swan.

C. Challenge: The Word Bank word *presumptuous* comes from the word *presume* and has the *-ous* suffix. Yet *presumptuous* does not follow the rule you learned earlier about words ending in silent *e*. (If it did, *presume* would become *presumous* or *presumious*.) In your own words, write a rule for changing *presume* to *presumptuous*.

_____

Name _____ Date _____

"The Third Wish" by Joan Aiken

Build Grammar Skills: Adjectives

An **adjective** is a word that modifies or describes a noun or pronoun. An adjective tells about a noun by answering the question *what kind? which one? how many?* or *how much?*

> **Examples:**   The man asked for <u>three</u> wishes. (how many?)
> A <u>young</u>, <u>beautiful</u> wife suddenly appeared. (what kind?)

A. Practice: Underline the adjective or adjectives in each sentence.

1. Mr. Peters drove along a straight, empty stretch of road.

2. He heard strange cries coming from a distant bush.

3. A great white swan suddenly changed into a little man.

4. The grateful stranger granted Mr. Peters several wishes.

5. Mr. Peters soon had a gorgeous wife with pretty blue-green eyes.

6. Leita was an obedient woman, yet she remained an unhappy person.

7. Kind Mr. Peters used a second wish to turn Leita into a swan again.

8. Eventually, Mr. Peters was found dead with a withered leaf and a white feather.

B. Writing Application: Write a sentence about each topic listed below, using the adjective or adjectives given. When you are finished, reread your sentences and underline any additional adjectives that you used.

1. Write a sentence about the author Joan Aiken, using the adjective *creative*.

   _____

   _____

2. Write a sentence about Mr. Peters, using the adjectives *lonely* and *quiet*.

   _____

   _____

3. Write a sentence about Leita, using the adjective *attractive*.

   _____

   _____

4. Write a sentence about the forest, using the adjectives *dark* and *remote*.

   _____

   _____

5. Write a sentence about your reaction to the story, using the adjective *interesting*.

   _____

   _____

"The Third Wish" by Joan Aiken

Reading Strategy: Clarifying Word Meanings

Only *you* know what you don't understand. When you read a passage that you don't completely grasp, stop to **clarify** the meaning. Here are techniques you can use:

- Pause to think about the meaning of a word or a detail.
- Reread a portion of the text to find clues you may have missed.
- Ask a question you can answer to resolve confusion.
- Read ahead to piece together meaning.
- Look up a word in the dictionary or other resource.

DIRECTIONS: Complete the chart below to clarify details as you read.

Detail to Clarify	Meaning of Detail	Strategy Used (Pause, Reread, Question, Read Ahead, Use Another Source)
. . . had become <u>entangled</u> in the thorns . . .		
. . . took it to the <u>verge</u> of the canal . . .		

Unit 3: What Matters

Name _____ Date _____

"The Third Wish" by Joan Aiken

Literary Analysis: Modern Fairy Tale

The elements of a **modern fairy tale** are the same as those of the traditional fairy tale with which you are familiar. Both contain mysterious and fantastic events, magic and wishes, and animals with unusual abilities. A modern fairy tale may also include details about contemporary life that reflect the modern-day world.

DIRECTIONS: Use the chart below to record details that qualify "The Third Wish" as a modern fairy tale. Enter each detail in its appropriate place on the chart. One example is provided.

Mysterious and Fantastic Events	Magic and Wishes	Unusual Animals	Details About Contemporary Life
	three wishes		

"A Boy and a Man" by James Ramsey Ullman
from *Into Thin Air* by Jon Krakauer

Build Vocabulary

Using the Prefix *mal-*

The prefix *mal-* means "bad." For example, a person suffering from *malnutrition* is someone who has poor nutrition or a bad diet.

A. DIRECTIONS: Match each word on the left with its definition on the right. Write the letter of the definition on the line next to the word it defines.

____ 1. malformation   a. a disease marked by bad chills and fever

____ 2. malaria   b. caused by bad or evil feelings for

____ 3. malcontent   c. to operate in a bad or wrong way

____ 4. malfunction   d. a faulty or bad shape

____ 5. malicious   e. feeling bad or unhappy about the way things are

Using the Word Bank

prone	taut	pummeled
malevolent	denigrate	reconnoiter

B. DIRECTIONS: Write the Word Bank word that best matches each clue.

1. A spy might do this behind enemy lines. _____

2. This describes a rope being pulled at both ends. _____

3. A jealous person may do this to another person's success. _____

4. People often sleep in this position. _____

5. This describes your worst enemy. _____

6. It's what the strong boxer did to his weaker opponent. _____

Analogies

C. DIRECTIONS: For each pair of words in CAPITAL LETTERS, choose the lettered pair that best expresses a *similar* relationship. Circle the letter of your choice.

1. DENIGRATE : PRAISE ::
   a. ask : question
   b. shout : whisper
   c. sneeze : sniffle
   d. wash : scrub

2. INVESTIGATOR : RECONNOITER ::
   a. police : badge
   b. singer : piano
   c. actor : actress
   d. teacher : instruct

3. TAUT : LOOSE ::
   a. heavy : light
   b. rope : string
   c. help : aid
   d. round : circle

4. FISTS : PUMMELED ::
   a. fingers : thumbs
   b. bandage : injured
   c. hand : foot
   d. feet : stamped

"A Boy and a Man" by James Ramsey Ullman
from *Into Thin Air* by Jon Krakauer

Build Spelling Skills: Hyphenate Words With Double Consonants

Spelling Strategy   When a word of two or more syllables has a double consonant, the word can be hyphenated between the consonants.

The Word Bank words *pummeled, reconnoiter,* and *allure* have double consonants. When you write, you may need to hyphenate (break into syllables) such words when they come at the end of a line. To hyphenate, divide each word between the double consonants.

Examples: pum-meled   recon-noiter

A. Practice: Write each of the following words. Place a hyphen between the double consonants to show where the word can be broken into syllables.

1. commute   _____
2. ballot   _____
3. rabbit   _____
4. riddle   _____
5. shuffle   _____

6. suppose   _____
7. horrid   _____
8. scissors   _____
9. dagger   _____
10. battle   _____

B. Practice: In each sentence, find a word that is hyphenated. If the hyphenation is wrong, cross out the word and hyphenate it correctly.

1. In "A Boy and a Man," the man was not sure exactly how far he was from the ~~bott~~ bottom
~~om~~ of the crevasse.

2. Rudi worked slowly for a long time to pull the man up from the cold, icy, sli-
ppery mountain.

3. When the man was finally rescued by Rudi, the boy was stunned, speechless, and embarrassed to discover who the man was.

4. In Jon Krakauer's account, the author describes how the icy surfaces that were supporting the ladder weren't always reliable.

5. Krakauer, an expert mountain climber, writes that the Icefall was both strenuous and te-
rrifying.

6. Finally, after great physical effort, the climber managed to arrive at the flat summ-
it of the Icefall.

Challenge: Many related English words have come to us from a single word in another language. In a dictionary that contains word origins, look up the meaning and origin of the follow-
ing words, and write them on the lines provided. Then write a sentence using each word in a way that demonstrates its meaning.

1. reconnoiter: Origin and Meaning: _____

2. reconnaissance: Origin and Meaning: _____

3. connoisseur: Origin and Meaning: _____

"A Boy and a Man" by James Ramsey Ullman
from *Into Thin Air* by Jon Krakauer

Build Grammar Skills: Placement of Adjectives

Adjectives are words that modify, or describe, nouns and pronouns. Often, an adjective comes just before the noun it modifies. At other times, the adjective follows a linking verb and modifies the subject of the sentence. Linking verbs include forms of *be* (*am, is, are, was, were, have/has/had been*), *seem, feel, appear*.

Examples: The man climbed a narrow crevice. (adjective before a noun)

The crevice was narrow. (adjective after a linking verb)

A. Practice: Underline the adjective or adjectives in each sentence. Draw an arrow from each adjective to the noun or pronoun that it modifies.

1. Rudi was calm during the entire operation.

2. The helpless climber turned out to be Captain John Winter.

3. Both hands were numb from the difficult climb.

4. Winter received good advice from the young boy.

5. Jon Krakauer was exhausted and terrified during the climb.

6. The expert climber also found great beauty in the challenge.

7. Safety was important during the risky adventure.

8. Krakauer was grateful after reaching the highest peak.

B. Writing Application: Imagine you are a mountain climber. Write sentences about your experience, using each adjective and placement specified below.

1. Use the adjective *dangerous* just before a noun.

_____

2. Use the adjective *steady* after a linking verb.

_____

3. Use the adjective *strong* just before a noun.

_____

4. Use the adjective *windy* after a linking verb.

_____

5. Use the adjective *entire* just before a noun and the adjective *beautiful* after a linking verb.

_____

"A Boy and a Man" by James Ramsey Ullman
from *Into Thin Air* by Jon Krakauer

Reading Strategy: Predicting

Have you ever watched a movie and said to yourself, "I bet I know what's going to happen next"? You're confident about taking a guess because of what you've already seen in the film. You can apply that same technique when reading a story. As you read, you can use story details to **predict**, or make an educated guess, about what will happen next. The more details you have to base your prediction on, the more likely you will be right. Of course, many stories hold surprises; therefore all your predictions may not come true. But it's still fun to see how close you come!

DIRECTIONS: Use the following chart to keep track of your predictions as you read "A Boy and a Man" and from *Into Thin Air*. First list details or clues, and then list the predictions you make from them. Later, list the actual outcomes. One example is provided.

Detail or Hint	My Prediction	Actual Outcome
The crevasse is steep and slippery.	Rudi will fall into the crevasse.	Rudi stays where he is.

© Prentice-Hall, Inc.

"A Boy and a Man" by James Ramsey Ullman
from *Into Thin Air* by Jon Krakauer

Literary Analysis: Conflict With Nature

In most stories, the main characters face some kind of problem that they struggle to overcome. Their struggle is called **conflict**. Sometimes, the conflict is with other characters. In these two selections, however, characters struggle not against each another but against forces of nature. They battle icy glaciers in a struggle for survival and conquest. Their struggle with nature creates suspense and excitement in the story.

DIRECTIONS: Read each of the following passages. On the lines provided, explain the exact nature of the conflict, and tell how it creates suspense and excitement in the story.

1. "Rudi looked up and down the crevasse. He was thinking desperately of what he could do."

   _____
   _____
   _____

2. "This time, as he lay down, the ice bit, cold and rough, into his bare chest, but he scarcely noticed it."

   _____
   _____
   _____

3. "The climber was close now. But heavy. Indescribably heavy. Rudi's hands ached and burned, as if it were a rod of hot lead that they clung to."

   _____
   _____
   _____

4. "At one point I was balanced on an unsteady ladder in the predawn gloaming, stepping tenuously from one bent rung to the next, when the ice supporting the ladder on either end began to quiver as if an earthquake had struck."

   _____
   _____
   _____

5. "A moment later came an explosive roar as a large serac somewhere close above came crashing down."

   _____
   _____

6. "As the glacier moved, crevasses would sometimes compress, buckling ladders like toothpicks . . ."

   _____
   _____

Unit 3: What Matters

"The Charge of the Light Brigade" by Alfred, Lord Tennyson

from *Henry V* by William Shakespeare

"The Enemy" by Alice Walker

Build Vocabulary

Using Homophones

Homophones are words that sound alike but have different meanings and often different spellings. For example, the words *hear* and *here* are homophones; so are the words *there, their,* and *they're.*

A. DIRECTIONS: Choose the correct homophone in parentheses to complete each sentence.

1. The (maid, made) _____ straightened the house before dinner.

2. The eagle (sword, soared) _____ high over the mountaintops.

3. I'd bake a cake, but I don't have enough (flour, flower) _____.

Now look back at the homophones that you did *not* choose from the parenthesis. Write your own sentences using each of those words.

4. _____

5. _____

6. _____

Using the Word Bank

dismayed	blundered	volleyed	reeled	sundered

B. DIRECTIONS: Write the Word Bank word that can replace the italicized word or phrase in each sentence.

1. The player *made a mistake* on the field and lost the game as a result. _____

2. The log cabin was *torn apart* by the explosion. _____

3. The bank teller felt *frightened* for several days after the robbery. _____

4. The dancer suddenly began to faint and *fell back* on stage. _____

5. We had to cover our ears when the rifles were *shot at the same time.* _____

Recognizing Antonyms

C. DIRECTIONS: Circle the letter of the word or phrase that is most *opposite* in meaning to the word in CAPITAL LETTERS.

1. DISMAYED: a. confident   b. dizzy   c. suspicious   d. dry

2. BLUNDERED: a. filled   b. quieted   c. dropped   d. corrected

3. SUNDERED: a. heated   b. joined   c. cooled   d. darkened

"The Charge of the Light Brigade" by Alfred, Lord Tennyson

from *Henry V* by William Shakespeare

"The Enemy" by Alice Walker

Build Spelling Skills: Adding *-ed* to a Verb

Spelling Strategy   The Word Bank words *dismayed, blundered,* and *sundered* each have the *-ed* ending. Many verbs in the past tense end in *-ed*. For example: *The player* blun-dered *and* dropped *the ball.* There are different rules for adding *-ed* to the end of verbs.

- When a word ends in vowel + consonant and the final syllable is stressed, double the final consonant before adding *-ed*.

   Examples: confer + ed = confe**rr**ed   expel + ed = expe**ll**ed

- When a word ends in vowel + consonant and the final syllable is *not* stressed, do not double the final consonant before adding *-ed*.

   Examples: label + ed = labeled   limit + ed = limited

- **Exceptions:** Words that end in *w, x,* and a vowel + *y* do not double their final consonant when an *-ed* ending is added.

   endow + ed = endowed   relax + ed = relaxed   delay + ed = delayed

A. Practice: Add *-ed* to each of the verbs. Write your new word.

1. prefer   _____
2. enjoy   _____
3. program   _____
4. travel   _____
5. permit   _____

6. allow   _____
7. rebel   _____
8. focus   _____
9. unwrap   _____
10. offer   _____

B. Practice: Complete each sentence by adding the *-ed* ending to the word in parentheses. Write the new word.

1. The soldiers (travel) _____ a great distance to the battle.

2. Soldiers never (confer) _____ with their superiors about their orders.

3. The British soldiers were (shatter) _____ by the devastating battle.

4. The gentlemen will think about what (occur) _____ on St. Crispian's Day.

5. The speaker in "Lonely Particular" recalls an earlier time before the General (control) _____ the troops.

6. The speaker in "The Enemy" describes how a tiny fist (unsnap) _____ and reveal a handful of crumpled flowers.

Unit 3: What Matters

"The Charge of the Light Brigade" by Alfred, Lord Tennyson
from *Henry V* by William Shakespeare
"The Enemy" by Alice Walker

Build Grammar Skills: Possessive Adjectives

A **possessive adjective** is an adjective that shows ownership. It answers the question *whose?* A possessive adjective is sometimes called a *personal pronoun.*
The following words are possessive adjectives:

my   your   his   her   our   their   its

Example: Our teacher told us about the Light Brigade.

A. Practice: Underline the possessive adjective in each sentence.

1. The Light Brigade faithfully followed its orders.

2. About 450 soldiers lost their lives in the battle.

3. The poem is our reminder of the tragedies of war.

4. Henry V said that the soldiers would be like his brothers.

5. Shakespeare's writing awakens my love of poetry.

6. The teacher offered her interpretation of the passage.

7. "The Enemy" implies that children should be our top priority.

B. Writing Application: In each sentence, replace the underlined word or phrase with a possessive adjective. Then write your new sentence.

1. The soldiers did not think it was the soldiers' duty to question orders.

_____

_____

_____

2. Tennyson's poem is one of Tennyson's most famous works.

_____

_____

_____

3. Some people have said that war is war's own worst enemy.

_____

_____

_____

"The Charge of the Light Brigade" by Alfred, Lord Tennyson

from *Henry V* by William Shakespeare

"The Enemy" by Alice Walker

Reading Strategy: Using Word Parts

Knowing the meaning of some word parts and the prefixes that may be affixed to them can help you determine the meaning of a longer word. Break apart a long word into smaller parts you can grasp. Use the familiar part to get a clue to the meaning of the whole word. Then see how that meaning is affected by the prefix. For example, in the word *outlive*, you see the familiar word part *live*. The prefix *out-* means to go beyond. Using these two word parts, you can figure out that "to outlive this day" is to live beyond today.

DIRECTIONS: The chart below contains phrases that appear in the poems in this grouping. In each phrase, identify the part that you recognize in the underlined word. List that part in the second column. Then identify the prefix or suffix affixed to the word part. In the last column, give your own meaning for the whole word. Check a dictionary, if necessary.

Phrase	Familiar Part	Prefix or Suffix	Overall Meaning
Half a league <u>onward</u>			
familiar as <u>household</u> words			
hold their <u>manhoods</u> cheap			
tiny fist <u>unsnapped</u>			
snatched <u>hurriedly</u> on the go			

Unit 3: What Matters

"The Charge of the Light Brigade" by Alfred, Lord Tennyson
from *Henry V* by William Shakespeare
"The Enemy" by Alice Walker

Literary Analysis: Repetition

In ordinary conversation, you may grow annoyed if friends tend to repeat information they have already told you. But in poetry, **repetition** has a much more positive effect. Poets very often choose to repeat particular words, rhythms, or rhymes. The repetition not only helps to emphasize ideas, but also creates a desired mood and tone, as well as a kind of "musical" feeling. As you read a poem aloud, notice where repetition occurs. As it sinks into your mind, think how the repetition affects your thoughts and feelings about the poem.

DIRECTIONS: Read each passage. Describe the repetition and how it affects your feelings about the poem.

1. "Half a league, half a league,/Half a league onward . . . "

   _____

   _____

2. "Into the jaws of Death,/Into the mouth of Hell . . . "

   _____

   _____

3. "Flashed all their sabers bare,/Flashed as they turned in air/Sab'ring the gunners there . . . "

   _____

   _____

4. "Honor the charge they made!/Honor the Light Brigade . . . "

   _____

   _____

5. "Stormed at with shot and shell,/While horse and hero fell,/They that had fought so well/ . . . Back from the mouth of Hell . . . "

   _____

   _____

6. "But we in it shall be remembered—/We few, we happy few, we band of brothers . . . "

   _____

   _____

"The Californian's Tale" by Mark Twain
"Valediction" by Seamus Heaney

Build Vocabulary

Using the Suffix -fy

The suffix -fy after a root word indicates that the word is a verb. For example, when you cause people to have glory, you *glorify* them. The suffix -fy means "to make or cause."

A. DIRECTIONS: Match each word on the left with its definition on the right. Write the letter of the definition on the line next to the word it defines.

____ 1. beautify   a. to cause a feeling of shock or disgust

____ 2. clarify   b. to make up a lie

____ 3. horrify   c. to make more attractive

____ 4. mystify   d. to make clear

____ 5. falsify   e. to cause to be puzzled

balmy	predecessors	abundant	desolation
furtive	gravity	humiliation	apprehensions

Using the Word Bank

B. DIRECTIONS: Write the Word Bank word that matches each clue.

1. This tells what you might feel after an embarrassing defeat. _____

2. This tells what you might see on a lonely desert island. _____

3. This could describe a pickpocket or a fox. _____

4. This word describes a pleasant spring day. _____

5. This tells what you might have before entering a strange, dark room. _____

6. This describes a banquet or feast. _____

7. This is the force that holds things on the Earth. _____

8. This names those who came before you. _____

Recognizing Synonyms

C. DIRECTIONS: Circle the letter of the word that is most similar in meaning to the word in CAPITAL LETTERS.

1. DESOLATION: a. fear   b. emptiness   c. water   d. togetherness

2. HUMILIATION: a. victory   b. pity   c. embarrassment   d. joy

3. APPREHENSIONS: a. fears   b. fasteners   c. helpers   d. collectors

4. ABUNDANT: a. evil   b. silly   c. deadly   d. plenty

5. FURTIVE: a. noisy   b. sneaky   c. furry   d. empty

Unit 3: What Matters

"The Californian's Tale" by Mark Twain
"Valediction" by Seamus Heaney

Build Spelling Skills: Words With Silent *l*

Spelling Strategy Some words in English have a silent *l*. For example, you do not pronounce the *l* sound in the Word Bank word *balmy*. The word is pronounced so that it rhymes with *mommy*.

A. Practice: Write each word with a silent *l* that matches the clues.

1. This word means the opposite of *nervous*. It starts with *c*. _____

2. This word names a part of your hand or a kind of tree. It starts with *p*. _____

3. This word names how you move with your legs. It starts with *w*. _____

4. This word means the same as *speak*. It starts with *t*. _____

5. This word means the same as "fifty percent." It starts with *h*. _____

6. This word is the name of a baby cow. It starts with *c*. _____

7. This word names what you use to write on a blackboard. It starts with *c*. _____

8. This word names a prayer that is sung. It starts with a *ps* and rhymes with *mom*. _____

B. Practice: In each sentence, find a word with a silent l that is misspelled. Cross it out and write it correctly.

1. The traveler roamed the lonely California territory one bommy afternoon.

2. He was surprised to find such a nice-looking house as he wocked along the dusty California roads.

3. The man accepted his host's invitation to come in, and the two tocked for quite a while.

4. Henry grew more nervous and less com as the time approached for his wife's arrival.

5. Henry's friends had to watch him the way a cowboy might watch a troublesome caff.

6. In "Valediction," it is clear that the speaker thinks of the lady more than haff the time.

Challenge: As used in "The Californian's Tale," *apprehension* means "fear" or "anxious feelings." However *apprehension* has other meanings not related to "fear." In a dictionary, find at least two other definitions of *apprehension*. Write down each definition and a sentence demonstrating that meaning of *apprehension*.

Definition: _____

Sentence: _____

Definition: _____

Sentence: _____

"The Californian's Tale" by Mark Twain
"Valediction" by Seamus Heaney

Build Grammar Skills: Adverbs

An **adverb** is a word that modifies or describes a verb, an adjective, or another adverb. An adverb answers the question *how? when? where? how often?* or *to what extent?*

Examples: The man walked <u>slowly</u> along the road. (tells how he walked)
People went <u>away</u> after the gold rush. (tells where, or the direction in which, they went)

A. Practice: Underline the adverb in each sentence and draw an arrow to the verb it modifies. The first one has been done for you.

1. The curious traveler <u>frequently</u> roams the deserted territory.

2. The surprised man looks admiringly at the cozy cottage.

3. The home owner eagerly invites his new guest into the house.

4. Henry speaks lovingly of his beautiful young wife.

5. Several of Henry's friends come to the house later.

6. Henry hopes that his wife will arrive soon.

7. The visitor eventually learns the truth about the situation.

8. In "Valediction," the speaker misses his companion terribly.

B. Writing Application: Imagine that the Californian traveler kept a log of his experiences. Write sentences that he might have written about his visit with Henry. Use the adverbs below.

1. quickly

_____

2. never

_____

3. gently

_____

4. always

_____

5. finally

_____

© Prentice-Hall, Inc.

"The Californian's Tale" by Mark Twain
"Valediction" by Seamus Heaney

Reading Strategy: Summarizing

As you read a story, it is also helpful to **summarize** one passage or section after completing it. You review all the main events and important details that were introduced in that section, and then you retell that part of the story in your own words. The summary helps you determine how well you understand the material.

DIRECTIONS: Use the chart below to record main events and important details from portions of "The Californian's Tale" and to write a summary of each section in your own words. One event and one detail are provided.

Main Events	Important Details	Summary of Section
The traveler stops at a cottage one afternoon.	The cottage is well kept, instead of having the usual deserted look.	

Write a one-sentence summary of "Valediction":

_____

_____

_____

Name _____ Date _____

"The Californian's Tale" by Mark Twain
"Valediction" by Seamus Heaney

Literary Analysis: Local Color

Local color is the use of details specific to a region, which adds authenticity to a story. For example, Mark Twain provides details specific to the California mining region where his story is set. Readers can envision the look of the landscape and hear the colorful language of the people.

DIRECTIONS: As you read, fill in this graphic organizer with details of local color that bring "The Californian's Tale" to life.

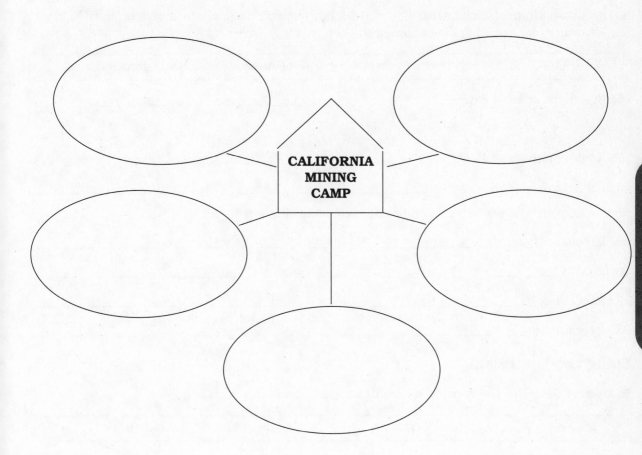

"Stopping by Woods on a Snowy Evening" by Robert Frost
"Miracles" by Walt Whitman
"Four Skinny Trees" by Sandra Cisneros

Build Vocabulary

Using Forms of *ferocious*

The word *ferocious* is an adjective that means "fierce" or "savage." As with most other words, the word *ferocious* has several related words that are other parts of speech. For example, the word *ferociously* is an adverb, and the words *ferociousness* and *ferocity* are nouns.

A. DIRECTIONS: In the blanks, write one of the following words to match each definition. Fill in one letter per blank, and discover something fierce in the circles.

ferocious	ferocity	ferociously	ferociousness

1. in a fierce or savage way   __ __ __ __ __ __ __ __ __ __ __

2. savagery   __ __ __ __ __ __ __ __ __

3. fierce or savage   __ __ __ __ __ __ __ __ __

4. fierceness   __ __ __ __ __ __ __ __ __ __

Now write your own sentences using each of the following words.

5. ferocious _____

6. ferocity _____

7. ferociously _____

8. ferociousness _____

Using the Word Bank

B. DIRECTIONS: Write the Word Bank word that best completes each sentence.

downy	ferocious	exquisite	distinct

1. A rotten egg has a _____ odor.

2. I fell asleep immediately on the large _____ pillow.

3. The house was designed with such _____ taste that several people wished to buy it.

4. The _____ tiger battled with the zebra until finally killing it.

Analogies

C. DIRECTIONS: For each pair of words in CAPITAL LETTERS, choose the lettered pair that best expresses a *similar* relationship. Circle the letter of your choice.

____ 1. EXQUISITE : UGLY ::
      a. sleepy : surprising   b. eye : see   c. heavy : weighty   d. exciting : boring

____ 2. DOWNY : QUILT ::
      a. sharp : razor   b. shell : turtle   c. bed : legs   d. flat : round

"Stopping by Woods on a Snowy Evening" by Robert Frost
"Miracles" by Walt Whitman
"Four Skinny Trees" by Sandra Cisneros

Build Spelling Skills: *z* Sound Spelled *s*

Spelling Strategy   In the Word Bank word *exquisite*, the letter *s* is pronounced *z*. Many other words contain the *z* sound spelled *s*. Learn them as you come across them in your reading.

Examples: composer   rose   desert   noise

A. Practice: Complete each sentence with a word in which the *z* sound is spelled *s*.

1. Bill made a sandwich with tomato, lettuce, and Swiss c_____.

2. Doctors can now perform surgery using a high-powered l_____ beam.

3. In most sports contests, there is a winner and a l_____.

4. Did you ever wake up early enough to watch the sun r_____ over the horizon?

5. I understand the rule, but I don't understand the r_____ for it.

6. I tried telephoning my friend, but the line was b_____ for hours.

7. When you are done with the ketchup bottle, I would like to u_____ it.

8. Did you know that r_____ are grapes that have been dried in the sun?

9. We're throwing a s_____ party for Ann next week, so don't tell her.

10. I can't study or concentrate because the classroom is too n_____.

B. Practice: In each sentence, find a word with the *z* sound that is spelled wrong. Cross out the word and write it correctly.

1. The traveler in the woods thinks he knowz who the owner is.

2. The fact that the traveler choozes to move on indicates that he is not lazy or irresponsible.

3. The girl thinks that each of the four skinny trees rezembles her in some way.

4. She says that the trees would droop if they ever forgot their reazon for being.

5. The speaker in "Miracles" obzerves miracles in every aspect of everyday living.

6. He watches honeybees that are buzy around the hive on a summer afternoon.

Challenge: The Word Bank word *exquisite* may be pronounced two different ways. Say the word aloud. Which syllable did you stress the hardest? Write the word with the stressed syllable in capital letters. _____

Now, try to guess the other pronunciation of *exquisite* that is acceptable, and write it with the stressed syllable in capital letters. _____

Check a dictionary to see if you were correct.

"Stopping by Woods on a Snowy Evening" by Robert Frost
"Miracles" by Walt Whitman
"Four Skinny Trees" by Sandra Cisneros

Build Grammar Skills: Adverbs Modifying Adjectives and Adverbs

An **adverb** is a word that modifies or describes a verb, but an adverb can also modify an adjective or another adverb. Adverbs that are commonly used to modify adjectives and other adverbs include *too, so, very, quite, more, most, rather, usually,* and *almost.*

> **Examples:** The woods were <u>so</u> beautiful. (modifies the adjective *beautiful*)
> I <u>very</u> slowly left the area. (modifies the adverb *slowly*)

A. Practice: In each sentence, underline any adverb that modifies an adjective or adverb. Draw an arrow to the word it modifies. Do not underline adverbs that modify verbs.

1. The traveler is most impressed by the beautiful woods.

2. He stares for quite some time at the falling snow.

3. The man shows himself to be a very responsible person.

4. Four rather skinny trees stand proudly in the concrete.

5. They have stood in the same spot for so many years.

6. Nothing is more inspiring than the four skinny trees.

7. The Manhattan walker almost always sees a miracle in the street.

8. The usually ignored sights are ones that the walker cherishes.

B. Writing Application: Write sentences about your favorite selection. Use the following adverbs in the ways that are specified.

1. Use the adverb *very* to modify an adjective.

_____

2. Use the adverb *very* to modify an adverb.

_____

3. Use the adverb *most* to modify an adjective.

_____

4. Use the adverb *quite* to modify an adverb.

_____

"Stopping by Woods on a Snowy Evening" by Robert Frost

"Miracles" by Walt Whitman

"Four Skinny Trees" by Sandra Cisneros

Reading Strategy: Interpreting Figures of Speech

Do you know people who "talk back" to their televisions? As they watch a program, they speak out to the people on the screen. They may give their opinion about something that was just said or make some comment about the program. Of course, the people on screen can't hear them, but that doesn't discourage the viewers from talking anyway.

When you read literature, you also react in specific ways. It might be a **figure of speech**—a statement that is not to be read literally—that triggers a reaction in you. Perhaps what you read reminds you of something that happened to you in real life. Perhaps you strongly agree or disagree with the author's opinion, or you find the writing style very pleasant or unpleasant. The thoughts that run through your head as you read are your response to the literature.

DIRECTIONS: Reread the three selections. Use the chart below to record figures of speech that evoke a reaction in you. For each entry, record your personal response—what the passage makes you think and feel.

Selection	Figure of Speech	Personal Response
"Stopping by Woods on a Snowy Evening"		
"Stopping by Woods on a Snowy Evening"		
"Stopping by Woods on a Snowy Evening"		
"Four Skinny Trees"		
"Four Skinny Trees"		
"Four Skinny Trees"		
"Miracles"		
"Miracles"		

Unit 3: What Matters

"Stopping by Woods on a Snowy Evening" by Robert Frost
"Miracles" by Walt Whitman
"Four Skinny Trees" by Sandra Cisneros

Literary Analysis: Levels of Meaning

When you peel an onion, you go through different layers. First you have the surface layer of skin. Next come the layers beneath the surface and, finally, the inner core. In a way, reading literature is like peeling an onion. You discover different **levels of meaning** as you read. You may find a literal meaning at the surface level, a deeper meaning for a character, and a still deeper personal meaning for yourself. For example, in "Stopping by Woods on a Snowy Evening," the speaker tells us that he has "miles to go before I sleep." On the surface, this statement can be taken literally. At a deeper level, the "miles" may be interpreted as responsibilities the speaker has to meet. On the deepest level, the miles may symbolize the road of life that all of us must travel.

DIRECTIONS: Use the circles below to record different levels of meaning you find in each of the three selections.

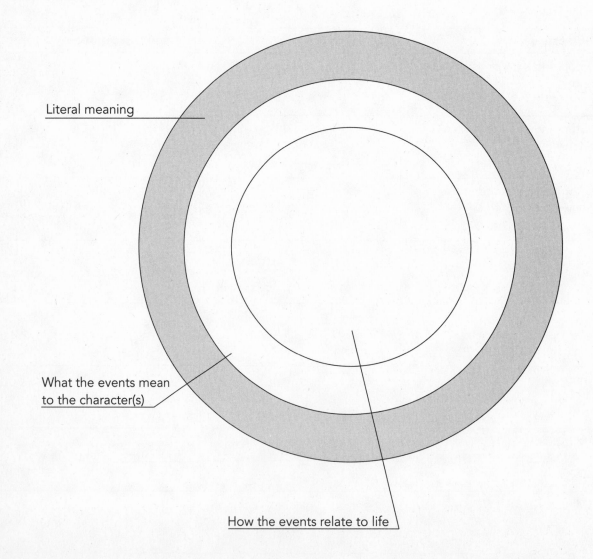

Literal meaning

What the events mean
to the character(s)

How the events relate to life

Name _____   Date _____

"The Night the Bed Fell" by James Thurber

Build Vocabulary

Using the Prefix *ex-*

A. DIRECTIONS: In each sentence, replace the phrase in parentheses with one of the following words beginning in *ex-*, meaning "out."

excavate   exceptional   exhausted   exiled   extend

1. After working for a full day, many people are (tired out) _____.

2. The builders planned to (dig out) _____ the hill in order to make the tunnel.

3. The traitor was (sent out) _____ from the country after being discovered.

4. The school board decided to (stretch out) _____ classes for two more days.

5. Dave is an (out of the ordinary) _____ student who gets straight A's.

Using the Word Bank

ominous	allay	fortitude	perilous
deluge	pungent	extricate	culprit

B. DIRECTIONS: Write the Word Bank word that completes each sentence correctly.

1. The _____ of rain caused the river to overflow its banks.

2. After a robbery, detectives always search for the _____.

3. The mayor tried to _____ the residents' fears about rising taxes.

4. The hikers took a _____ walk across the old, rotted bridge.

5. The _____ smell of chili sauce filled the small diner.

6. The robbery victims tried to _____ themselves from the rope that bound them.

7. The dark clouds were an _____ sign that a storm was approaching.

8. Getting on with their lives after the accident took lots of _____.

Recognizing Synonyms

C. DIRECTIONS: Circle the letter of the word that is most *similar* in meaning to the word in CAPITAL LETTERS.

1. PERILOUS: a. happy   b. tired   c. safe   d. dangerous

2. FORTITUDE: a. weakness   b. honesty   c. strength   d. connection

3. PUNGENT: a. sharp   b. silly   c. serious   d. light

4. EXTRICATE: a. erase   b. untangle   c. appear   d. tangle

5. ALLAY: a. hide   b. excite   c. mix   d. calm

6. CULPRIT: a. judge   b. criminal   c. jury   d. lawyer

Name _____ Date _____

"The Night the Bed Fell" by James Thurber

Build Spelling Skills: *j* Sound Spelled *g*

Spelling Strategy In certain words, the *j* sound is spelled *g*. This happens mainly when the letter *g* is followed by an *e*, an *i*, or a *y*.

Examples: deluge pungent magic fragile geology

A. Practice: Use the clues below to write words that contain the *j* sound spelled *g*. The first letter of each word is given to you. Use a dictionary for help if necessary.

1. A school that students attend after high school: c ___ ___ ___ ___ ___ ___

2. Another name for a small town: v ___ ___ ___ ___ ___ ___

3. The study of plants and animals: b ___ ___ ___ ___ ___ ___

4. What we must breathe in order to live: o ___ ___ ___ ___ ___

5. Another word for trash: g ___ ___ ___ ___ ___ ___

6. Where a pet bird is often kept: c ___ ___ ___

7. What actors stand on to do a play: s ___ ___ ___ ___

8. A set of suitcases used for traveling: l ___ ___ ___ ___ ___ ___

9. Very big: h ___ ___ ___

10. The device that runs a car: e ___ ___ ___ ___ ___

B. Practice: In each sentence, find a word or words with the *j* sound. If a word is spelled wrong, cross it out and write it correctly.

1. James Thurber's father slept in the attic one night to take advantaje of the peace and quiet there.

2. His wife thought it was too danjerous to sleep on the attic bed because it was wobbly.

3. When James's cot toppled over, it was lojical for his mother to believe that her husband's bed had collapsed instead.

4. The resulting activity and confusion caused some damaje in the Thurber home and gave James a big laugh.

5. Briggs probably needed a bandaje for his injured hand.

Challenge: The Word Bank word *deluge* becomes a completely different word when you change the letter *g* to a *d*. Then you have the word *delude*, meaning "to fool."

1. Can you think of another word to make by changing a single letter in *deluge*? (Here's a hint: It means "very fancy" or "elegant.") _____

2. Can you make a new word by changing a single letter in the Word Bank word *allay*? (Hint: It refers to a passageway or narrow back street.) _____

"The Night the Bed Fell" by James Thurber

Build Grammar Skills: Prepositions

A **preposition** is a word that shows the relationship of a noun or a pronoun to another word in the sentence.

> **Example:** Mr. Thurber slept <u>in</u> the attic.

In the above example, the preposition *in* shows the relationship between the noun *attic* and the verb *slept*.

These are some of the most common prepositions. Notice that a few of them consist of more than one word.

about	behind	from	of	through
above	below	in	off	to
across	beneath	inside	on	toward
after	between	instead of	out	under
around	by	in front of	out of	until
at	concerning	into	over	up
because of	during	like	past	with
before	for	near	since	without

A. Practice: Write the preposition in each sentence. Then write the first letter of each preposition below. The message tells you where part of Thurber's story takes place.

1. The attic was above the other rooms. _____

2. Briggs slept near his cousin James. _____

3. James's bed collapsed after a while. _____

4. Mother ran to the attic. _____

5. Briggs headed toward the window. _____

6. Confusion reigned inside the house. _____

7. Thurber wrote this story concerning his family. _____

Message: ___ ___ ___ ___ ___ ___ ___
           1   2   3   4   5   6   7

B. Writing Application: Using each of the prepositions shown in parentheses, describe a funny thing that once happened to you.

1. (during) _____

2. (on) _____

3. (until) _____

4. (after) _____

5. (because of) _____

Unit 4: Resolving Conflicts

Name _____ Date _____

Reading Strategy: Picturing Events

To understand a work of literature fully, you must go beyond a simple scan of the page to put the writer's ideas together in your own mind. One way to construct meaning while you read is to **picture,** or envision, the **events** in the text. Use details that the author provides to help you picture in your mind the people, places, and events in a piece of writing. Don't limit yourself just to your sense of sight. Use your imagination to experience sounds, tastes, smells, and physical sensations as well.

DIRECTIONS: Complete the following chart to help you to more fully picture events that take place in "The Night the Bed Fell." Record sensory details from the text that help you to form a clear picture in your mind, and list the senses to which they appeal.

Person, Place, or Event	Sensory Details	Senses Used
the bed in the attic	old, wooden, unsafe, wobbly, heavy headboard	sight, physical sensation

"**The Night the Bed Fell**" by James Thurber

Literary Analysis: Humorous Essay

A **humorous essay** is nonfiction written for the purpose of amusing an audience. Often in a humorous essay, the amusement is based on *irony*—a situation that is the opposite of what might be expected. In "The Night the Bed Fell," irony exists because each member of the family had a very wrong impression of what was actually happening at the time of all the chaos and confusion. For example, Mrs. Thurber believed that her husband's bed had crashed when, in reality, it was her son's bed that had fallen.

DIRECTIONS: Use the following chart to record all the contrasting views of events in Thurber's story. First, describe briefly the events that actually happened. Then, for each character listed, tell what he or she thought was happening.

What Grandfather thought:	What Briggs thought:	What Mother thought:
_____ _____ _____ _____ _____	_____ _____ _____ _____ _____	_____ _____ _____ _____ _____
What the narrator thought:	**What Really Happened:**	**What Herman thought:**
_____ _____ _____ _____ _____	_____ _____ _____ _____ _____	_____ _____ _____ _____ _____
What Father thought:		**What Roy thought:**
_____ _____ _____ _____ _____ _____		_____ _____ _____ _____ _____ _____

Unit 4: Resolving Conflicts

"All Summer in a Day" by Ray Bradbury

Build Vocabulary: Using the Word Root -vita-

A. DIRECTIONS: Each of the following words contains the word root -vita-, meaning "life." Choose the word that completes each sentence correctly.

vitality   vitamin   vital statistics   revitalize

1. Your _____ include your age, height, weight, gender, and date of birth.

2. Well-balanced meals help give you the _____ to be active and alert all day long.

3. The mayor wanted to _____ the downtown area, which had grown shabby in recent years.

4. Riboflavin, a _____ found in milk, cheese, fish, poultry, and green vegetables, helps the body cells use oxygen.

Using the Word Bank

concussion	slackening	vital	surged
tumultuously	resilient	savored	

B. DIRECTIONS: Circle the letter of the word or phrase that is most *similar* in meaning to the word in CAPITAL LETTERS.

1. VITAL
   a. difficult
   b. sickening
   c. essential
   d. causing disease

2. CONCUSSION
   a. outcome
   b. violent shaking
   c. agreement
   d. argument

3. SAVORED
   a. disappeared
   b. burned lightly
   c. mixed
   d. greatly enjoyed

4. TUMULTUOUSLY
   a. noisily
   b. happily
   c. slowly
   d. dangerously

5. SLACKENING
   a. tightening
   b. cleaning
   c. passing on
   d. easing up

6. SURGED
   a. rushed forward
   b. fell apart
   c. begged
   d. spent recklessly

7. RESILIENT
   a. losing strength
   b. springing back into shape
   c. not making sense
   d. surprisingly amusing

"All Summer in a Day" by Ray Bradbury

Build Spelling Skills: Words in Which the *choo* Sound Is Spelled *tu*

Spelling Strategy The *choo* sound is often spelled *tu* in a word that is derived from a base word ending with the *t* sound. In the Word Bank word *tumultuously*, the third syllable has the *choo* sound spelled *tu*. Here are two more examples.

    fact—fac*tu*al   rite—ri*tu*al

- The *choo* sound at the beginning of a word is never spelled *tu*.

    choose   chew

- The letters *tu* at the beginning of a word do not have the *choo* sound.

    tune   tuba

A. Practice: Read each pair of words. Complete the spelling of the *choo* sound in the second word. Write the entire word on the line.

1. act   ac___ally   _____

2. spirit spiri___al   _____

3. event even___ally _____

4. site   si___ation   _____

5. tumult tumul___ous _____

6. sate   sa___rate   _____

B. Practice: In each sentence, find a word with the *choo* sound that is spelled wrong. Cross out the word and write it correctly. The first one has been done for you.

                                              factual

1. Bradbury's story is science fiction rather than ~~fakchual~~.

2. On Venus, there is no richual of watching a sunrise or a sunset.

3. Instead, it is nachooral to watch a steady rainfall for years.

4. Margot is a timid girl who stands as motionless as a stachoo.

5. She is the target of a prank played by immachure classmates.

6. Before the sun appears, the children agree mutchually to lock Margot in a closet.

7. Unforchunately, the teacher is unaware of what is happening.

8. The sun makes a punkchual appearance after seven years.

9. Scientists must have congrachulated themselves on predicting when the sun would appear.

10. But for Margot, the sun's appearance was a sad sichooation.

Challenge: Choose at least three words from this page in which the *choo* sound is spelled *tu*. Write an original sentence that uses all three.

_____

_____

Name _____ Date _____

"All Summer in a Day" by Ray Bradbury

Build Grammar Skills: Prepositional Phrases

A **prepositional phrase** is a group of words beginning with a preposition and ending with a noun or pronoun. The noun or pronoun is called the **object of the preposition.**

preposition   object of preposition

Example: The children lived on another planet.

Some commonly used prepositions include:

about	before	for	near	past
above	below	from	of	to
across	between	in	off	toward
after	by	inside	on	under
against	down	into	out	until
along	during	like	over	with

A. Practice: Find the prepositional phrase or phrases in each sentence. Enclose each phrase in parentheses. Underline the preposition once and the object of the preposition twice. Notice that many sentences have more than one prepositional phrase. The first one is done for you.

1. The children (in the classroom) gazed (out the large window).

2. The pouring rain finally stopped after seven years.

3. They waited with excitement for the appearance of the sun.

4. The boys and girls ran from the room and into the jungle.

5. Poor Margot was locked inside the closet during the event.

6. The teacher didn't know about Margot throughout her ordeal.

B. Writing Application: Imagine you are Margot or another student in her class. Write sentences that tell about your experience. In each sentence, include the prepositional phrases below.

1. without the sun _____

_____

2. on Venus _____

_____

3. through the tunnels _____

_____

4. for seven years _____

_____

"All Summer in a Day" by Ray Bradbury

Reading Strategy: Comparing and Contrasting Characters

The **characters** are the people or animals who take part in the action of a literary work. The main character is the most important character in the story. Minor characters are involved in the action, and may provoke it, but they are not the focus of attention. Writers often work to create characters with conflicting traits. These contrasting traits often contribute to the central conflict of the story.

The central character of "All Summer in a Day" is Margot. Her classmates on Venus collectively form a set of minor characters. Margot and her classmates share some characteristics, but they also possess great differences. These differences lead to the story's conflict.

DIRECTIONS: Complete the following Venn diagram to compare and contrast Margot with her classmates. In the outer portions of the rings, list character traits that are unique to Margot and to her classmates. Where the rings intersect, list traits that Margot and her classmates share.

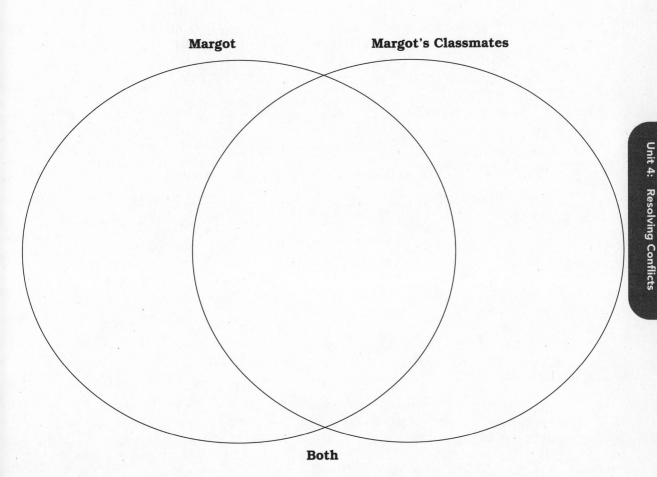

Unit 4: Resolving Conflicts

"All Summer in a Day" by Ray Bradbury

Literary Analysis: Setting

The **setting** of a story is the time and place in which the events occur. The author portrays the setting by offering vivid words and phrases that enable you to envision the time and place in your mind. For example, when describing the jungle on planet Venus, author Bradbury writes:

> It was a nest of octopi, clustering up great arms of fleshlike weed, wavering, flowering in this brief spring. It was the color of rubber and ash, this jungle, from the many years without sun. It was the color of stones and white cheeses and ink, and it was the color of the moon.

Sometimes a story has more than one setting. As the story continues, the location of the action changes, as does the time when the action occurs. In Bradbury's story, several indoor locations are described, including the classroom, the underground tunnel, and the closet. Also, several outdoor locations are described, including the jungle and the sun-filled sky.

A. DIRECTIONS: Go through the story carefully to find words and phrases that describe either an indoor or an outdoor setting. In the chart, list the descriptive words and phrases that you feel are most effective in helping you to envision each setting.

Indoors	Outdoors

B. DIRECTIONS: On another piece of paper, draw a picture of one of the above settings, using your list of details to help you.

"The Highwayman" by Alfred Noyes
"The Real Story of a Cowboy's Life" by Geoffrey C. Ward

Build Vocabulary

Using Compound Nouns

A. DIRECTIONS: The Word Bank word *landlord* is an example of a compound noun—a noun made by combining two smaller words. Use one of the following compound nouns to complete each sentence correctly.

mountainside   bookstore   seashell   airplane

1. At the beach, the collector found a _____ shaped like a spiraled horn.

2. Our local _____ also sells newspapers and magazines.

3. The _____ landed in order to refuel before completing its flight.

4. Many skiers found it difficult getting down the steep _____.

Using the Word Bank

torrent	cascade	tawny	strive
bound	brandished	landlord	

B. DIRECTIONS: Write the Word Bank word that best matches each clue.

1. You might pay this person monthly. _____

2. This travels in a rushing stream. _____

3. It may be the color of a deer or duck. _____

4. You may have used rope if you did this. _____

5. The robber did this with his gun. _____

6. This moves from top to bottom. _____

7. This is what you do to reach a goal. _____

Analogies

C. DIRECTIONS: For each related pair of words in CAPITAL LETTERS, choose the pair that best expresses a similar relationship. Circle the letter of your choice.

1. TAWNY : BROWN ::
   a. black : sky   b. duck : cow   c. pink : red   d. paint : green

2. CASCADE : FALL ::
   a. wind : blow   b. rocket : missile   c. rain : snow   d. water : dry

3. LANDLORD : APARTMENT ::
   a. house : home   b. grocer : supermarket   c. car : driver   d. pen : pencil

Unit 4: Resolving Conflicts

"The Highwayman" by Alfred Noyes
"The Real Story of a Cowboy's Life" by Geoffrey C. Ward

Build Spelling Skills: Use a Hyphen in Compound Adjectives

Spelling Strategy   To form a compound adjective using an adjective and a noun, add
-*ed* to the noun. Use a hyphen to separate the two words in the compound adjective. In "The
Highwayman," black-eyed demonstrates this rule.

Examples:	Adjective	Noun				Compound Adjective
	black	eye	+ ed	=	black-eyed (daughter)
	two	side	+ ed	=	two-sided (argument)

A. Practice: Form a compound adjective from each adjective and noun. Then write a sentence
that uses your compound adjective.

1. quick foot   Compound adjective: _____

   Sentence: _____

2. six leg   Compound adjective: _____

   Sentence: _____

3. thin skin   Compound adjective: _____

   Sentence: _____

4. empty hand   Compound adjective: _____

   Sentence: _____

B. Practice: In each sentence, find one or more compound adjectives. If any are written incorrectly, cross them out and write them correctly.

1. The highwayman was a thickskin man who didn't seem to fear anyone.

2. He was deeply in love with Bess, the landlord's black-eyed and red lipped daughter.

3. Bess was a kindhearted soul who longed to be with the highwayman.

4. The mean spirited British redcoats carefully planned an ambush.

5. A real cowboy is a welltravel worker who goes on long cattle drives.

Challenge: The Word Bank word *landlord* is a compound noun that begins with the word *land*.
How many other compound words do you know that begin with the word *land*? (For example:
landmark) Make a list of your compound words. Then look in a dictionary and see how many
more words you can add to your list.

_____

_____

"The Highwayman" by Alfred Noyes
"The Real Story of a Cowboy's Life" by Geoffrey C. Ward

Build Grammar Skills: Mechanics: Dashes and Hyphens

The **dash** (—), a long, horizontal mark made above the writing line, is used to set off material in text. It signals an abrupt change of thought or sets off an interrupting idea or a summary statement. See the following examples from the selections.

> **Examples:** . . . some tribes charged tolls for herds crossing their land—payable in money or beef.
>
> I know that if you wasn't singing, any little sound in the night—it might be just a horse shaking himself—could make them leave the country . . .

Hyphens (-) are used to connect words. They connect two-word numbers and fractions used as adjectives; they join certain compound words and compound modifiers that come before nouns; and they show that a word has been broken at the end of a line. See the following examples from the selections.

> **Examples:** the landlord's black-eyed daughter
> wine-red was his velvet coat
> forty-two head of cattle

A. Practice: Insert one or more dashes in each statement to indicate a dramatic break in the text.

1. The letter arrived exactly on time an amazing fact since it was mailed in rural Mexico!

2. It took herds this may be hard to imagine about fifty days to get from Texas to Nebraska.

3. Two railway centers Omaha and St. Louis were main destinations of cattle drives.

B. Practice: In the phrases below, insert hyphens where necessary.

1. nearly forty five inches across

2. won by a three fifths majority

3. an all American scene

4. is an ex rancher

C. Writing Application: Write four sentences that describe the daily life of a cowboy. Two of the sentences should include hyphens, and two should include dashes.

1. _____

_____

2. _____

_____

3. _____

_____

4. _____

_____

Unit 4: Resolving Conflicts

"The Highwayman" by Alfred Noyes
"The Real Story of a Cowboy's Life" by Geoffrey C. Ward

Reading Strategy: Identify Cause and Effect

In stories, as in real life, very few events happen for no reason. Each event usually has a **cause**, or reason why it occurs. The event that follows as a result the cause is called the **effect**. For example, in "The Highwayman," Tim is jealous of the highwayman. Jealousy causes him to inform the British redcoats of the highwayman's planned arrival. Tim's jealousy is the cause, and his informing is the effect. Later, his informing becomes the cause of a new effect—the ambush by the British.

In a story, each effect may eventually becomes a cause for the next event, linking causes and effects and propelling the action forward.

DIRECTIONS: Use the following chart to show the flow of important events in each of the selections. One example is provided.

"The Highwayman"

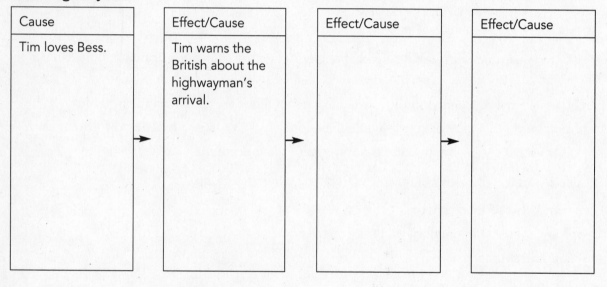

Cause	Effect/Cause	Effect/Cause	Effect/Cause
Tim loves Bess.	Tim warns the British about the highwayman's arrival.		

"The Real Story of a Cowboy's Life"

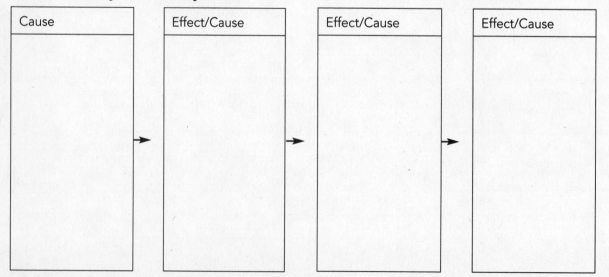

Cause	Effect/Cause	Effect/Cause	Effect/Cause

"The Highwayman" by Alfred Noyes
"The Real Story of a Cowboy's Life" by Geoffrey C. Ward

Literary Analysis: Suspense

Suspense in a story is created when the author arouses your curiosity about characters and events but then makes you wait to find out how the story will end. The more eager you become to know the ending, the greater the suspense. Good writers know how to draw out a story, introducing new and interesting details along the way in order to delay the ending. As long as you remain interested in the outcome, the suspense continues to build. The author's challenge is to hold your interest before the outcome is finally revealed.

DIRECTIONS: For each selection, think about the story details that arouse your interest and make you curious to know the ending. Use the chart below to record those details. Then list the information you want revealed by the end of the story.

"The Highwayman"

Details that arouse your interest	What you want the end to reveal

"The Real Story of a Cowboy's Life"

Details that arouse your interest	What you want the end to reveal

Unit 4: Resolving Conflicts

"Justin Lebo" by Phillip Hoose
"The Rider" by Naomi Shihab Nye
"Amigo Brothers" by Piri Thomas
"The Walk" by Thomas Hardy

Build Vocabulary

Using the Prefix *re-*

A. DIRECTIONS: The prefix *re-* means "again." Use one of the following words to complete each sentence correctly:

reseal   reread   redial   reset

1. If you don't understand a story the first time, you might _____ it.

2. Sharon had to _____ the envelope with glue after it accidentally opened.

3. On the first day of spring, you need to _____ your clock one hour ahead.

4. If you call a wrong number, check in the phone book and then _____.

Using the Word Bank

| realign | yield | coalition | devastating |
| superimposed | perpetual | dispelled | evading |

B. DIRECTIONS: Write the Word Bank Word that best matches each clue.

1. Nations or neighbors might form this. _____

2. It's what the losers in a battle do. _____

3. This might describe one picture covering another in a collage. _____

4. It describes a motion that never stops. _____

5. It might describe an earthquake or tornado. _____

6. You may need to do this to car wheels. _____

7. It's what you're doing when you hide. _____

8. It might describe the fog after a wind blows. _____

Recognizing Antonyms

C. DIRECTIONS: Circle the letter of the word or phrase that is most *opposite* in meaning to the word in CAPITAL LETTERS.

1. YIELD   a. attack   b. grow   c. ask   d. answer

2. DEVASTATING   a. confusing   b. appearing   c. harmful   d. helpful

3. PERPETUAL   a. permanent   b. temporary   c. strong   d. wide

"Justin Lebo" by Phillip Hoose
"The Rider" by Naomi Shihab Nye
"Amigo Brothers" by Piri Thomas
"The Walk" by Thomas Hardy

Build Spelling Skills: Use No Hyphen After the Prefix *re-*

Spelling Strategy   In most cases, do not use a hyphen when adding the prefix *re-* to a word.

Right: realign   **Wrong:** re-align
Example: re- + cook = *recook*

Use a hyphen after the prefix *re-* only when your new word might be confused with another word having the same spelling.

Example: re- + creation = *re-creation* (meaning "the remaking," not to be confused with the word *recreation*, meaning "play" or "fun")

A. Practice: Add the prefix *re-* to each word below. Then use the new word in a sentence to reflect its meaning.

1. examine _____

2. read _____

3. sharpen _____

4. subscribe_____

5. sent _____

B. Practice: In each sentence, find the word (or words) with the prefix *re-*. If the word is spelled wrong, cross it out and write it correctly.

1. Justin Lebo is able to repair and recycle the parts of old bicycles to make new ones.

2. Justin reviews the situation and re-considers how many bikes to build after seeing how many children want them.

3. The narrator in "The Rider" re-thinks the idea of roller-skating as it relates to bicycling.

4. Felix and Antonio are unable to relax as they plan and re-plan their big fight.

5. The two men resume and re-strengthen their friendship after their boxing bout.

6. In "The Walk," the narrator recalls how he used to walk with his friend, re-playing the scene in his mind.

Challenge: Without a hyphen, the word *resent* means "to feel bitter about." But with a hyphen, *re-sent* means "sent again." Use the clues below to guess the word pairs.

1. Without a hyphen, this word means "to take away." With a hyphen, it means "to move again." What are the two words? _____   _____

2. Without a hyphen, this word means "to decide." With a hyphen, it means "to solve again." What are the two words? _____   _____

Selection Support   **97**

Unit 4: Resolving Conflicts

"**Justin Lebo**" by Phillip Hoose
"**The Rider**" by Naomi Shihab Nye
"**Amigo Brothers**" by Piri Thomas
"**The Walk**" by Thomas Hardy

Build Grammar Skills: Coordinating Conjunctions

A **coordinating conjunction** is a word that connects words, phrases, or entire sentences. Coordinating conjunctions include *and*, *but*, *for*, *nor*, *or*, *so*, and *yet*.

Connecting two words: Boys <u>and</u> girls rode Justin's bikes.
Connecting two phrases: You can skate either on the driveway <u>or</u> in the street.
Connecting two sentences: The boys boxed each other, <u>yet</u> they remained friends.

A. Practice: Circle the coordinating conjunction in each sentence. Underline the two words, phrases, or sentences connected by the conjunction.

1. Mr. Lebo and Justin worked on the boy's two racing bikes after every race.

2. Justin made some bicycles, but more people wanted them.

3. Justin needed help, so a neighbor wrote a letter to the newspaper.

4. Justin got great results, for many people saw the letter.

5. When you bicycle, you don't feel loneliness or pain.

6. Antonio and Felix were close friends who didn't talk much about the fight.

7. Each boy boxed hard and exercised daily to prepare for the bout.

8. The friends fought each other and left the ring together.

9. They stayed friends, for they knew what was really important.

10. The man did not walk or speak with his friend on his way to the tree.

B. Writing Application: Imagine you are a character in one of the selections you read. Write sentences that describe your experiences or express your thoughts. In each sentence, use the coordinating conjunction in the way that is described.

1. Join two nouns with the conjunction *and*. _____

_____

2. Join two verbs with the conjunction *or*. _____

_____

3. Join two sentences with the conjunction *but*. _____

_____

4. Join two phrases with the conjunction *or*. _____

_____

5. Join two sentences with the conjunction *yet*. _____

_____

"Justin Lebo" by Phillip Hoose
"The Rider" by Naomi Shihab Nye
"Amigo Brothers" by Piri Thomas
"The Walk" by Thomas Hardy

Reading Strategy: Make Inferences

When you **make an inference** in a story, you make a guess about a character, event, or situation. You supply information that the author did not state directly in the selection. However, inference is not created out of thin air. It is based on details supplied by the author and those supplied by you from your knowledge of the world.

For example, in "Justin Lebo" you learn that a neighbor writes a letter to the newspaper. The next day, a hundred people call to help Justin. From these details, you can infer that many people in Justin's town read the newspaper.

DIRECTIONS: Use graphic organizers such as those below to record inferences that you make in each of the selections. List at least one detail that each inference is based on.

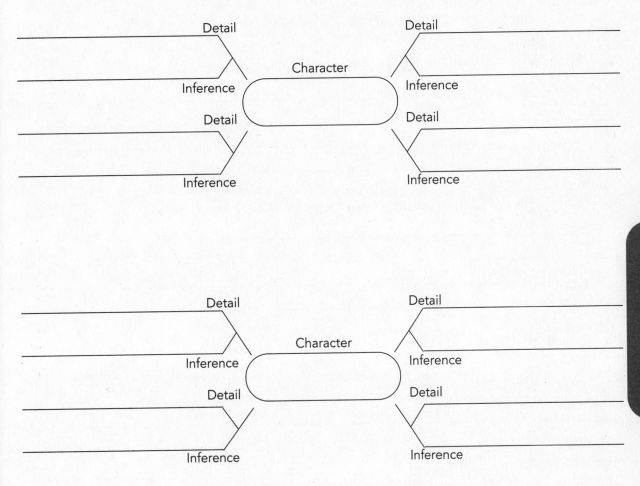

Unit 4: Resolving Conflicts

"Justin Lebo" by Phillip Hoose
"The Rider" by Naomi Shihab Nye
"Amigo Brothers" by Piri Thomas
"The Walk" by Thomas Hardy

Literary Analysis: Third-Person Point of View

Point of view in a story refers to the person who is telling you about the characters and events. Most stories are told from a **third-person point of view**, which means the narrator is someone outside the story, not a character who takes part in the events. Both "Justin Lebo" and "Amigo Brothers" are told from a third-person point of view. On the other hand, "The Rider" and "The Walk" are *not* narrated in third person but rather by a person taking a direct part in the action.

The advantage of having a story told in third person is that the narrator can tell you what each character thinks, feels, and does. When the narrator is a character in the story, you learn only what that one character tells you and see everything from only that character's view.

DIRECTIONS: On the lines below, record important details from "Justin Lebo" and "Amigo Brothers" that only a third-person narrator could provide. Then describe how "The Rider" and "The Walk" might be different if they were told from third-person point of view.

"Justin Lebo"
Important details only a third-person point of view could provide:

_____

_____

_____

_____

"Amigo Brothers"
Important details only a third-person point of view could provide:

_____

_____

_____

_____

"The Rider"
How it might be different told from a third-person point of view:

_____

_____

_____

_____

"The Walk"
How it might be different told from a third-person point of view:

_____

_____

_____

_____

"**Our Finest Hour**" by Charles Osgood

Build Vocabulary

Using the Suffix -*ment*

The suffix -*ment* means "a state or condition of." By adding the suffix -*ment* to a verb, you create a noun: *excite* + -*ment* = *excitement* ("a state of being excited").

A. DIRECTIONS: Add -*ment* to the following verbs, and complete the sentences below.

enjoy   amaze   punish   equip   ship

1. The criminal received a _____ of three years in prison.

2. The _____ of goods was delivered to the store by truck.

3. To everyone's _____, it didn't rain the entire year.

4. Skilled workers know how to use each piece of _____.

5. I get a great deal of _____ from listening to music.

Now write an original sentence using each word below.

6. (appointment) _____

7. (improvement) _____

8. (movement) _____

Using the Word Bank

correspondent	bewilderment

B. DIRECTIONS: Write the Word Bank word that best completes each sentence.

1. The _____ checked all facts before reporting the story.

2. The gifted magician left the audience in a state of _____.

Analogies

C. DIRECTIONS: For each related pair of words in CAPITAL LETTERS, choose the pair that best expresses a *similar* relationship. Circle the letter of your choice.

1. CORRESPONDENT : NEWS ::
   a. storm : weather
   b. writer : pencil
   c. athlete : sport
   d. doctor : nurse

2. CONFUSED : BEWILDERMENT ::
   a. pleased : enjoyment
   b. laugh : cry
   c. sing : statement
   d. appointment : office

Unit 5: Just for Fun

"Our Finest Hour" by Charles Osgood

Build Spelling Skills: Words With a Double *r*

Spelling Strategy   The Word Bank word *correspondent* contains a double *r*. There are many other words in English in which the *r* sound is also spelled with a double *r*.

Examples: correction   interrupt   furry   irregular

A. Practice: Write the word with a double *r* that matches each set of clues.

1. This word rhymes with *bearable*, starts with a *t*, and means "awful." The word is
   _____.

2. You do this when you take something with the intention of giving it back. It starts with a *b*. The word is _____.

3. This is a compound word. It names something round that is often seen on someone's ear. The word is _____.

4. This word describes the kind of movie that contains monsters or ghosts. It starts with an *h*. The word is _____.

5. This word names the ceremony that joins a man and a woman as husband and wife. It starts with an *m*. The word is _____.

B. Practice: In each sentence below, find a misspelled word that is supposed to have a double *r*. Cross out the word and write it correctly. The first one is done for you.

1. Charles Osgood described a broadcast that turned out to be ~~terible~~. **terrible**

2. Osgood was working at the time as a corespondent for CBS News.

3. One night, he stared on the evening news as the substitute anchor.

4. A number of technical erors were made that night during the broadcast.

5. These occurences happened because many of the crew were substitutes.

6. The broadcast was a horible experience for the entire crew.

7. One mistake after another kept interupting the flow of the show.

8. The crew didn't know how to corect any of the mistakes.

9. Osgood was embarassed because visitors from China were in the studio.

10. Osgood now views the experience more with humor than with sorow.

Challenge: The Word Bank word *correspondent* has the smaller word *den* within it, although the two words are not related. How many other smaller words can you find in *correspondent*? See if you can find five, then write them down.

_____   _____   _____   _____   _____

"Our Finest Hour" by Charles Osgood

Build Grammar Skills: Subjects and Predicates

The simple sentence is the most common type of sentence. Simple sentences can vary in length, but they must contain a subject and a predicate, and they must express a complete thought.

The **subject** part of a sentence tells who or what the sentence is about. The **simple subject** is the noun or pronoun in the subject part that answers the questions *who?* or *what?*

simple subject

Example: Many (people) in the news room made embarrassing mistakes.

└── subject ──────────┘

The **predicate** of a sentence tells something about the subject. The **simple predicate** is the verb in the predicate part that tells what the subject does.

simple predicate

Example: Many people in the news room (made) embarrassing mistakes.

└── predicate ──────┘

A. Practice: In each sentence, underline the subject once and the predicate twice. Then circle the simple subject and the simple predicate. The first one is done for you.

1. The news (correspondent) (substituted) for the absent anchor.

2. The first report of the night appeared on the monitor.

3. It was the wrong story by a different reporter.

4. A second mistake occurred right after the first.

5. Charles Osgood felt bad about all the technical errors.

6. The confused president of the network visited Osgood at his desk.

B. Writing Application: Imagine you were Charles Osgood during the error-filled broadcast. Write sentences that tell what happened. Use each simple sentence and simple predicate listed below. Add more words to make a complete subject and complete predicate.

1. broadcast, began

_____

2. reporter, announced

_____

3. crew, worked

_____

4. story, described

_____

5. visitors, watched

_____

"**Our Finest Hour**" by Charles Osgood

Reading Strategy: Recognizing Author's Purpose

Authors generally write to achieve a purpose, such as the following:

- to entertain
- to inform
- to call readers to action
- to reflect on experiences

Notice the author's choice of words and the details he or she includes. These clues will help you **recognize the author's purpose**.

DIRECTIONS: A piece of writing may have more than one purpose. Use the chart to identify the author's purpose in each passage from "Our Finest Hour." Then, select two other passages from the essay and identify the author's purpose in each.

Passage	Author's Purpose
1. Anchoring, you understand, means sitting there in the studio and telling some stories into the camera and introducing the reports and pieces that other reporters do. It looks easy enough. It is easy enough, most of the time . . .	
2. It was back when I was relatively new at CBS News. I'd been in the business a while, but only recently had moved over to CBS News. I was old, but I was new.	
3. In the "fishbowl," the glassed-in office where the executive producer sits, there were at least three people yelling into telephones.	
4. I could hear him perfectly clearly, and so could half of America.	
5.	
6.	

"Our Finest Hour" by Charles Osgood

Literary Analysis: Humor

Humor is often based on the unexpected. For example, in "Our Finest Hour," Charles Osgood details all the unexpected things that go wrong the night he substitutes as anchor on a live news broadcast. One of the reasons the description is humorous is that you begin to read the selection not expecting anything to go wrong. The fact that so many things go wrong—the unexpected—ultimately makes you laugh at the situation along with Osgood.

DIRECTIONS: Complete the following chart with examples of humor from "Our Finest Hour." For each example you give, explain why it is humorous. One example is provided.

Example of Humor	Why It Is Funny
The regular news anchor, executive producer, cameraman, editor, and director all are on vacation.	You don't expect so many people who work on a live television broadcast to be away at the same time.

"Cat on the Go" by James Herriot

Build Vocabulary

Using the Prefix *in-*

You can create the opposite of some adjectives by placing the prefix *in-*, meaning "not," before the word. For example, the prefix *in-* before the word *sincere* forms its antonym, *insincere.*

A. DIRECTIONS: Turn the underlined word into its opposite by adding the prefix *in-*.

1. One medicine was <u>effective</u>, but the other one proved to be _____.

2. One's behavior should always be <u>appropriate</u>, never _____.

3. The judge considered some evidence <u>admissible</u> and other evidence _____.

4. Tomorrow it will be <u>convenient</u> for me to help you; today it is _____.

Using the Word Bank

grotesquely	emaciated	inevitable	sauntered
distraught	despondent	intrigued	surreptitiously

B. DIRECTIONS: Write the Word Bank word that matches each meaning below.

1. extremely upset _____

2. extremely thin _____

3. fascinated _____

4. in a strange way _____

5. in a sly or secret way _____

6. certain to happen _____

7. lacking hope; depressed _____

8. strolled _____

Recognizing Antonyms

C. DIRECTIONS: Choose the word that is most *opposite* in meaning to the word in CAPITAL LETTERS. Fill in the letter of your choice.

____ 1. EMACIATED: a. thin   b. smart   c. fat   d. slow

____ 2. DESPONDENT: a. confident   b. writing   c. sad   d. confused

____ 3. DISTRAUGHT: a. missing   b. discovered   c. shallow   d. peaceful

____ 4. INTRIGUED: a. trapped   b. bored   c. alert   d. away

____ 5. INEVITABLE: a. avoidable   b. eatable   c. washable   d. likable

"**Cat on the Go**" by James Herriot

Build Spelling Skills: Silent *gh*

Spelling Strategy   Many words in English, such as the Word Bank word *distraught*, contain a silent *gh*. You must learn these words as you come across them.

Examples: night   thought   through

A. Practice: Write a word with a silent *gh* that matches each clue.

1. It's the opposite of *wrong.* _____

2. It's the number after *seven.* _____

3. It's the opposite of *sold.* _____

4. It's the opposite of *threw.* _____

5. It's what the teacher did. _____

6. It's the opposite of *crooked.* _____

7. It's what a scale tells you. _____

8. It's the opposite of *low.* _____

9. It's the opposite of *heavy.* _____

10. It's the time when you see the stars. _____

B. Practice: In each sentence below, find a misspelled word that is supposed to have a silent *gh*. Cross out the word and write it correctly. The first one is done for you.

brought

1. Tristan was interested in the stray cat that was ~~brout~~ in one night.

2. The cat looked as if it had been in a terrible fite.

3. The veterinarian gave a deep si and began to work on the cat.

4. Tristan thot that the cat might have a chance to be saved.

5. The cat Oscar managed to live throo the night and beyond.

6. The Herriots cared for Oscar and discovered how brite he was.

7. The cat would go out at night but would return strait home after visiting.

8. Oscar brought the Herriots a great deal of pleasure and delit.

Challenge: The Word Bank word *inevitable* has the smaller word *table* within it, although the two words are not related in meaning. What other small words can you find in the word *inevitable*? If you look hard, it is inevitable that you will find five more. Write them down.

_____   _____   _____   _____   _____

"Cat on the Go" by James Herriot

Build Grammar Skills: Compound Subjects and Predicates

A **compound subject** is two or more simple subjects that have the same verb.

compound subject

Example: The veterinarian and his assistant worked on the cat.

A **compound predicate** is two or more verbs that have the same subject.

compound predicate

Example: The cat roamed the neighborhood and returned later.

A. Practice: Read the sentences. Underline compound subjects once. Underline compound predicates twice.

1. A neighborhood girl and a stray cat appeared at the doctor's door.

2. The veterinarian washed the cat and stitched its torn body.

3. James and Helen kept the cat as a pet in their own home.

4. The cat left the house at night and visited other places in town.

5. Friends and neighbors told the Herriots about the cat.

6. The Herriots laughed at the stories and enjoyed their new pet.

7. A stranger arrived after a while and reclaimed his lost cat.

8. The doctor and his wife missed the cat and visited it later.

B. Writing Application: Imagine you are Oscar the cat. Write sentences that describe your adventures around town. Use the following compound subjects and compound predicates in your sentences.

1. men, women

_____

2. sat, listened

_____

3. ate, drank

_____

4. adults, children

_____

5. snooped, crept

_____

"Cat on the Go" by James Herriot

Reading Strategy: Interpreting Idioms

Writers often add authenticity and flavor to their work by including idioms. An **idiom** is an expression with a unique meaning that differs from what the specific words literally mean. For instance, to say that the test was "easy as pie" is an idiom that means that the test was extremely easy. Idioms from a place or time other than your own may be unfamiliar to you. When you encounter an unfamiliar idiom, use context clues to determine its meaning.

DIRECTIONS: The chart below contains several idioms that appear in "Cat on the Go." In the second column, write an interpretation of the idiom. Then, in the last row, enter another idiom from the story and interpret its meaning.

Idiom	Its Meaning
1. You'll be going *to put him out of his misery.*	
2. All things were possible with cats because some people seemed to *regard them as fair game* for any cruelty.	
3. He's *a skeleton.*	
4. He *had a soft spot* for cats.	
5. I had a nasty feeling of *sweeping undesirable things under the carpet.*	
6. *Right bonny* 'e was.	
7.	

Name _____ Date _____

"Cat on the Go" by James Herriot

Literary Analysis: Character Traits

Character traits are the qualities found in a story character, whether a human being or an animal. You discover a character's traits in many ways. Often you discover the traits through things the character says, does, or thinks. Sometimes you discover them through things the narrator tells you about the character. In "Cat on the Go," James Herriot works very hard to help Oscar when the cat is brought to him. His actions reveal that he is caring, dedicated, and compassionate.

DIRECTIONS: For each main character, fill out a graphic organizer like the one below. In each circle, write an adjective that describes the character.

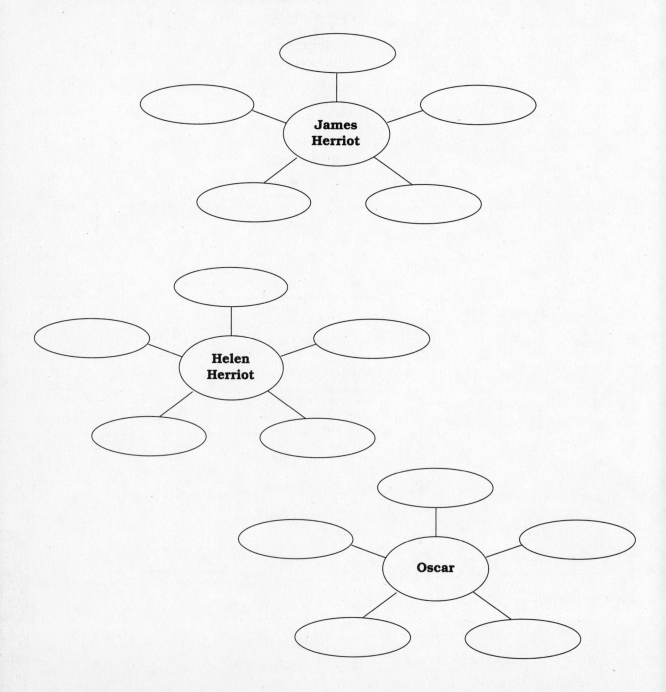

"The Luckiest Time of All" by Lucille Clifton
"Father William" by Lewis Carroll
"The Microscope" by Maxine Kumin
"in Just-" by E. E. Cummings
"Sarah Cynthia Sylvia Stout Would Not Take the Garbage Out" by Shel Silverstein

Build Vocabulary

Using Words with Multiple Meanings

Many words in English have more than one meaning. For example, the word *rose* may be a noun that refers to a kind of flower, or it may a verb that means "went up." You can tell which meaning of the word is intended by understanding how the word is used in a sentence.

A. DIRECTIONS: Circle the letter of the correct meaning for the word in italics. Then write an original sentence with each word, using the definition you did *not* choose.

1. The canoe was swept away by the river's *current.*

   a. most recent; up-to-date   b. a flow of water

2. The *patient* was rushed to the hospital.

   a. one under a doctor's care   b. able to endure calmly

3. (current)_____

4. (patient) _____

Using the Word Bank

incessantly	sage	supple	withered	curdled	rancid

B. DIRECTIONS: Write the Word Bank word that can replace the italicized group of words.

1. Many people came to the *very wise man* for advice. _____

2. The milk *thickened and clotted* as it turned into yogurt. _____

3. The noise went on *without stopping* for several hours. _____

4. We had to throw out the *spoiled and bad-smelling* butter. _____

5. Without water, the flower *dried up* and eventually died. _____

6. The gymnast had a *flexible* body that could bend quickly and easily. _____

Recognizing Antonyms

C. DIRECTIONS: Circle the letter of the word or phrase that is most opposite in meaning to the word in CAPITAL LETTERS.

1. SUPPLE: a. unbearable   b. unbendable   c. unteachable   d. understandable

2. CURDLED: a. cried   b. gave comfort   c. thickened   d. thinned

3. RANCID: a. fresh   b. costly   c. free   d. smooth

"The Luckiest Time of All" by Lucille Clifton
"Father William" by Lewis Carroll
"The Microscope" by Maxine Kumin
"in Just-" by E. E. Cummings
"Sarah Cynthia Sylvia Stout Would Not Take the Garbage Out" by Shel Silverstein

Build Spelling Skills: Words With -cess-

Spelling Strategy   The sound *ses* is sometimes spelled *cess*, as in the Word Bank word *incessantly*. This spelling is usually associated with the root *-cess-*, which means "to go" or "to yield." **Examples:** inter<u>cess</u>ion; ne<u>cess</u>ary

A. Practice: Fill in the missing *cess* in each word. Write the entire word and its meaning. Use a dictionary for help.

1. pro____ ____ ____ ____ ion _____

   Meaning: _____

2. ____ ____ ____ ____ ation _____

   Meaning: _____

3. se____ ____ ____ ____ ion _____

   Meaning: _____

4. ne____ ____ ____ ____ ity _____

   Meaning: _____

B. Practice: Complete each sentence by adding the root *-cess-* to the prefix in parentheses.

1. In "The Luckiest Time of All," Grandmama describes her (suc) _____

   in meeting the man that eventually became her husband.

2. In "The Microscope," the narrator describes the long and hard (pro) _____

   that Leeuwenhoek went through in order to invent the microscope.

3. In "Father William," the young man asks questions to such (ex) _____

   that his father ultimately becomes annoyed by them.

4. In "in Just-" the children play, as if they were enjoying a school (re) _____.

5. In "Sarah Cynthia Sylvia Stout Would Not Take the Garbage Out," the garbage piles up so

   much that the girl eventually loses (ac)_____ to her own house.

Challenge: The Word Bank word *supple* begins with the letters *supp*. How many more words can you think of that begin with those same letters? (*Supply* is one.) Write them on the lines.

_____   _____   _____

_____   _____

Name _____ Date _____

Build Grammar Skills: Complete and Incomplete Sentences

A **complete sentence** contains both a subject and predicate and expresses a complete thought.

> **Examples:** The great-grandmother told an interesting story. Tee listened.

An **incomplete sentence** does not contain both a subject and predicate and does not express a complete thought.

> **Examples:** The curious boy. (missing a predicate)
> Invented the microscope. (missing a subject)

A. Practice: Write whether each sentence is **complete** or **incomplete.** If it is complete, underline the subject part once and the predicate part twice.

_____ 1. Rocked slowly on her porch.

_____ 2. Grandmama met her husband-to-be.

_____ 3. Father William laughed.

_____ 4. Many annoying questions.

_____ 5. Scorned the Dutch inventor.

_____ 6. His work paid off.

_____ 7. The balloonman whistles.

_____ 8. Dancing in the spring.

_____ 9. Would not take the garbage out.

_____ 10. The garbage piled up.

B. Writing Application: Rewrite each of the following incomplete sentences so that they become complete. You will have to add either a subject or a predicate.

1. Threw a stone at the dog. _____

2. The rude son. _____

3. Looked through the lens. _____

4. The lame balloonman. _____

5. Stank up the whole neighborhood. _____

Unit 5: Just for Fun

"The Luckiest Time of All" by Lucille Clifton
"Father William" by Lewis Carroll
"The Microscope" by Maxine Kumin
"in Just-" by E. E. Cummings
"Sarah Cynthia Sylvia Stout Would Not Take the Garbage Out" by Shel Silverstein

Reading Strategy: Clarifying Word Meanings

When you read, you often encounter unfamiliar words, or words used in uncommon ways. There are several strategies you can use to help you **clarify word meanings,** or explain their usage in a particular work of literature:

- Use context clues to determine meaning.
- Rephrase passages to uncover the meaning.
- Reorder words in poetry to make their meaning easier to grasp.
- Consult a dictionary for words whose meanings you cannot determine in any other way.

DIRECTIONS: The chart below contains words from these selections that you might find unfamiliar. Use one of the suggested strategies to clarify the meaning of each word in italics. Then, in the second column, write the meaning in your own words. Finally, add to the chart another unfamiliar word and use one of the strategies to determine its meaning.

Word	Meaning
. . . we *plaited* our hair . . .	
He had a length of *twine* in his hand . . .	
By the use of this *ointment* . . .	
He sold *pincushions*, cloth, and such.	
She'd *scour* the pots . . .	
Gristly bits of beefy roasts . . .	

"The Luckiest Time of All" by Lucille Clifton
"Father William" by Lewis Carroll
"The Microscope" by Maxine Kumin
"in Just-" by E. E. Cummings
"Sarah Cynthia Sylvia Stout Would Not Take the Garbage Out" by Shel Silverstein

Literary Analysis: Hyperbole

Hyperbole is exaggeration for effect. A good example of hyperbole is a parent saying to a child, "I've told you a thousand times not to do that!" The number one thousand, of course, is an exaggeration, but it is spoken for effect.

At times, writers use hyperbole either to make something sound funny or to emphasize a point. For example, in "The Luckiest Time of All" when Grandmama describes Mr. Pickens as "the finest fast runnin hero in the bottoms of Virginia," she is using hyperbole to make her point clear: Mr. Pickens was a very fast runner.

DIRECTIONS: Use the chart below to record examples of hyperbole in each of the selections.

Selection	Examples of Hyperbole
1. "The Luckiest Time of All"	
2. "Father William"	
3. "The Microscope"	
4. "in Just-"	
5. "Sarah Cynthia Sylvia Stout . . . "	

Unit 5: Just for Fun

"Zoo" by Edward D. Hoch
"The Hippopotamus" by Ogden Nash
"How the Snake Got Poison" by Zora Neale Hurston

Build Vocabulary

Using Forms of *wonder*

The words *wonderful, wondrous, wonderland, wonderstruck, wonderment,* and *wonderworker* are related to wonder. All concern the idea of surprise and amazement.

A. DIRECTIONS: Match each word on the left with its definition on the right.

____ 1. wondrous   a. struck with wonder or surprise

____ 2. wonderland   b. a person who performs miracles or wonders

____ 3. wonderstruck   c. wonder or amazement

____ 4. wonderment   d. an imaginary place full of wonders

____ 5. wonderworker   e. full of wonder

Using the Word Bank

interplanetary	awe	immensity	wonderment

B. DIRECTIONS: Write the Word Bank word that best completes each sentence below.

1. The cabinet was of such _____ that it didn't fit through the door.

2. The space shuttle began its _____ trip from Earth to Mars.

3. The citizens felt very much in _____ of their powerful king.

4. The confusing series of strange events left the whole town in _____.

C. DIRECTIONS: Circle the letter of the word or phrase that is most similar in meaning to the word in CAPITAL LETTERS.

1. INTERPLANETARY
   a. above planets   b. below planets   c. before planets   d. between planets

2. IMMENSITY
   a. smallness   b. largeness   c. brightness   d. darkness

3. AWE
   a. fear and wonder   b. courage   c. curiosity   d. death and destruction

"**Zoo**" by Edward D. Hoch
"**The Hippopotamus**" by Ogden Nash
"**How the Snake Got Poison**" by Zora Neale Hurston

Build Spelling Skills: Add -ity to Nouns Ending in e

Spelling Strategy   When adding the suffix -ity to a word that ends in e, drop the final e. The Word Bank word immensity is formed by adding the suffix -ity to the word immense. Notice that the final e in immense is dropped when -ity is added.

Other examples: commune + ity = community   dense + ity = density

A. Practice: Change each word below to a noun with the suffix -ity. Write your new word in the puzzle.

1. universe

2. insane

3. pure

4. intense

5. obese

6. cave

B. Practice: Complete each sentence below by changing the word in parentheses to a noun that ends in -ity. Write your new word on the line.

1. The twist at the end of "Zoo" shows the author's (creative) _____.

2. "Zoo" teaches us that the (sensible) _____ of our beliefs is dependent upon our point of view.

3. In "Hippopotamus," the speaker contemplates the (immense) _____ of the animal.

4. In "How the Snake Got Poison," the poisonous snake gets a rattle after other animals complain about the (grave) _____ of their situation.

Challenge: The Word Bank word *awe* is a three-letter word that starts and ends with a vowel. How many other three-letter words can you think of that start and end with a vowel? Make a list, and then compare it with the lists of your classmates.

_____   _____   _____   _____   _____

"Zoo" by Edward D. Hoch

"The Hippopotamus" by Ogden Nash

"How the Snake Got Poison" by Zora Neale Hurston

Build Grammar Skills: Direct and Indirect Objects

A **direct object** is a noun or pronoun that receives the action of a verb. It answers the question *whom* or *what* after the verb.

direct object

Examples: The visitors paid a <u>dollar</u>. (paid *what?*)

direct object

The citizens greeted <u>Professor Hugo</u>. (greeted *whom?*)

A sentence with a direct object may also contain an indirect object. An **indirect object** names the person or thing that something is given to or is done for. It answers the question *To or for whom?* or *To or for what?* Often the word *to* is understood, as in the first example below.

indirect object   direct object

Examples: The visitors paid [to] the <u>Professor</u> a *dollar*. (*to whom* paid *what?*)

direct object   indirect object

They paid the *money* to <u>him</u>. (paid *what to whom?*)

A. Practice: Read the sentences. Underline each direct object. Draw a circle around each indirect object.

1. Thousands of people saw the strange animals.

2. The animals told their parents the story.

3. People offer the hippopotamus funny looks.

4. Few works of literature mention the hippopotamus.

5. In the folk tale, God created the wily snake.

6. The varmints climb the ladder to talk with God.

7. The snake receives poison.

8. God also gives the snake a rattle.

B. Writing Application: Write sentences using the nouns below as indicated.

1. Use *zoo* as a direct object. _____

2. Use *hippopotamus* as an indirect object. _____

3. Use *poison* as a direct object. _____

4. Use *snake* as a direct object. _____

"Zoo" by Edward D. Hoch
"The Hippopotamus" by Ogden Nash
"How the Snake Got Poison" by Zora Neale Hurston

Reading Strategy: Evaluate an Author's Message

Most writing, whether serious or humorous, contains some sort of message. Once you've read a selection, it's important that you **evaluate the author's message.** Begin by asking yourself, What observation is the writer making about the people or the subject in the writing? Then ask yourself, What do I think of the author's message? Has the writer supported it well with specific details? Do I agree or disagree with the message? Why?

For example, in "Zoo," the author's message is that, like people on Earth, people from other worlds are afraid of the unknown. You may or may not agree with the message, based on how persuasively the details that support this message are presented.

DIRECTIONS: Use the chart below to evaluate the author's message in each selection. State the message, give details to show how it is supported, and tell if you agree or disagree with it.

Selection	Author's Message	Supporting Details	Agree/Disagree
1. "Zoo"			
2. "The Hippopotamus"			
3. "How the Snake Got Poison"			

Name _____ Date _____

Literary Analysis: Character's Point of View

In a story, a **character's point of view** is the position from which that character views and judges an event. Point of view makes the character interpret the event a certain way, which may be different from the way other characters interpret it. The character may then take action, based on his or her special viewpoint.

DIRECTIONS: Use the diagram below to record examples of characters' points of view in the selections. For each example, first tell whose point of view it is. Then describe that character's understanding of events, and list the actions the character takes as a result.

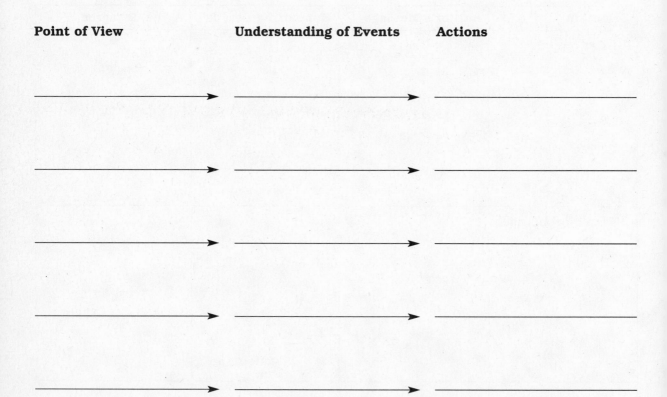

Point of View   **Understanding of Events**   **Actions**

"After Twenty Years" by O. Henry

Build Vocabulary

Using the Word Root -spec-

A. DIRECTIONS: The word root -spec- means "see" or "look." It is used in the Word Bank word *spectators*, which means "people who watch an event without taking part in it." Apply what you know about -spec- and use context clues to match the underlined word to its definition.

____ 1. The fireworks were <u>spectacular</u>.

____ 2. The soldier got ready for the <u>inspection</u> by polishing his boots.

____ 3. Maureen showed <u>respect</u> by calling her boss "Sir."

____ 4. The police questioned the <u>suspect</u>.

____ 5. Would you care to <u>speculate</u> about the future of the company?

a. high regard

b. striking to the eye

c. one seen as possibly being guilty

d. make a prediction based on what one has seen or observed

e. the act of viewing closing or looking over

Using the Word Bank

spectators	intricate	destiny	dismally	absurdity	simultaneously

B. DIRECTIONS: Read each clue. Then write the correct word on the puzzle. When complete, the shaded boxes will spell a word related to the story.

Clues

1. watchers
2. miserably
3. detailed
4. at the same time
5. nonsense
6. fate

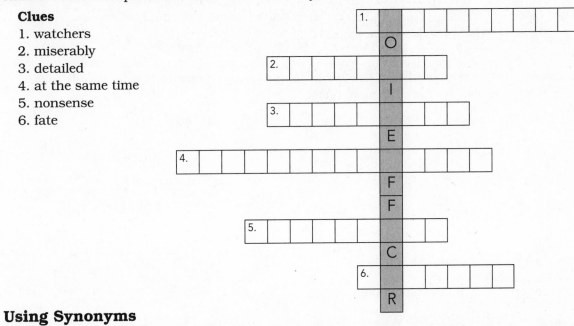

Using Synonyms

C. DIRECTIONS: Circle the letter of the word most similar in meaning to the word in CAPITAL LETTERS.

1. ABSURDITY
   a. beauty
   b. ugliness
   c. meaning
   d. nonsense

2. INTRICATE
   a. tiny
   b. complicated
   c. simple
   d. intelligent

3. DISMALLY
   a. daily
   b. cheerfully
   c. gloomily
   d. partly

"After Twenty Years" by O. Henry

Build Spelling Skills: *-er* and *-or*

Spelling Strategy   The ending *-er* or *-or* can be added to some verbs to form a noun meaning "one who." Usually, use the *-or* ending for verbs that end in *-ate, ct,* or *-ess*. Otherwise, use the *-er* ending.

Examples: spectate + -or = spectator   garden + -er = gardener

Notice that if the verb ends in *ate*, drop the final *e* before adding *or*.

A. Practice: Add *-er* or *-or* to each of the following words. Cross out any silent *e's* that have to be dropped. Then use the words to complete the sentences that follow.

act_____, one who acts

instruct_____, one who instructs

manage_____, one who manages

operate_____, one who operates

write_____, one who writes

1. The _____ finished the story and sent it to the publisher today.

2. The _____ helped the caller with the long-distance connection.

3. The _____ needed for this role must be about thirty years old.

4. The office _____ is very strict about the length of breaks.

5. The driving _____ showed the students how to start the engine.

B. Practice: Add *-er* or *-or* to each of the following words, and then use the new words to complete the sentences below. Use each word once.

read   edit   prison   embezzle   tell   travel   contribute

1. After a series of odd jobs, O. Henry worked as a bank _____ in Texas.

2. It was there that he was accused of being an _____.

3. He fled to Central America, not as a _____ but as a fugitive.

4. After giving himself up, he spent thirty-nine months as a _____ in Ohio.

5. While in prison, he became a frequent _____ of stories to magazines.

6. His stories made an impression on _____ and _____ alike.

Challenge: The following words, which are synonyms of the Word Bank word *destiny*, are probably unfamiliar to you. Look up the origin of each word in a dictionary that gives word origins. Write the origin of the word on the line.

1. kismet _____

2. karma _____

"After Twenty Years" by O. Henry

Build Grammar Skills: Clauses

A **clause** is a group of words that has a subject and a verb. An **independent clause,** or **main clause,** is one that makes sense when it stands alone. A **subordinate clause,** or **dependent clause,** is one that cannot stand alone. A subordinate clause is usually introduced by a **subordinating conjunction.** These are some common subordinating conjunctions: *although, as, as long as, because, before, if, since, so that, that, unless, when, whenever, wherever, while*

Sentence: As the policeman walked up to him, the man spoke up quickly.
Independent clause: the man spoke up quickly
Subordinate clause: As the policeman walked up to him

A. Practice: For each sentence, write the independent clause in the first box and write the subordinate clause in the second box. Then underline each subject once, underline each verb twice, and draw a circle around the subordinating conjunction.

Sentence	Independent Clause	Subordinate Clause
1. Haven't you heard from your friend since you left?		
2. Jimmy will meet me here if he's alive.		
3. It was exactly ten o'clock when we parted at the restaurant door.		
4. When they came into the glare, each turned to gaze at the other's face.		

B. Writing Application: Use each of these clauses in a sentence about "After Twenty Years." If the clause is independent, add a subordinate clause. If the clause is subordinate, add an independent clause.

1. the policemen twirled his club _____

_____

2. that we would meet here in twenty years _____

_____

3. if Jimmy is still alive _____

_____

4. the police in Chicago sent a message _____

_____

"**After Twenty Years**" by O. Henry

Reading Strategy: Breaking Down Sentences

O. Henry wrote at a time when long, complex sentences were more common. As you read this story, you will better understand it if you get in the habit of **breaking down sentences** to grasp their meaning. Here are some useful approaches:

- Don't read a long sentence word by word. Look for groups of meaningful words. Use punctuation clues, such as commas or brackets, to find manageable sections.

- Find the subject—the person, place or object that is the focus of the sentence. Also, find key words about the subject.

- Find the verb—what the subject is doing or feeling. Look for key words about the action.

Be aware that the subject and verb may not appear close together, as in this example:

Trying doors as he went, twirling his club with many intricate and artful movements, turning now and then to cast his watchful eye down the pacific thoroughfare, the officer, with his stalwart form and slight swagger, made a fine picture of a guardian of the peace.

Notice that the subject, *the officer*, appears in mid-sentence; the verb *made* appears farther along.

Break Down Sentences: The chart below contains some long sentences from the story. For each one, identify the subject and the verb. Indicate groups of meaningful words that shed more light on the subject and verb.

Long Sentence	Subject	Verb	Meaningful words about the subject and verb
The light showed a pale, square-jawed face with keen eyes, and a little white scar near his right eyebrow.			
The few foot passengers astir in that quarter hurried dismally and silently along with coat collars turned high and pocketed hands.			
And in the door of the hardware store the man who had come a thousand miles to fill an appointment, uncertain almost to absurdity, with the friend of his youth, smoked his cigar and waited.			
The man from the West, his egotism enlarged by success, was beginning to outline the history of his career.			

"After Twenty Years" by O. Henry

Literary Analysis: Surprise Ending

A **surprise ending** in a story is just what it sounds like—something the reader is not quite expecting. In "After Twenty Years," since the story is told through the eyes of an outside observer, the reader does not know what is going on in the mind of the police officer. When Bob finds out who the police officer is, the reader shares his surprise. For a surprise ending to work, it must be believable—meaning that there should be some clues along the way to prepare a careful reader for the surprise.

DIRECTIONS: After you read "After Twenty Years," think back on the details of the characters' actions, appearance, and conversation. Fill in the following chart to compare the two characters. A sample entry has been given.

	Actions	Appearance	Conversation
Police Officer	Tries doors, twirls club, looks down street		
What It Suggests	He takes his job seriously.		
Man in Doorway			
What It Suggests			

"Rikki-tikki-tavi" by Rudyard Kipling

Build Vocabulary

Using the Word Root -viv-

A. DIRECTIONS: The word root -viv- means "life." When used with the prefix re-, which means "again," it forms the Word Bank word revived, "returned to life." Use these defined words to complete the sentences that follow.

> **vivid:** creating clear, lifelike images in the mind
> **survive:** to remain alive
> **vivacious:** full of life; lively
> **vivarium:** an enclosed place for keeping animals and plants for observation

1. To _____ in the wilderness, you'll need proper clothing.

2. Betty's _____ personality kept the party going.

3. Michael has a colorful poison-dart frog in his _____ .

4. Chris gave us a _____ description of his fishing-trip adventure.

Using the Word Bank

revived	draggled	flinched	mourning	consolation	cunningly

B. DIRECTIONS: Match each word in the left column with its definition in the right column. Write the letter of the definition on the line next to the word it defines.

____ 1. consolation a. feeling sorrow for the death of a loved one

____ 2. draggled   b. cleverly

____ 3. flinched   c. something that makes you feel better

____ 4. cunningly   d. wet and dirty

____ 5. mourning   e. brought back to life

____ 6. revived   f. moved back, as if away from a blow

Analogies

C. DIRECTIONS: Each question below consists of a related pair of words in CAPITAL LETTERS, followed by four lettered pairs of words. Circle the letter of the pair that best expresses a relationship similar to that expressed by the pair in capital letters.

1. SORROW : MOURNING
   a. tear : cry
   b. hunger : food
   c. joy : laughter
   d. pain : injury

2. LIFELESS : REVIVED
   a. thirsty : water
   b. food : hungry
   c. sleeping : wakened
   d. lively : quiet

3. FLINCHED : ATTACKED
   a. sang : shouted
   b. strong : weak
   c. retreated : ran
   d. pulled : pushed

Name _____ Date _____

"**Rikki-tikki-tavi**" by Rudyard Kipling

Build Spelling Skills: Homophones

Spelling Strategy The Word Bank word *mourning* and the word *morning* are **homophones,** or words that sound alike but are spelled differently and have different meanings. The spellings of homophones must be memorized.

A. Practice: In each numbered box, write a sentence using one of the homophones in each pair. Use each homophone once.

1. _____	real, reel	2. _____

3. _____	tail, tale	4. _____

5. _____	nose, knows	6. _____

7. _____	piece, peace	8. _____

B. Practice: Use the following homophones to complete each sentence below. Use each word once.

   meet, meat   write, right   one, won   feet, feat

1. _____ day, a summer flood washed a mongoose out of his home.

2. A family brought him _____ into their house to revive him.

3. They fed the mongoose a piece of raw_____.

4. The mongoose watched the man _____ at his desk.

5. Soon the mongoose went to _____ the other animals in the yard.

6. He heard about Nag, a dangerous animal that had no _____.

7. The mongoose later _____ a great victory over the snakes.

8. This was quite a_____ for such a small animal.

Challenge: The name of the mongoose, Rikki-tikki-tavi, comes from the sound he made, "Rikki-tikk-tikki-tikki-tchk." Words that are based on sounds are called **onomatopoeia.** For each of the following sounds, write a word that sounds like it. You may use real words or new words that you make up yourself.

   The sound made by

1. bees in a hive _____   5. a snake _____

2. a duck _____   6. a balloon breaking _____

3. a car backfiring _____   7. burgers on a grill _____

4. a campfire _____   8. a fish falling back in the water _____

"Rikki-tikki-tavi" by Rudyard Kipling

Build Grammar Skills: Simple and Compound Sentences

A **sentence** is a group of words containing a subject and a verb and expressing a complete thought. A **simple sentence** is made up of one independent, or main, clause and no subordinate clauses. A **compound sentence** is made up of two or more independent clauses joined by a coordinating conjunction (*and, or, nor, but, so, for, yet*) or separated by a semicolon (;).

Simple sentence: They gave him a little piece of raw meat.

Compound sentences: Rikki-tikki came to breakfast, **and** they gave him banana and some boiled egg.

His eyes and the end of his restless nose were pink; he could scratch himself anywhere.

When trying to decide if a sentence is a compound sentence, do this: In your mind, cross out the comma and "and" or the semicolon. Then ask yourself if each remaining part can stand on its own and make sense. If the answer is yes, the sentence is a compound sentence.

A. Practice: Write *S* if the sentence is a simple sentence. Write *C* if it is a compound sentence.

1. Rikki-tikki did the real fighting. _____

2. Rikki-tikki went out into the verandah, and he sat in the sunshine. _____

3. He fluffed up his fur; then he felt better. _____

4. He nearly drowned himself in the bathtub. _____

5. He put his nose into the ink on a writing table. _____

6. Teddy's mother and father came in to look at their boy, and Rikki-tikki was awake on the pillow. _____

B. Writing Application: For each character in column 1, write a simple sentence in column 2 and a compound sentence in column 3.

Topic	Simple sentence	Compound sentence
Rikki-tikki		
Teddy		
Nag		

"Rikki-tikki-tavi" by Rudyard Kipling

Reading Strategy: Predict

Do you ever find yourself predicting what will happen when you watch a movie or a TV show? You can do the same thing when you read stories. When you **predict,** you make an educated guess, based on existing evidence, about what will happen. Your predictions will be more accurate if you pay attention to the clues that the author includes.

As you read "Rikki-tikki-tavi," make predictions about what will happen next. Then compare your predictions with what actually happens. Use this chart to help you keep track of your predictions. One example has been given.

Clue	What I Predict Will Happen	What Actually Happened
Teddy's mother says, "Perhaps he isn't really dead."	The mongoose will turn out to be alive.	The mongoose lived and became a good friend to Teddy.

Name _____ Date _____

"Rikki-tikki-tavi" by Rudyard Kipling

Literary Analysis: Plot

The **plot** is the sequence of events in a story. Most plots follow a similar pattern, beginning with the **exposition,** which introduces the characters and the basic situation. Then the central **conflict,** or problem faced by the characters, is presented. In the next stage, the **rising action,** the conflict increases until it comes to a **climax.** After that, the story slows down in the **falling action** until it comes to the **resolution.** This is where the reader learns the outcome of the conflict.

DIRECTIONS: Use this plot diagram to record the main elements of the plot of "Rikki-tikki-tavi."

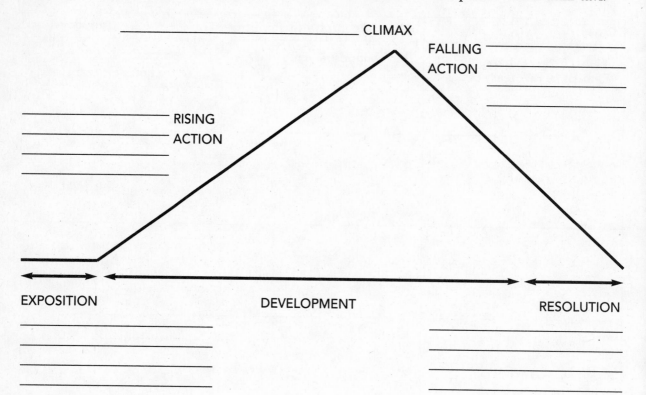

CLIMAX

FALLING
ACTION

RISING
ACTION

EXPOSITION

DEVELOPMENT

RESOLUTION

"Papa's Parrot" by Cynthia Rylant

Build Vocabulary

Word Analysis: Suffix -ment

A. Practice: The suffix -ment has several meanings. It can mean "the state or quality of," as in *amusement* or *bewilderment*. It can mean an "action or process," as in *development* or *government*. It can also mean a "product or thing," as in *instrument* or *ornament*. Apply what you know about the suffix -ment to answer the following. What word would describe:

1. The state of being content? _____

_____

2. The process of enjoying? _____

_____

3. The product of the process of paving? _____

_____

4. The state of resenting someone? _____

_____

5. The process of being enchanted? _____

_____

6. The quality of feeling befuddled? _____

_____

7. The process of becoming engaged to be married? _____

_____

Using New Words

B. Writing Application: Use each of the defined words in the sentences that follow:

merely, only

stroll, walk for pleasure in a slow, quiet way

cling, stick or hold fast

1. Harry and his friend would sometimes_____
past the candy shop on their way to the video arcade or the burger joint.

2. Harry was alarmed, but it was _____
his father's parrot, Rocky, excited to see someone.

3. When Harry shouted, the startled parrot shrieked and decided to _____
tightly to his wooden perch.

"Papa's Parrot" by Cynthia Rylant

Build Spelling Skills: Unusual Spellings

Some words you encounter in your reading include silent letters whose sounds are not pronounced. For example, in "Papa's Parrot," you will find the word *sign*. This word has a silent *g*. The spelling of words with silent letters must be memorized—words like these do not follow typical spelling rules.

A. Practice: For each word given below, identify its silent letter. Write that letter on the line.

1. talked   _____

2. stomach   _____

3. would   _____

4. school   _____

5. answered   _____

6. dumb   _____

7. knew   _____

8. rheumatism   _____

9. catch   _____

10. science   _____

B. Practice: Each sentence below contains a word with an unusual spelling. Look for a word that has a silent letter. Circle that word, and on the line following the sentence, write the silent letter.

1. At the end of church services yesterday, we got to sing my favorite hymn. _____

2. When I reach the twelfth grade, I hope to apply to become a foreign exchange student. _____

3. The City Council has voted to condemn the old post office because it is too old. _____

4. The story sounded true at first, but the more I considered it, the more I doubted it. _____

5. We're taking a class trip to see an exhibit of Pablo Picasso's paintings at the museum. _____

6. My mother encourages me to gain all the knowledge I can. _____

7. I prefer listening to the radio to watching television. _____

8. You must present the original sales receipt whenever you wish to exchange a gift. _____

C. Writing Application: Use each of these unusually spelled words in its own sentence: *people, scene, wrench.*

1. _____

_____

2. _____

_____

3. _____

_____

"**Papa's Parrot**" by Cynthia Rylant

Build Grammar Skills: Complex Sentences

A **complex sentence** is made up of one independent clause and one or more subordinate clauses. Remember that an independent clause can stand by itself as a complete sentence, but a subordinate (or dependent) clause cannot. A subordinate clause begins with a word or words that make it impossible for the clause to stand by itself as a sentence. Here are some words that can introduce subordinate clauses: *after, although, as, as if, because, before, if, so that, until, what, when, where, which, while.*

Subordinate Clause

Complex sentence: Though his father was fat and merely owned a candy

Independent Clause

and nut shop, Harry Tillian liked his papa.

A. Practice: For each item, write *C* if it is a complex sentence, write *I* if it is an independent clause, and write *S* if it is a subordinate clause.

1. For years, Harry had always stopped in to see his father at work. _____

2. Because they were older and had more spending money. _____

3. Harry's father talked to the parrot as if the parrot understood. _____

4. Harry and his papa joked together at home as they always had. _____

5. One day, Mr. Tillian became ill. _____

6. While Harry was sorting the candy. _____

B. Writing Application: Write complex sentences based on "Papa's Parrot." Use the word in the circle as part of each independent clause. Use the words on the lines as part of each subordinate clause. An example has been given.

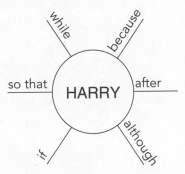

1. After he turned twelve, Harry stopped going to the candy store.

2. _____

3. _____

4. _____

5. _____

6. _____

Selection Support **133**

"Papa's Parrot" by Cynthia Rylant

Reading Strategy: Identify with a Character

When you **identify with a character,** you imagine how you would feel if you were in the character's place. This kind of imagining can make a story seem more like real life. In a way, you get inside the character's skin and look out from the character's eyes. Then you ask, "What would I do if I were here?"

DIRECTIONS: As you read the story, fill out the chart to help you identify with the main characters.

"Papa's Parrot"		
Event	**Character's Reaction**	**How I Would React**

"Papa's Parrot" by Cynthia Rylant

Literary Analysis: Characterization

Writers give information about characters in two main ways: **direct characterization** and **indirect characterization.** In the first of these, the writer tells you about the character's traits. In the second, the writer shows you what kind of person the character is through the words, actions, and thoughts of the character and those of others who interact with the character.

DIRECTIONS: As you read "Papa's Parrot," complete the character chart. Two examples have been given.

"Papa's Parrot"			
Character	**Characteristic**	**Quotation**	**Direct or Indirect?**
Harry Tillian			
Mr. Tillian			

Name _____ Date _____

"**Suzy and Leah**" by Jane Yolen

Build Vocabulary

Using the Suffix -ee

A. DIRECTIONS: The Word Bank word *refugee* uses the suffix -*ee,* which means "one who." It also means "a person who benefits from an action." Once you know that *refuge* means "a safe place," you can figure out that *refugee* means "one who seeks or has come to a safe place." Use what you know about the suffix -*ee* to define the following words.

1. payee _____

2. standee _____

3. absentee _____

4. escapee _____

5. appointee _____

B. Using New Words

Use each of the defined words in the sentences that follow.

refugee (noun): person who flees home or country to seek refuge from war or persecution

porridge (noun): soft food made of oatmeal or other cereal boiled until thick

rickety (adj.): shaky, weak, likely to fall or break down

steel (verb): to make hard or tough

permanent (adj.): intended to last; not for a short time only

porthole (noun): opening in a ship's side to let in light and air

1. After a warm meal of _____ and milk, the children felt satisfied and sleepy.

2. During the long voyage, the passengers peered out of the round _____ to catch glimpses of sunshine and to breathe some fresh air.

3. Thanks to help from relief agencies, Leah will now be making her _____ home in America.

4. It would be easy for the crowds to break down the _____ fence to escape.

5. Maya had to _____ herself to face her oral report.

6. The young _____, far from home, was confused and frightened.

Name _____ Date _____

"**Suzy and Leah**" by Jane Yolen

Build Spelling Skills: Adding -ee

Spelling Strategy When adding the suffix -ee to a word that ends in the letter e, drop the final e before adding the suffix. If the word ends in a consonant, just add the suffix.

mortgage + -ee = mortgagee   address + -ee = addressee

A. Practice: Add the suffix -ee to each of the following words. Write the new word on the line.

1. select _____

2. grant _____

3. examine _____

4. refuge _____

B. Practice: Add -ee to the following words. Then write each new word in the blank in which it makes the most sense.

devote _____   honor _____

employ _____   attend _____

1. Accomplished author Jane Yolen is a true _____
   of the art of storytelling. Listening to a story told aloud reminds her of the "music" in words.

2. As a child, Jane Yolen was an _____
   of the School of American Ballet in New York City, with hopes of becoming a professional dancer.

3. For a time, she was an _____
   of Smith College, where she taught courses in children's literature.

4. Yolen is proud to have been an _____
   of the Educational Press Association. She received their Distinguished Achievement Award for her story, "Suzy and Leah."

Challenge: In "Suzy and Leah," Leah wears a blue pinafore that had been donated by Suzy's mother. A pinafore was worn over another dress, like an apron, and pinned to the dress in the front. Because of this, it was sometimes called a *pin-before,* which gradually changed to *pinafore.* Here are some other clothing items. Describe them in a way that shows how each got its name.

1. overalls _____

2. turtleneck _____

3. sneakers _____

Name _____ Date _____

Build Grammar Skills: Adverb Clauses

Like an adverb, an **adverb clause** modifies a verb, an adjective, or another adverb, answering the question *when? where? how? why? under what condition?* or *to what extent?* The difference between an adverb and an adverb clause is this: An adverb is just one word, whereas an adverb clause is a group of words with a subject and a verb. In the following sentence, the adverb clause modifies the verb *would (not) find*, and answers the question "*under what condition?*"

adverb clause

If a whole snowdrift were to fall on him, . . . he would not find it necessary to shake the snow off himself.

Remember that an adverb clause begins with a subordinating conjunction, such as *after, as, although, because, if, since, when, unless,* and *until.*

When an adverb clause introduces a sentence, use a comma to separate it from the rest of the sentence. It is usually unnecessary to use a comma before an adverb clause that ends a sentence.

A. Practice: Underline the adverb clause in each sentence. On the line, write the word or words it modifies.

1. When I looked back, she was gone. _____

2. I wouldn't have minded so much if she had only asked. _____

3. At least, that's the way she writes it. _____

4. If I write all this down, I will not forget the appointment. _____

5. I didn't answer "Nothing," though that would have been true. _____

B. Writing Application: Based on the short story "Suzy and Leah," write ten sentences using adverb clauses that answer each of the questions.

When?   Where?   How?   Why?   To what extent?

1. _____

2. _____

3. _____

4. _____

5. _____

6. _____

7. _____

8. _____

9. _____

10. _____

"Suzy and Leah" by Jane Yolen

Reading Strategy: Drawing Inferences

In everyday life, you **draw inferences** all the time. For instance, if your neighbors' newspapers are piling up by the front door, you can infer that they are not at home. You can use clues like these to make inferences about characters in stories, too. For example, when you read about the "angularity of shape" and "stick-like straightness" of Iona's horse, you can infer that Iona is too poor to feed his horse well.

As you read "Suzy and Leah," fill in the chart. In the first column, write details from the story. In the second column, write what those details tell you about the characters or situation.

"Suzy and Leah"	
Detail(s)	**Inference**

"Suzy and Leah" by Jane Yolen

Literary Analysis: Setting

The **setting,** or the time and place in which a story takes place, includes all the aspects of that time and place, such as social customs and culture, geography, weather, and historical period. Sometimes the setting is the driving force of the story; in other words, the story could happen only in that time and place. Other times, the setting acts merely as the background for the plot; in other words, the story could happen just about anywhere.

As you read "Suzy and Leah," fill out this chart.

	"Suzy and Leah"
1. When does the story take place?	
2. Where does the story take place?	
3. Which parts of the story could have happened only then and there?	
4. Which parts of the story could have happened elsewhere?	
5. How important is setting in this story?	

"Ribbons" by Laurence Yep
"The Treasure of Lemon Brown" by Walter Dean Myers

Build Vocabulary

Using the Word Root -sens-

A. DIRECTIONS: The word root -sens-, which means "feel," appears in many words, such as the Word Bank word *sensitive*. Use the following defined words to complete the sentences below.

insensitivity, lack of feeling
desensitize, to make less able to feel
extrasensory, beyond the normal range of the five senses
sensational, outstanding enough to arouse strong feeling

1. This medicine will _____ your gums so the dentist can work.

2. The magician claimed to have _____ powers.

3. The child laughed at his friend's problem, which showed his _____.

4. The fireworks display was _____, and everyone cheered.

Using the Word Bank

sensitive	coax	laborious	exertion
meek	ajar	tentatively	impromptu

B. DIRECTIONS: Match each word in the left column with its definition in the right column.

____ 1. ajar   a. easily hurt or irritated; touchy

____ 2. coax   b. taking much work or effort; difficult

____ 3. exertion   c. humble, shy

____ 4. impromptu   d. open

____ 5. laborious   e. unscheduled; unplanned

____ 6. meek   f. hesitantly; with uncertainty

____ 7. sensitive   g. to influence through pleasant words

____ 8. tentatively   h. effort; struggle

Using Antonyms

C. DIRECTIONS: Circle the letter of the word that means the opposite of the word in CAPITAL LETTERS.

1. IMPROMPTU
   a. sudden
   b. rehearsed
   c. immediate
   d. unplanned

2. LABORIOUS
   a. easy
   b. difficult
   c. slow
   d. effective

3. MEEK
   a. frightened
   b. squinting
   c. loud
   d. bold

"Ribbons" by Laurence Yep
"The Treasure of Lemon Brown" by Walter Dean Myers

Build Spelling Skills: Adding the Suffix *-ious*

Spelling Strategy   You can add the suffix *-ious* to some nouns to change them into adjectives. If the noun ends in the letter *y* or *e*, drop the *y* or *e* before adding *-ious*.

A. Practice: Add the suffix *-ious* to each of the following words. Write the new word on the line.

1. labor _____

2. envy _____

3. grace _____

B. Practice: Add *-ious* to the following words. Then write each new word in the blank where it makes the most sense.

glory _____   fury _____

victory _____   space _____

1. Stacy's room was not _____ enough for all Grandmother's things.

2. Stacy was angry but not _____ about the way Grandmother treated her.

3. Ballet gave Stacy a _____ feeling.

4. Stacy's mom had finally been _____ in her efforts to get Grandmother to move to San Francisco.

Challenge: Lemon Brown's hands are described as "gnarled." When the letters *gn* are used in the beginning of a word, the *g* is silent. In a dictionary, look up the meanings of these words that begin with *gn*. Write the definitions on the lines.

1. gnash _____

2. gneiss _____

3. gnome _____

4. gnat _____

Name _____ Date _____

"Ribbons" by Laurence Yep
"The Treasure of Lemon Brown" by Walter Dean Myers

Build Grammar Skills: Adjective Clauses

An **adjective clause** does the same thing that an adjective does. That is, it modifies a noun or a pronoun, answering the question *which one? what kind?* or *how many?* The difference between an adjective and an adjective clause is this: An adjective is just one word, whereas an adjective clause is a group of words with a subject and a verb. In the following example, the adjective clause modifies *Ian.*

> Instead, she stumped up the stairs after Mom, trying to coax a smile from Ian,
>
> **adjective clause**
> who was staring at her over Mom's shoulder.

Adjective clauses are usually introduced by relative pronouns such as *who, whom, whose, which,* and *that.* The relative pronoun not only introduces the clause, it is also often the subject of the clause.

A. Practice: Underline the adjective clause in each sentence. On the line, write the word or words it modifies.

1. Dad had taken away the one hope that had kept me going . . . _____

2. Now I got out the special box that held my satin toe shoes. _____

3. Then she looked down at my bare feet, which were callused from three years of daily

   lessons. _____

4. When she looked back at the satin ribbons, it was with a hate and disgust that I had

   never seen before. _____

5. Her feet were like taffy that someone had stretched out and twisted. _____

6. Each foot bent downward in a way that feet were not meant to . . . _____

7. Naturally, Ian chose the fattest story, which was my old collection of fairy tales by

   Hans Christian Andersen. _____

B. Writing Application: Rewrite each sentence, adding an adjective clause to it. Circle the word the adjective clause modifies.

1. The dark sky reflected Greg Ridley's mood.

   _____

2. Greg's father said ball-playing would depend on Greg's report card.

   _____

3. Down the block was an old tenement building.

   _____

4. From the couch, Greg could see the blinking neon sign.

   _____

"Ribbons" by Laurence Yep
"The Treasure of Lemon Brown" by Walter Dean Myers

Reading Strategy: Ask Questions

One way to get more out of what you read is to stop from time to time and **ask questions** about it. For example, you might ask why a character does something, says something, or wants something. You also might ask why the author gives you certain details. As you read "Ribbons" and "The Treasure of Lemon Brown," fill out these charts. A sample question has been given for each story.

"Ribbons"	
Question	Answer
Why does Ian rush to the window?	He's expecting his grandmother.

"The Treasure of Lemon Brown"	
Question	Answer
Why is Greg in such a bad mood?	His father won't let him play ball unless his math grade improves.

Name _____   Date _____

"Ribbons" by Laurence Yep
"The Treasure of Lemon Brown" by Walter Dean Myers

Literary Analysis: Theme

The **theme** of a story is its central underlying message, usually about life or human nature. A theme is sometimes stated directly, but more often it is suggested through the title, the words and experiences of the characters, the events and conflict in the story, and other details. For example, if a person in a story overcomes great obstacles to win a race, the theme might be the importance of determination in accomplishing goals.

DIRECTIONS: Complete this diagram for either "Ribbons" or "The Treasure of Lemon Brown." In the center circle, write what you see as the theme of the story. In the boxes, write details that led you to this conclusion.

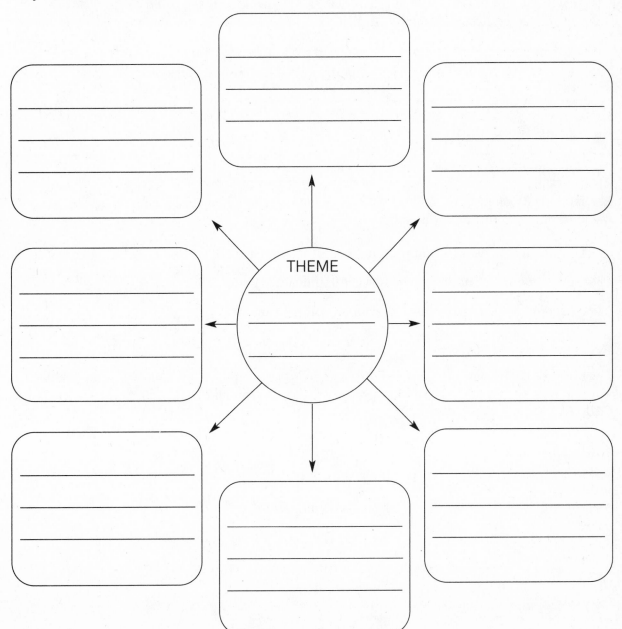

"Stolen Day" by Sherwood Anderson

Build Vocabulary

Using the Latin Root -*flam*-

A. DIRECTIONS: The Word Bank word *inflammatory* has the Latin word root -*flam*-, which means "flame" or "burn." Apply what you know about the word root -*flam*- and answer the following questions.

1. Why is kerosene considered highly inflammable?

   _____

2. How do you think the flamingo (a bird with a long neck, long legs, and bright reddish-orange feathers) got its name?

   _____

3. Why do you think an injury or infection in part of the body is called an inflammation?

   _____

Using the Word Bank

inflammatory	rheumatism	solemn

B. DIRECTIONS: Complete each of the following sentences to demonstrate your understanding of the underlined Word Bank words.

1. To make it look as if he had <u>rheumatism</u>, the narrator _____

2. The <u>inflammatory</u> nature of the disease could cause joints to _____

3. You could tell that Earl was a <u>solemn</u> person because he_____

Recognizing Synonyms

C. Practice: Each question below consists of a word in capital letters, followed by four lettered words. Circle the letter of the word or phrase that is most similar in meaning to the word in CAPITAL letters.

1. SOLEMN
   a. joyful
   b. silent
   c. serious
   d. cheerful

2. INFLAMMATORY
   a. relaxed
   b. feeble
   c. calming
   d. swollen and painful

Name _____ Date _____

"Stolen Day" by Sherwood Anderson

Build Spelling Skills: The Spelling *mn*

Spelling Strategy

A. Practice: Complete each of the defined words by adding *mn* in the blank. Then use the words to complete the sentences that follow. Write each word on the line.

autu___, the season of the year between summer and winter

colu___, a tall post shaped like a cylinder

conde___, to declare unfit for use

hy___, a song of praise, usually religious

sole___, serious, somber

li___, draw, paint

1. One _____ on the building needs to be repaired.

2. The children sang a short _____ before the ceremony.

3. Arthur could _____ so well that he earned money as an artist.

4. The friends made a _____ promise to meet again in one year.

5. Tasha traveled to Connecticut in the _____ to see the colorful trees.

6. The inspector will certainly _____ this old building.

condemn	solemn	column	hymn	autumn	limn

B. Practice: Complete the puzzle with words from the box.

Across
    3. a cylindrical pillar
    4. to draw or paint
    5. serious, somber

Down
    1. a song of praise
    2. one of the seasons
    3. to declare unsafe

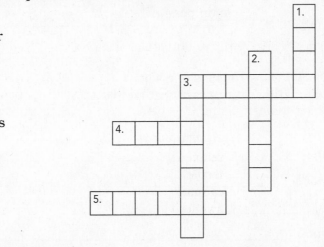

Challenge: A carp is featured in this story. Here is a list of fish whose names are scrambled. Unscramble them, and write the name of the animal on the line.

1. nimown _____   4. rutot _____

2. namsol _____   5. digfohls _____

3. naut _____   6. lenrudof _____

Build Grammar Skills: Subject and Verb Agreement

A **verb** must agree with its **subject** both in person (first, second, or third) and in number (singular or plural).

	Singular	**Plural**
First Person	I am, I walk	we are, we walk
Second Person	you are, you walk	you are, you walk
Third Person	he/she/it is; he/she/it walks	they are, they walk

Notice that the verb *walk*, in third-person singular, ends with an *s*.

A **collective noun** names a group. Some collective nouns are *family, flock, class, gang, company, corps,* and *crowd.* A collective noun may be considered either singular or plural, depending on its use in a sentence. It takes a singular verb when it refers to the group *as a whole.* It takes a plural verb when it refers to the group *as individual members.*

Examples: The crowd is eagerly watching the game. (refers to the group as a whole)

The crowd are yelling different slogans. (refers to the group as individuals)

A. Practice: In each sentence, the subject and verb do not agree. Rewrite the sentence, correcting the verb form so that it agrees with the subject in number and person.

1. She come right over to me. _____

2. I is getting more and more hungry. _____

3. The band meet after school on Tuesdays. _____

4. They arrives home for supper. _____

5. The class play outside at recess. _____

6. Everyone have always been saying we ought to have a party. _____

B. Writing Application: Imagine that Sarah Suggett, the narrator's teacher, records observations about her students. Write some sentences that Ms. Suggett might write, using a subject in the person and number indicated, and the correct verb form. Keep your sentences in the present tense.

1. First-person singular _____

2. Third-person plural _____

3. First-person plural _____

4. Third-person singular _____

5. Second-person singular _____

6. Second-person plural _____

"Stolen Day" by Sherwood Anderson

Reading Strategy: Understanding Author's Purpose

As you know, authors have many purposes. Some authors write to amuse, to explore a character's behavior, to inform, to capture a special time or place, to prompt the reader's sympathy, or to make the reader think. If you can determine an author's purpose, you can develop a richer understanding of a piece of writing.

Look for clues to the author's purpose or purposes in "Stolen Day." The chart that follows contains quotations from the story. To complete the chart, suggest why the author may have included each quotation.

QUOTATION	AUTHOR'S PURPOSE
1. [Walter] had been able to walk down there all right.	
2. I kept on crying and it worked all right.	
3. They did laugh at me pretty often and I didn't like that at all.	
4. "I might just suddenly die right here; my heart might stop beating."	
5. We were up at the fairgrounds after school and there was a half-mile track.	
6. "If she really knew the truth, that I have inflammatory rheumatism and I may just drop down dead at any time, I'll bet she wouldn't care about that either," I thought.	
7. I was having a grand time, having died.	
8. He was a big one all right. He was nearly half as big as myself.	

"Stolen Day" by Sherwood Anderson

Literary Analysis: Point of View

Point of view is the perspective, or vantage point, from which a story is told. Most stories are told from the **third-person point of view.** Narratives told from this point of view have a narrator who is someone outside the story, not a character who takes part in the events. The narrator uses third-person pronouns, such as "he" and "she," to refer to the characters. There is no "I" telling the story.

Some stories are told in the **first-person point of view.** Narratives told from this point of view have a narrator who is a character in the story, and takes a direct role in the action. The first-person narrator refers to himself or herself with the first-person pronoun "I."

The advantage of having a story told in third person is that the narrator can tell you what each character thinks, feels, and does. When the narrator is a character in the story, you learn only what that one character tells you, and you see everything from only that character's vantage point.

DIRECTIONS: On the lines below, answer the questions relating to point of view used to tell the story of "Stolen Day".

1. Who narrates the story? _____
   _____
   _____
   _____

2. What details prove that this story is told in the first-person point of view? _____
   _____
   _____
   _____

3. Why can't a first-person narrator tell the reader everything about how other characters are feeling or what they are thinking? _____
   _____
   _____
   _____

4. What additional details might be provided if this story were told in the third-person point of view? _____
   _____
   _____
   _____

5. Why do you think the author chose to use the first-person point of view? _____
   _____
   _____
   _____

"How to Enjoy Poetry" by James Dickey

Build Vocabulary

Using the Prefix *inter-*

A. DIRECTIONS: In each sentence, replace the italicized phrase with one of the following words that start with the prefix *inter-*, meaning "between" or "among":

interstate   interfere   intergalactic   intermission

1. A play usually has at least one (*break between acts*) _____.

2. Do not (*come between*) _____ in our personal business.

3. Road workers completed the (*between states*) _____ highway.

4. Scientists hope one day to achieve travel that is (*between galaxies*) _____.

Write an original sentence using each word below.

5. interrupt _____

6. interracial _____

7. intersection _____

8. intertwine _____

Using the Word Bank

prose	inevitability	interacts	vital

B. DIRECTIONS: Write the Word Bank word that completes each sentence.

1. A writer's work may be poetry or _____.

2. A hopeful person believes in the _____ of a happy ending.

3. Fresh air is _____ for any human being to survive.

4. When water _____ with fire, the fire goes out.

Analogies

C. DIRECTIONS: Circle the letter next to the word or phrase that is most similar in meaning to the word in CAPITAL LETTERS.

1. PROSE
   a. structure   b. paragraph   c. spoken language   d. nonpoetic language

2. INEVITABILITY
   a. success   b. certainty   c. strength   d. caution

3. VITAL
   a. very necessary   b. very pretty   c. very active   d. very quiet

4. INTERACTS
   a. runs from   b. sews up   c. mixes   d. denies

"**How to Enjoy Poetry**" by James Dickey

Build Spelling Skills: Change the Adjective Ending *-able* to the Noun Ending *-ility*

Spelling Strategy To change an adjective that ends in *-able* to a noun that ends in *-ility*, drop the final *-le* and add *-ility*. The adjective *inevitable* can be turned into the noun *inevitability* by changing its ending from *-able* to *-ability*.

Other Examples: reliable – le + ility = reliability   probable – le + ility = probability

A. Practice: Change each adjective in the left column into a noun by adding *-ility*. Write your new word on the line.

Adjective	Noun	Adjective	Noun
1. believable	_____	6. detectable	_____
2. liable	_____	7. bendable	_____
3. lovable	_____	8. workable	_____
4. flammable	_____	9. traceable	_____
5. washable	_____	10. wearable	_____

B. Writing Application: Complete each sentence below by changing the adjective in parentheses to a noun that ends in *-ility*. Write your new word on the line.

1. According to James Dickey, poetry has special qualities that give it a (durable) _____.

2. Dickey says that readers have the (capable) _____ of making poetry a lively and meaningful experience for themselves.

3. The writer maintains that the rhythm of language has a special kind of (unforgettable) _____.

4. The effects of a poem can affect the soul in ways that have no (predictable) _____.

5. Every good poem has a satisfying (readable) _____ if readers make the effort to interact with the writing.

6. Dickey implies that a well-written poem has the power and (able) _____ to change a person who truly delves into it.

Challenge: Since the prefix *in-* means "not," you might think that *inevitable* means "not evitable." However, there is no such word as *evitable* in the English language. Use a dictionary to discover the meanings of *inept*, *incessant*, and *indelible*. Do they mean "not ept," "not cessant," and "not delible"? Write their meanings on the lines provided.

1. inept _____

2. incessant _____

3. indelible _____

"How to Enjoy Poetry" by James Dickey

Build Grammar Skills: The Four Functions of Sentences

A sentence can perform one of four functions:

A **declarative** sentence makes a statement and ends with a period.

> A poet writes poetry.

An **interrogative** sentence asks a question and ends with a question mark.

> Is James Dickey a poet?

An **imperative** sentence gives a command and may end with either a period or an exclamation point.

> Read this poem by him. Don't miss it!

An **exclamatory** sentence shows emotion and ends with an exclamation point.

> How nice it is!

A. Practice: Read each sentence. In the blanks at the right, write whether the sentence is *declarative*, *interrogative*, *imperative*, or *exclamatory*. Then copy the circled letters in the blanks beneath the activity. You will spell out a message from James Dickey.

1. What is poetry? ___ ___ ___ ___ ___[_]___ ___ ___ ___ ___ ___

2. Reach for the poet from your gut out. ___ ___ ___[_]___ ___ ___ ___ ___ ___

3. Words and feelings go together. ___ ___ ___ ___[_]___ ___ ___ ___ ___ ___

4. Your response gives the poem its magic. [_]___ ___ ___ ___ ___ ___ ___ ___ ___ ___

5. Find your own way to open yourself. ___ ___[_]___ ___ ___ ___ ___ ___ ___ ___

6. It is quite a list! ___ ___ ___ ___ ___ ___ ___[_]___ ___ ___

7. What moss do you see? ___ ___ ___[_]___ ___ ___ ___ ___ ___

8. Writing poetry is like a contest. ___ ___ ___ ___ ___ ___[_]___ ___ ___ ___

9. What brambles are your brambles? ___ ___ ___ ___[_]___ ___ ___ ___ ___ ___

10. Well, would you look at that! ___ ___ ___ ___ ___ ___ ___ ___ ___[_]___ ___

Message: ___ ___ ___ ___ ___ ___ ___ ___ ___ ___!

B. Writing Application: Read each sentence. Then write a related sentence that performs the function shown in parentheses.

> **Example:**   The most beautiful constellation is Orion.
> (show emotion)   What a beautiful constellation Orion is!

1. If you give to a poem, it will give to you. (ask a question)

_____

2. Reading a poem takes special concentration. (give a command)

_____

3. What do you think about when you read a poem? (make a statement)

_____

4. The language of the poem is beautiful. (show emotion)

_____

Reading Strategy: Identifying Main Ideas

You're bombarded with facts and ideas at all times and from every direction. When you scan a cereal box, read a textbook, or surf the Internet you must make decisions about which information in your reading is most significant.

- **Identify main ideas.** In general, nonfiction authors want to convey one or two main ideas. The rest of the information you will encounter is there to support the main ideas. Look for the main ideas that are suggested or stated directly in the beginning or at the end of the work. You may find additional clues in headings or questions that can help to focus your thinking about main ideas. Other clues may include signal words like *in summary*, *in conclusion*, *the central concept*, *the principal item*, or *a key feature*.

When you read nonfiction, look for passages that sum up the main ideas. Search in the passage for hints that can help you grasp the main points. Then state the main idea in your own words.

DIRECTIONS: Use the following chart to help you determine the author's main idea in different sections of the essay "How to Enjoy Poetry." One example has been provided for you.

Section	Hint in Passage	Author's Main Idea
Introduction	But that is not what poetry is or why it is still around.	Poetry does not exist just to challenge students.
Where Poetry is Coming From		
Your Connection With Other Imaginations		
Which Sun? Whose Stars?		
Where to Start		
The Poem's Way of Going		
Some Things You'll Find Out		
How It Goes With You		

Name _____   Date _____

"How to Enjoy Poetry" by James Dickey

Literary Analysis: Expository Essay

An **expository essay** is one that explains a subject. Dickey's essay, as the title indicates, explains how a reader can enjoy poetry. By reading this expository essay carefully, you can find many instructions on how to appreciate a poem. Each instruction is accompanied by details that help explain to readers what to do.

DIRECTIONS: In the chart below, map out the instructions that Dickey presents for enjoying a poem. Supply important details to support each instruction.

Instruction	Important Details
Don't let the poet write down to you; reach up to him.	Reach for him from your gut out; the heart and muscles will come into it, too.
1.	
2.	
3.	
4.	

"**No Gumption**" by Russell Baker
"**The Chase**" by Annie Dillard

Build Vocabulary

Using the Root *-pel-*

A. DIRECTIONS: The root *-pel-* means "to push" or "to drive." Complete each sentence below with one of the following words:

expelled   repelled   dispelled   propelled

1. The principal _____ the student for bad behavior.

2. The rocket was _____ into the sky by liquid fuel.

3. The wind _____ the fog that had filled the air.

4. A skunk's enemies are _____ by its terrible odor.

Using the Word Bank

gumption	paupers	crucial	aptitude
translucent	compelled	perfunctorily	

B. DIRECTIONS: Match each Word Bank word on the left with its definition on the right. Write the letter of the definition on the line next to the word it defines.

____ 1. gumption   a. talent or ability

____ 2. paupers   b. without enthusiasm

____ 3. crucial   c. people who are poor

____ 4. aptitude   d. forced

____ 5. translucent   e. courage and boldness

____ 6. compelled   f. very important

____ 7. perfunctorily   g. letting light pass in a hazy way

Analogies

C. DIRECTIONS: For each related pair of words in CAPITAL LETTERS, choose the lettered pair that best expresses a similar relationship. Circle the letter of your choice.

1. PAUPERS : POOR ::
   a. babies : adults
   b. geniuses : smart
   c. students : schools
   d. rich : winners

2. COWARD : GUMPTION ::
   a. fool : intelligence
   b. hero : bravery
   c. doctor : nurse
   d. runner : energy

3. SLAVE : COMPELLED ::
   a. teacher : class
   b. swimmer : swimming
   c. reader : book
   d. volunteer : chosen

4. EMERGENCY : CRUCIAL ::
   a. telephone : number
   b. story : character
   c. comedy : humorous
   d. happy : sad

"No Gumption" by Russell Baker
"The Chase" by Annie Dillard

Build Spelling Skills: Doubling the Final Consonant When Adding -*ing*

Spelling Strategy   In a two-syllable word ending in a single vowel followed by a single consonant and having *the accent on the final syllable*, double the final consonant before adding -*ing*.

Examples: com**PEL** + ing = compelling   ad**MIT** + ing = admitting

Notice that if the word is accented on the first syllable, you do not double the final consonant.

Examples: **TRA**vel + ing = traveling   **PRO**gram + ing = programing

A. Practice: Add -*ing* to each word in the left column below. In the right column, write the word by putting one letter in each blank.

1. control + ing   =   __ __ __ __ __ __ __ __ __ __
2. expel + ing   =   __ __ __ __ __ __ __ __
3. prefer + ing   =   __ __ __ __ __ __ __ __ __
4. commit + ing   =   __ __ __ __ __ __ __ __
5. permit + ing   =   __ __ __ __ __ __ __ __ __

B. Practice: In each sentence, find a word with the -*ing* ending that is spelled wrong. Cross out the word and write it correctly.

1. Russell Baker is admiting that he did not have much gumption when he was a young boy.

2. His seeming lack of ambition was upseting his mother, who decided that her son should sell magazine subscriptions.

3. In time, Russell chose writting, which he prefered to any other type of job because it required no gumption.

4. In "The Chase," when the man in the black Buick got out of his car, he was begining a race that would last for many blocks.

5. Annie says that as the stranger chased the children, he was impeling them forward, just as they were compeling him to follow.

Challenge: There are several words in English that start with *perf*, the first four letters in the Word Bank word *perfunctorily*. See how many words you can list that start with the letters *perf*. Then check in a dictionary to find other words you may have overlooked. Write your words on the lines provided.

_____   _____   _____

_____   _____   _____

"**No Gumption**" by Russell Baker
"**The Chase**" by Annie Dillard

Build Grammar Skills: Participles and Participial Phrases

A **participle** is a verb form that often acts as an adjective to modify a noun or pronoun. Present participles end in *-ing*. Many past participles end in *-ed*. In the following examples, notice that the present participle *working* modifies the noun *youth*, and the past participle *discouraged* modifies the noun *worker*.

Examples: Russell Baker was a working youth who sold magazines.

He quickly became a discouraged worker on the job.

A **participial phrase** contains a participle plus other words that go with it. Like a participle, a participial phrase modifies a noun or pronoun. In this example, the participial phrase *Working at the same job* modifies the noun *sister*.

Examples: Working at the same job, his sister did much better.

A. Practice: In the following sentences, underline any participial phrases once and all participles twice. Circle the noun or pronoun that the participle or participial phrase modifies. The first one has been done for you.

1. Sitting behind a desk, a writer never had to trudge through town.

2. Mrs. Baker was a concerned mother who worried about her son.

3. Russell eventually found that to be a writer was a more enchanting profession.

4. In "The Chase," Annie was a valued player on the boys' football team.

5. Throwing snowballs at passing cars, Annie angered one driver.

6. The fuming driver got out of his car and chased the girl for many blocks.

B. Writing Application: Write sentences about the characters in "No Gumption" or "The Chase." In each sentence, use the participle or participial phrase shown below. Remember to use the participles and participial phrases to modify nouns or pronouns.

1. excited _____

2. upsetting _____

3. Looking for a way out _____

4. relieved _____

5. Thinking about it later _____

Name _____ Date _____

"No Gumption" by Russell Baker
"The Chase" by Annie Dillard

Reading Strategy: Understand the Author's Purpose

Authors write with different reasons, or **purposes**, in mind. For example, politicians often write speeches in order to *persuade* listeners to agree with their views and opinions. Newspaper reporters write articles in order to *inform* readers about a subject. Humorists write pieces that they hope will *entertain* their audiences.

Sometimes a writer may have more than one purpose in mind. In "No Gumption," for example, author Russell Baker wishes to entertain his audience. You can tell that by humorous passages such as this one: "I was enchanted. Writers didn't have to have any gumption at all." At the same time, Baker also wishes to educate his readers, as he does in this passage: "It was 1932, the bleakest year of the Depression."

DIRECTIONS: Choose brief passages from "No Gumption" and "The Chase." Decide what the author's purpose is in writing each passage. Record the information in the chart below. One example is given.

Selection	Passage	Author's Purpose
"No Gumption"	"My mother was present during one of these interrogations."	to entertain
"No Gumption"		
"No Gumption"		
"The Chase"		
"The Chase"		
"The Chase"		

"No Gumption" by Russell Baker
"The Chase" by Annie Dillard

Literary Analysis: Autobiography

An **autobiography** is the story of a person's life as written by that person. Authors of autobiographies want you to come away with certain impressions of them based on the stories they tell and how they tell them. For example, in "No Gumption," Russell Baker wants you to picture him as someone who has little ambition or drive. He helps paint this picture by explaining how, as a child, he did not wish to become President of the United States. Later, he reinforces the impression by saying that he was "enchanted" upon discovering a job that required no gumption at all.

DIRECTIONS: In the charts below, list impressions you get about the author of each selection. Then give examples to show how you formed those impressions.

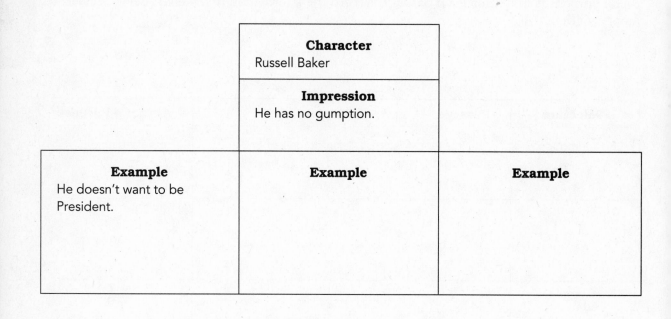

Character
Russell Baker

Impression
He has no gumption.

| **Example** | **Example** | **Example** |
| He doesn't want to be President. | | |

Character
Annie Dillard

Impression

| **Example** | **Example** | **Example** |
| | | |

"Nolan Ryan, Texas Treasure" by William W. Lace

Build Vocabulary

Using the Prefix *sub-*

A. DIRECTIONS: Each word below on the left contains the prefix *sub-*, meaning "under" or "below." Match each word with its definition. Write the letter on the line next to the word it matches.

_____ 1. subsoil   a. a ship that travels under the water

_____ 2. subside   b. dirt that is below the surface layer of dirt

_____ 3. submarine   c. a train that travels under the ground

_____ 4. subway   d. to decrease, become lower in intensity

_____ 5. substandard   e. to split into smaller sections

_____ 6. subentry   f. a secondary plot in a play, a novel, a film, etc.

_____ 7. subdivide   g. below customary quality

_____ 8. subplot   h. entry listed under a main entry

Using New Words

B. DIRECTIONS: Use each of the defined words in the sentences that follow:

excel, to surpass, stand out, outclass   **franchise,** team or sports organization

keenly, eagerly, intensely   **memento,** souvenir, keepsake, reminder

reserved, distant, detached, standoffish   **wholesome,** healthy, nutritious

1. Earlier in his career, Nolan Ryan played for the Mets, the Angels, and the Astros. But it

   was with the Arlington (near Dallas) Texas Ranger _____
   that he truly made his mark in sports history.

2. Sports fans during the Nolan Ryan era became quite accustomed to _____
   following his every game and marveling at his growing list of accomplishments.

3. He was a quiet and ordinary person at home, but on the mound Ryan wanted to _____
   in every aspect of the pitcher's game.

4. To maintain top-notch physical and mental condition, Nolan Ryan ate _____
   meals and avoided foods high in fat and empty calories.

5. Some lucky baseball fans still brag that they possess a unique _____
   from the Nolan Ryan years—a foul ball that a hapless batter popped up into the stands.

6. Nowadays, as a retired Hall-of-Famer and one of the sports greats of the twentieth century,

   Nolan Ryan comes across as a middle-aged man who is very calm and _____.

"**Nolan Ryan, Texas Treasure**" by William W. Lace

Build Spelling Skills: Add Suffixes to Words Ending With *e*

Spelling Strategy When adding a suffix to a word ending with *e*, you usually drop the *e* if the suffix begins with a vowel. You usually keep the *e* if the suffix begins with a consonant.

Examples: hostile + ity = hostility   use + age = usage   use + ful = useful

A. Practice: For each word below, add the suffix that is shown. Write the entire word. Then write its meaning. Use a dictionary for help if necessary.

1. home + less = _____

   Meaning: _____

2. serene + ity = _____

   Meaning: _____

3. serve + ile = _____

   Meaning: _____

B. Practice: Supply the missing word in each sentence by joining the word and suffix in parentheses to form a new word.

1. Nolan Ryan's family offered him lots of (encourage + ment) _____ once they realized how important baseball was to him.

2. Ryan attributes his enduring success in baseball to a (combine + ation) _____ of great physical conditioning and positive mental attitudes.

3. During his long baseball career, Nolan Ryan has either set or (broke + en) _____ many different kinds of sports records.

4. One of Nolan Ryan's teammates said that there wasn't anything more (excite + ing) _____ than coming to a game to see Ryan pitch.

5. Ryan learned the importance of a balanced, healthy diet from his mother, who served him only (whole +some) _____ meals when he was a child.

Challenge: Do you realize that the letters in the Word Bank word *subtle* can be rearranged to spell two other words: *bustle* and *bluest*? Different words that are spelled with the same letters are called **anagrams.** How many anagrams can you find in the word *star*? Try to spell three other words with those same four letters, and write them on the lines provided. Then have fun making up your own anagrams. Try it using the letters in your own first or last name.

_____   _____   _____

Name _____ Date _____

"**Nolan Ryan, Texas Treasure**" by William W. Lace

Build Grammar Skills: Appositives and Appositive Phrases

An **appositive** is a noun placed near another noun or a pronoun to identify or give additional information about it.

Example: Nolan Ryan loved to play his favorite sport, <u>baseball</u>.

An **appositive phrase** is an appositive and the words that modify it.

Example: Steve Buchele, <u>a southern California native</u>, praised Ryan.

In the preceding examples, "baseball" is an appositive of "sport," and "a southern California native" is an appositive phrase that gives additional information about Steve Buchele. Note that appositives and appositive phrases are usually set off by commas and occasionally by dashes (—).

A. Practice: In each sentence, identify the appositive or appositive phrase. Then identify the noun or pronoun that the appositive or appositive phrase explains.

1. After Ryan's biggest game, a no-hitter, he was up early the next day.

   Appositive or phrase: _____ Word explained: _____

2. Ryan avoids high-fat foods—bacon, sausage, and cream soups.

   Appositive or phrase: _____ Word explained: _____

3. Some gave Nolan Ryan a special title, America's greatest pitcher.

   Appositive or phrase: _____ Word explained: _____

4. Ryan, a Texan at heart, retired there 1993.

   Appositive or phrase: _____ Word explained: _____

5. In his later life, Ryan, the player people came to see, dominated his team.

   Appositive or phrase: _____ Word explained: _____

B. Writing Application: Write each sentence, inserting the bracketed appositive phrase in a suitable place. Remember to set off phrases with commas or dashes.

1. [a player who tries hard in every game] Ryan wants to be remembered as a "gamer."

   _____

2. [Texas] He is possibly the best-known ball player in his home state.

   _____

3. [most strikeouts and most no-hitters] Ryan's records include two very impressive ones.

   _____

Unit 7: Nonfiction

"Nolan Ryan, Texas Treasure" by William W. Lace

Reading Strategy: Distinguishing Fact and Opinion

The careful reader's job is to distinguish facts from opinions to help better understand the author's point of view. A **fact** is a statement that can be proven true by an outside source. An **opinion,** on the other hand, is an expression of someone's personal feelings; an opinion cannot be proven to be true, even if the reader happens to agree with it. An opinion reflects a unique viewpoint, which may be based on admiration, interpretation, or bias, but is not grounded in verifiable fact.

For example, in "Nolan Ryan, Texas Treasure," author William W. Lace first expresses his opinion in the title of his essay. It may be that he hopes to convince you to agree with his viewpoint. Still, it is his personal opinion, supported with a careful choice of examples that he believes will support his case.

DIRECTIONS: Complete the chart below to record different examples of facts and opinions you discover in "Nolan Ryan, Texas Treasure." One example has been provided.

Facts	Opinions
A generation has passed since Nolan Ryan threw his first major league pitch.	"There wasn't anything more exciting than coming to the games and watching Nolan Pitch."

"**Nolan Ryan, Texas Treasure**" by William W. Lace

Literary Analysis: Biography

A **biography** is the story of one person's life as told by another person. Biographers usually do more than just offer facts about their subject. They try to present the subject from a particular point of view. In the article on Nolan Ryan, the author portrays his subject as the best pitcher ever in baseball.

DIRECTIONS: In the chart below, describe William Lace's view of his subject, Nolan Ryan. Then give examples the author uses to support those views.

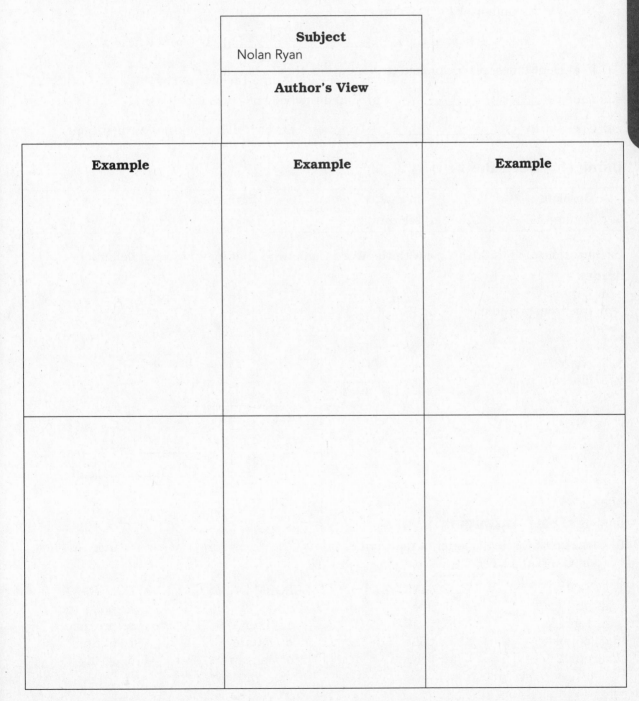

Subject
Nolan Ryan
Author's View

Example	Example	Example

© Prentice-Hall, Inc.

from *Barrio Boy* by Ernesto Galarza
"I Am a Native of North America" by Chief Dan George
"Rattlesnake Hunt" by Marjorie Kinnan Rawlings
"All Together Now" by Barbara Jordan

Build Vocabulary

Using the Root *-mort-*

A. DIRECTIONS: The root *-mort-* means "death." Complete each sentence below with one of the following words:

immortal   mortician   mortuary   immortalize

1. The dead body was kept at the _____ before the funeral.

2. In ancient times, people prayed to gods whom they believed were _____.

3. The _____ prepared the body before it was buried.

4. One way to _____ heroes is by building statues in their honor.

Using the Word Bank

desolate	mortality	formidable
communal	tolerant	

B. DIRECTIONS: Fill in the puzzle with the Word Bank word that matches each definition.

Across
4. impressive
5. free from prejudice

Down
1. death
2. shared by all
3. lonely or empty

Recognizing Antonyms

C. DIRECTIONS: Circle the letter of the word or phrase that is most *opposite* in meaning to the word in CAPITAL LETTERS.

1. DESOLATE
   a. strange
   b. hungry
   c. populated
   d. quiet

2. COMMUNAL
   a. late
   b. warlike
   c. polite
   d. private

3. FORMIDABLE
   a. small
   b. great
   c. square
   d. dangerous

4. TOLERANT
   a. pressured
   b. prejudiced
   c. injured
   d. loving

from *Barrio Boy* by Ernesto Galarza
"I Am a Native of North America" by Chief Dan George
"Rattlesnake Hunt" by Marjorie Kinnan Rawlings
"All Together Now" by Barbara Jordan

Build Spelling Skills: *it* Sound Spelled *ate*

Spelling Strategy When spelling the *it* sound at the end of multisyllable adjectives, you often use the letters *ate*. The Word Bank word *desolate* demonstrates this rule.

Examples: temper<u>ate</u>   moder<u>ate</u>

A. Practice: Fill in the missing letters in each word. Write the entire word. Then use the word as an adjective in a sentence. Use a dictionary for help if necessary.

1. delic ___ ___ ___   _____

   Sentence: _____

2. intric ___ ___ ___   _____

   Sentence: _____

3. separ ___ ___ ___   _____

   Sentence: _____

B. Practice: In each sentence, find a word with the *it* sound that is spelled wrong. Cross out the word and write it correctly.

1. Before her first rattlesnake hunt, Marjorie Kinnan Rawlings worried that her courage for

   the adventure might not be adequit.

2. By the end of his first year in school, Ernesto Galarza felt at home and not separit from the

   rest of his classmates.

3. Barbara Jordan knows that getting people to accept differences in others can be a delikit

   task.

Challenge: The Word Bank word *communal* comes from the Latin word *communis*, meaning "shared by all or many." How many other words do you know that start with the letters *commun*? Make a list on the lines provided. Then see if you can tell how each word's meaning is related to the idea of "shared by all or many."

_____   _____

_____   _____

Unit 7: Nonfiction

from _Barrio Boy_ by Ernesto Galarza
"I Am a Native of North America" by Chief Dan George
"Rattlesnake Hunt" by Marjorie Kinnan Rawlings
"All Together Now" by Barbara Jordan

Build Grammar Skills: Infinitives

An **infinitive** is a verb form that can be used as a noun, an adjective, and an adverb. An infinitive may act as a noun, an adjective, or an adverb.

Examples: Ross wanted me to write an article about his work.

Ernesto has learned how to pronounce _butterfly!_

Today the nation seems to be suffering from compassion fatigue . . .

Remember that the word _to_ can also be a preposition, as in _to the north_ or _wrestled to the ground._ Do not confuse _to_ when it appears as a preposition with _to_ followed by a verb form. Only the second choice is the true infinitive.

A. Practice: Most of the sentences that follow contain one or more examples of infinitives. Circle all the infinitives you find. If you find a sentence _without_ an infinitive, write NO INFINITIVE.

1. I leaned over to pick a white violet.

2. They pay no attention to a man standing perfectly still.

3. It made no effort to strike.

4. Ernesto was ready to attend school but not yet to speak English.

5. I was soon able to match Ito's progress as a sentence reader.

6. When we came to know each other better, I tried interrupting to tell Miss Ryan how we said it in Spanish.

7. In houses like these, people learned to live with one another, learned to serve one another.

8. This is why I find it hard to accept many of the things I see around me.

9. It is possible for us to work on human relationships in every area of our lives.

10. Parents can actively encourage their children to be in the company of people who are of other racial and ethnic backgrounds.

B. Writing Application: Review the five essays included in this grouping. Write one sentence— with an infinitive—that captures your reactions to each essay.

1. _____

_____

2. _____

_____

3. _____

_____

4. _____

_____

from *Barrio Boy* by Ernesto Galarza
"I Am a Native of North America" by Chief Dan George
"Rattlesnake Hunt" by Marjorie Kinnan Rawlings
"All Together Now" by Barbara Jordan

Reading Strategy: Determining Main Points

In most essays, the author makes one or more main points. Often, the main points are stated directly or hinted at in the beginning or end of the essay. The rest of the essay offers details to support the main points.

For example, near the beginning of "All Together Now," Barbara Jordan writes, "But much remains to be done, and the answer does not lie in more legislation." This statement signals one of the author's main points: There is much to be done apart from passing new laws. Elsewhere in the essay, Jordan explains what needs to be done and gives her proposals for accomplishing some of these goals.

When you read an essay, look for passages that sum up the main idea of the entire essay. Search in the passage for hints that help you understand the main point. Then state what that main point is.

DIRECTIONS: Use the following chart to help you determine the author's main point in each of the four essays you read. One example is provided.

Selection	Passage	Hint in Passage	Author's Main Point
"I Am a Native . . . "	"My culture is like a wounded deer . . ."	A wounded deer is helpless.	Indians will be doomed without help from others.
from *Barrio Boy*			
"Rattlesnake Hunt"			
"All Together Now"			

from *Barrio Boy* by Ernesto Galarza
"I Am a Native of North America" by Chief Dan George
"Rattlesnake Hunt" by Marjorie Kinnan Rawlings
"All Together Now" by Barbara Jordan

Literary Analysis: Essay

An **essay** is a brief prose piece that presents an author's views on a subject. Here are several different types of essays:

- A **narrative** essay is a real-life story.

- A **descriptive** essay is a description of people or places.

- A **personal** essay is an informal account of the author's own life.

- A **reflective** essay presents thoughts about ideas and experiences.

- A **persuasive** essay presents arguments for believing or acting a certain way.

DIRECTIONS: In the chart below, briefly explain why each essay is categorized as it is.

from *Barrio Boy* is a personal essay because	"Rattlesnake Hunt" is a descriptive essay because

"I Am a Native of North America" is a reflective essay because	"All Together Now" is a persuasive essay because

Name _____ Date _____

A Christmas Carol: Scrooge and Marley, Act I
by Charles Dickens, dramatized by Israel Horovitz

Build Vocabulary

Using the Word Root *-bene-*

Words that contain the root *-bene-* have something to do with good. *Benevolence*, for example, means "goodness" or "kindness."

A. DIRECTIONS: Match each word on the left with its definition on the right. Write the letter of the definition on the line next to the word it defines. If you are not sure of the meaning of a word, check a dictionary.

____ 1. benevolent   a. one who does good by giving help

____ 2. benefit   b. good or kind

____ 3. benefactor   c. a prayer asking for a blessing or goodness

____ 4. benediction   d. to profit by receiving something good

Using the Word Bank

implored	morose	destitute	misanthrope
void	ponderous	benevolence	

B. DIRECTIONS: Write the Word Bank word that best completes each sentence.

1. The horse nearly collapsed under the _____ weight of its load.

2. People can tell that you are _____ when you wear a frown or scowl.

3. The wealthy _____ refused to give charity to anyone.

4. The loss of his wife left a _____ in the man's life.

5. Many charities rely on the public's _____ in order to continue their work.

6. The beggars _____ the king and queen to give them some food.

7. The gambler lost all his money and was left _____.

Recognizing Antonyms

C. DIRECTIONS: Circle the letter of the word or phrase that is most *opposite* in meaning to the word in CAPITAL LETTERS.

1. MOROSE: a. sad   b. happy   c. confused   d. dry

2. PONDEROUS: a. dangerous   b. safe   c. heavy   d. light

3. DESTITUTE: a. rich   b. poor   c. steady   d. shaky

4. BENEVOLENCE: a. group   b. individual   c. nastiness   d. giving

5. VOID: a. straight   b. fullness   c. open   d. shut

6. MISANTHROPE: a. loser   b. winner   c. lover   d. teacher

A Christmas Carol: Scrooge and Marley, Act I
by Charles Dickens, dramatized by Israel Horovitz

Build Spelling Skills: Add *-stitute*

Spelling Strategy The letter group *-stitute* comes from a Latin word meaning "place" or "stand." Many words are formed by adding a prefix to *-stitute*. The Word Bank word *destitute* is just one example.

A. Practice: Write the word that matches each clue and starts with the prefix shown in parentheses. Enter one letter in each blank.

1. Someone who takes over temporarily
   for the regular person. (sub)
   __ __ __ __ __ __ __ __ __ __

2. To set up or establish (in)
   __ __ __ __ __ __ __ __ __

3. Very poor (de)
   __ __ __ __ __ __ __ __ __

4. To make up, form, or compose (con)
   __ __ __ __ __ __ __ __ __ __

B. Practice: Complete each sentence below by adding the letters *-stitute* to the prefix shown in parentheses. Write your new word on the line.

1. Ebenezer Scrooge is a wealthy but stingy individual who has no pity or compassion for the
   (de) _____ people of the world.

2. Meanness and selfishness are the two main qualities that (con) _____
   Scrooge's personality.

3. Jacob Marley visits Scrooge in an effort to get him to (in) _____ a new policy of care and concern for others.

4. Marley wants Scrooge to realize that money is not a comforting (sub) _____
   for the love of another human being.

Challenge: The word *misanthrope* contains the smaller word *ant*, although the two words are not related in meaning. What other smaller words can you find within the word *misanthrope*? Can you find at least five more words? Write them on the lines provided.

_____   _____   _____

_____   _____

A Christmas Carol: Scrooge and Marley, Act I
by Charles Dickens, dramatized by Israel Horovitz

Build Grammar Skills: Active Voice

A verb is in the **active voice** if the subject *performs* the action. By contrast, a verb is in the **passive voice** if the subject *receives* the action. Note in the examples of passive voice that a form of the verb *be* is used. Not every use of the verb *be* is passive, but passive voice always uses a form of the verb *be*. Though passive voice can be useful and appropriate, modern writers generally prefer to use the active voice most of the time, because it is more direct and concise.

Verbs in Active Voice	Verbs in Passive Voice
Dialogue develops the characters in a play.	The characters in a play are developed by dialogue.
Scrooge signed the register of my burial.	The register of my burial was signed by Scrooge.
They owe me money.	Money is owed to me.

A. Practice: Underline the verb in each sentence. Then, identify the verb as *active* or *passive* by writing *A* or *P* on the line.

1. In *A Christmas Carol,* the audience meets the mean-spirited Ebenezer Scrooge. _____

2. Late one night, Scrooge is visited by the ghost of his business partner, Marley._____

3. Joe, an old second-hand goods dealer, appears in Act I. _____

4. Ebenezer Scrooge was Jacob Marley's sole friend and sole mourner. _____

5. Once again, the ghostly bell rings far off in the distance. _____

6. Ebenezer Scrooge is made angry by the upbeat and optimistic views of his nephew. _____

7. Mr. Jacob Marley died seven years ago on this very night. _____

8. Marley has been mightily dragged down by his ponderous chain. _____

B. Writing Application: Each sentence that follows has a verb in the *passive* voice. Rewrite each sentence to express its idea in the *active* voice.

1. Scrooge was warned by the angry ghost of Jacob Marley._____

_____

2. You will be haunted by Three Spirits._____

3. The darkness was searched by his ferret eyes. _____

_____

4. The audience is spoken to by Marley. _____

5. Careful attention must be paid by the reader to Scrooge's pain._____

_____

Name _____ Date _____

A Christmas Carol: Scrooge and Marley, Act I
by Charles Dickens, dramatized by Israel Horovitz

Reading Strategy Picturing the Action

As you read "A Christmas Carol," it is important that you be able to **picture** in your mind, how the play would look if performed on stage. The stage directions—italicized details supplied in brackets—help you do just that. Stage directions help you "see" exactly what each setting looks like. They also help you picture how characters move on stage.

Often, stage directions give you valuable information that you can't get from the actors' dialogue. For example, in Act I, Scene 1, as Marley speaks, the stage directions indicate that he stands right next to Scrooge. Knowing that Scrooge does not react to Marley's presence, we understand that although the audience can see Marley at this point, Scrooge cannot.

DIRECTIONS: Use the following chart to record important stage-direction details that help you picture the action, the setting, and the characters. One example is provided.

Scene	Character	Stage Direction
Scene 1, Scrooge's offices	Jacob Marley	Ghostly music in auditorium. A single spotlight on JACOB MARLEY, D.C. He is ancient: awful, dead-eyed. He speaks straight out to the auditorium.

Name _____ Date _____

A Christmas Carol: Scrooge and Marley, Act I
by Charles Dickens, dramatized by Israel Horovitz

Literary Analysis: Elements of Drama

The two main **elements of drama** are dialogue and stage directions. The **dialogue** is everything that the characters say to one another. The **stage directions,** which appear in italics in square brackets, explain how the characters move and speak on stage. They also provide important details about the costumes, sets, props, and lighting.

In Act I, Scene 2, for example, the dialogue between Scrooge and the people in his office immediately establishes Scrooge as a miserly grouch. This portrayal of Scrooge is reinforced in the stage directions, which describe Scrooge as "furious." When a clerk applauds the nephew's speech about the goodness of Christmas time, the stage directions read, "SCROOGE yells at him." These important details help paint a vivid picture of Scrooge and his conflicts with other characters.

DIRECTIONS: Explain the significance of each passage below. Explain what it reveals about a character or how it helps your understanding of the play.

1. **PORTLY MAN.** [*Offers his calling card*] **SCROOGE.** [*Handing back the card; unlooked at*]

    _____

    _____

2. **SCROOGE.** Are there no prisons?

    _____

    _____

3. [*SCROOGE puts his key in the door's keyhole . . . The door knocker changes and is now MARLEY's face . . . SCROOGE stares wordlessly here. The face, before his very eyes, does deliquesce. It is a knocker again . . .*]

    _____

    _____

4. **YOUNG SCROOGE.** He is the best, best, the very and absolute best! If ever I own a firm of my own, I shall treat my apprentices with the same dignity and the same grace.

    _____

    _____

5. **SCROOGE.** Remove me! I cannot bear it! Leave me! Take me back! Haunt me no longer!

    _____

    _____

6. [*There is a sudden flash of light: a flare. The GHOST OF CHRISTMAS PAST is gone.*]

    _____

    _____

Name _____ Date _____

A Christmas Carol: Scrooge and Marley, Act II
by Charles Dickens, dramatized by Israel Horovitz

Build Vocabulary

Using the Word Root *-aud-*

Words that contain the root *-aud-* have something to do with hearing. For example, an *audible* sound is one that is able to be heard.

A. DIRECTIONS: Complete each sentence with one of the following words.

auditorium   audition   audiocassette   audit

1. When you _____ a college class, you sit in and listen but don't take tests or get credit for it.

2. The director judged the actress's singing voice at her _____.

3. The _____ was packed with people who wanted to hear the speaker.

4. When you listen to an _____ recording of a play, you need to picture in your mind what is happening on stage.

Using the Word Bank

astonish	compulsion	meager	severe
audible	gnarled	dispelled	threadbare

B. DIRECTIONS: Write the Word Bank word that best matches each clue.

1. It names what a gambling or drug addict has. _____

2. A whisper is this, but just barely. _____

3. It's what surprises do to people. _____

4. This could describe knotty and twisted hands. _____

5. This could describe an old, worn-out piece of cloth.

6. This is what the wind did to the fog. _____

7. This might describe a portion of food that is too small. _____

8. This could describe an especially harsh winter. _____

Recognizing Synonyms

C. DIRECTIONS: Circle the word that is most *similar* in meaning to the word in CAPITAL LETTERS.

1. GNARLED: a. sharp   b. dull   c. twisted   d. straight

2. DISPELLED: a. gathered   b. scattered   c. spelled   d. spoke

3. MEAGER: a. little   b. plenty   3. selfish   d. important

4. ASTONISH: a. report   b. return   c. arrest   d. amaze

A Christmas Carol: Scrooge and Marley, Act II
by Charles Dickens, dramatized by Israel Horovitz

Build Spelling Skills: Silent *g* in *gn*

Spelling Strategy   The Word Bank word *gnarled* starts with the letters *gn*. The *g* is silent; it is not pronounced when you say the word. Several words in English start with the letters *gn*. In each word, the *g* is silent; only the *n* sound is heard. Note these words when you come across them in your reading.

A. Practice: Write the word that matches each clue. Each word starts with the letters *gn*. Place one letter in each blank.

1. This word names a large African antelope.
   It rhymes with *flu*.   ___ ___ ___

2. This word names a dwarf-like character in
   folk tales. It rhymes with *home*.   ___ ___ ___ ___ ___

3. This word names a small, two-winged insect.
   It rhymes with *hat*.   ___ ___ ___ ___

4. This word tells what a dog might do to a bone.
   It rhymes with *saw*.   ___ ___ ___

5. This word names a knot on the trunk or branch
   of a tree. It rhymes with *snarl*.   ___ ___ ___ ___ ___

6. This word tells what you do when you grind
   your teeth together. It rhymes with *cash*.   ___ ___ ___ ___ ___

B. Practice: In each sentence, find a word starting with silent *g* that is misspelled. Cross out the word and write it correctly.

1. If "A Christmas Carol" had been a folk tale, Scrooge might have been led around by nomes.

2. In the future, Scrooge sees three scoundrels attacking a dead man's possessions the way a

   nat might attack someone's skin.

3. Scrooge nashes his teeth in anger when he realizes how foolishly he has been behaving.

4. Feelings of guilt and shame begin to naw at Scrooge.

Challenge: When a word starts with the letters *gn*, the *g* is always silent. The same rule applies when a word ends in *gn*, as in the word *sign*. How many other words can you think of that end in the letters *gn*? Write your list on the lines provided. Then say each word. Is the *g* silent in each one?

_____   _____   _____

_____   _____   _____

Selection Support   **177**

A Christmas Carol: Scrooge and Marley, Act II
by Charles Dickens, dramatized by Israel Horovitz

Build Grammar Skills: Pronoun and Antecedent Agreement

An **antecedent** is the word for which a pronoun stands. A pronoun's antecedent may be a noun, a group of words acting as a noun, or even another pronoun. Personal pronouns must always agree with their antecedents in person, number, and gender.

> Tell <u>Martha</u> not to forget **her** books.
> Tell <u>Bill</u> I won't be going with **him** when **he** leaves.
> Tell <u>Martha</u> and <u>Bill</u> that **they** need to remember **their** homework.

Sometimes, agreement is not so obvious. Use a singular personal pronoun to refer to two or more singular antecedents joined by *or* or *nor*. Use a singular personal pronoun if the antecedent is a singular indefinite pronoun (*each, everyone,* etc.). And if the gender of a third-person-singular antecedent is unknown, use *he or she, him or her,* or *his or hers,* not *they, their,* or *theirs.*

> Either <u>Kim Lee</u> *or* <u>Sheri</u> should read **her** paper.
> <u>One</u> of the boys will need to bring **his** own equipment.
> <u>Each</u> of the students finished **his or her** project.

A. Practice: Complete each sentence with a pronoun that agrees with its antecedent in person, number, and gender. Write your pronoun on the line.

1. The Ghost of Christmas present appears; Scrooge has never seen anything like _____.

2. When the bells clang, Scrooge wonders where _____ are.

3. Those merry revelers carry _____ own dinners to work with them.

4. The singers enter the buildings, shutting the doors behind _____.

5. When Scrooge sees Mrs. Cratchit, _____ is preparing Christmas dinner.

6. One of Bob Cratchit's sons wants _____ share of the plum pudding.

7. Each of Cratchit's children finds _____ place around the table.

8. Everyone in the family sits at the table, where _____ bow their heads to pray.

B. Writing Application: Imagine that you have seen a staged performance of *A Christmas Carol.* Write sentences that might describe your reactions. In each sentence, use pronouns of the person, number, and gender specified. Underline the antecedent to which pronouns refer.

1. (third person, masculine, singular) _____

_____

2. (third person, feminine, singular) _____

_____

3. (third person, plural) _____

_____

4. (first person, plural) _____

_____

A Christmas Carol: Scrooge and Marley, Act II
by Charles Dickens, dramatized by Israel Horovitz

Reading Strategy: Asking Questions

As you read "A Christmas Carol," you may have questions about the events that occur. You may not understand immediately what a character means by a particular comment, or why a character behaves as he or she does. Good playwrights often try to puzzle you on purpose in order to raise your curiosity and hold your attention. As you continue reading, however, you should eventually find the answers to your questions.

For example, in Act II, Scene 4, three businessmen are talking together about someone who has died. You might ask yourself, "Who died?" By reading further, you will discover the answer: Scrooge has died, and this scene is telling about his future.

DIRECTIONS: Use the following chart to record questions you have as you read Act II. Then, once you discover the answers, record them on the chart as well. One example is provided.

Questions	Answers
Who is the dead man that the three businessmen are discussing?	The dead man is Ebenezer Scrooge.

Selection Support   **179**

A Christmas Carol: Scrooge and Marley, Act II
by Charles Dickens, dramatized by Israel Horovitz

Literary Analysis: Characterization in Drama

Characterization is the way in which a writer reveals a character's personality. In a drama, you learn about characters mainly by the things they say and do, and by what others say about them. For example, in Act II, Scene 3, when the Ghost of Christmas Present tells Scrooge about Cratchit's many children, Scrooge says, "On his meager earnings! What foolishness!" This comment reveals that Scrooge is unable to appreciate the human pleasures that a family can bring, acknowledging only the financial burden.

DIRECTIONS: Complete the following chart. Provide examples of dialogue from five characters in the play, and tell what each example reveals about the character.

Character	Example of Dialogue	What the Lines Reveal

"The Monsters Are Due on Maple Street" by Rod Serling

Build Vocabulary

Using the Word Root -sist-

Words that contain the root -sist- have something to do with standing. For example, a *persistent* person is one who stands firm and doesn't give in.

A. DIRECTIONS: Match each word on the left with its definition on the right. Write the letter of the definition on the line next to the word it defines.

____ 1. assistant   a. a force that stands against or in opposition to something

____ 2. resistance   b. standing in agreement with

____ 3. consistent   c. to take a firm stand and demand something

____ 4. insist   d. someone who stands ready to help

Using the Word Bank

flustered	sluggishly	assent	persistently
defiant	scapegoat	metamorphosis	

B. DIRECTIONS: Write the Word Bank word that can replace the italicized word or phrase in each sentence.

1. Caterpillars undergo a (*change*) _____ in order to become butterflies.

2. One student became the (*person blamed*) _____ for all the others in class.

3. The runner in last place moved (*as if lacking energy*) _____.

4. Soldiers are taught never to be (*boldly resisting*) _____ to their superiors.

5. There was (*agreement*) _____ between the enemies that finally ended the fighting.

6. The farm animals were (*made nervous*) _____ by the thunder.

7. The workers (*firmly and steadily*) _____ drilled into the thick stone.

Analogies

C. DIRECTIONS: For each related pair of words in CAPITAL LETTERS, choose the pair that best expresses a *similar* relationship. Fill in the letter of your choice.

____ 1. SCAPEGOAT : BLAMED ::
  a. teacher : taught
  b. hero : praised
  c. enemy : helped
  d. player : team

____ 2. ASSENT : DISAGREEMENT ::
  a. shout : speak
  b. yes : maybe
  c. entrance : exit
  d. today : tomorrow

____ 3. SLUGGISHLY : TIRED ::
  a. foolishly : silly
  b. quickly : slowly
  c. loudly : speaker
  d. instantly : soon

____ 4. METAMORPHOSIS : CHANGE ::
  a. appearance : disappearance
  b. arrival : station
  c. weather : cool
  d. conversation : talk

Unit 8: Drama

"The Monsters Are Due on Maple Street" by Rod Serling

Build Spelling Skills: *f* Sound Spelled *ph*

Spelling Strategy In some words in English, the *f* sound is spelled *ph*. This spelling may appear in the beginning, middle, or end of a word. Notice that the Word Bank word *metamorphosis* contains the *f* sound spelled *ph*.

Examples: physician   telephone   phase

A. Practice: Complete each sentence with a word that contains the *f* sound spelled *ph*. The first letter of the word is given as a clue.

1. Video games display exciting computer g_____s.

2. Your second year of high school or college is called your so _____ year.

3. If you want to speak to an out-of-town friend, just pick up the t_____.

4. A picture that you take with a camera is called a p_____.

5. The words *on Maple Street* are an example of a prepositional p_____.

6. If you write a person's life story, you write his or her b_____.

7. A terrible disaster such as an earthquake is called a ca_____.

8. A championship team often receives a silver cup as its t_____.

9. When you study the locations of countries, you are studying g_____.

10. A g_____ is a rodent that lives underground.

B. Practice: In each sentence, find a word with the *f* sound spelled *ph* that is spelled wrong. Cross out the word and write it correctly.

1. Everyone on Maple Street develops a fobia of monsters after a strange light appears in the sky.

2. Next, lights mysteriously go out in the neighborhood—a fenomenon that nobody is able to explain.

3. When someone walks along the sidewalk in darkness, residents fear it may be some sort of fantom or monster.

4. Neighbors begin to fear that one of the residents on Maple Street may be a fony human being who is really a monster or alien.

5. The play describes in grafic detail how long-time neighbors turn on each other.

6. In the end, two shadowy figures in a space craft discuss their filosofy of how easily fear and panic can be spread on Earth.

Challenge: One reason the name Maple Street was chosen for the story is that it is a street name found in many "typical" American towns and cities. Many other American streets are also named for trees, such as Elm or Oak. Look at a map of your city or town. List all the streets you find that are named for trees.

"The Monsters Are Due on Maple Street" by Rod Serling

Build Grammar Skills: Pronoun References

A **pronoun reference** is the antecedent to which a pronoun refers. Sometimes a pronoun reference is unclear. This lack of clarity occurs when a pronoun could refer to more than one antecedent, or when a pronoun is too far away from its antecedent for the connection to be determined. A sentence with unclear or distant pronoun references can be confusing and hard to understand. Always make sure that the antecedent for a pronoun is clear, either by keeping the pronoun close enough to its antecedent to prevent confusion, or by making sure that pronouns might not appear to refer to more than one antecedent.

Unclear: Carlos told Ian about finding the book he was looking for.
Clear: Carlos told Ian about finding the book Ian was looking for.
Unclear: Zheng asked his father if he could go to the store when he got home.
Clear: Zheng asked his father if he could go to the store when his father got home.
Unclear: Get your book, find a pencil, then go to your desk and open it to the lesson.
Clear: Get your book, find a pencil, then go to your desk and open your book to the lesson.

Practice and Writing Application: Rewrite the following sentences to make the unclear pronoun references more clear.

1. There's something wrong with the stove. There was a flash of light when that meteor struck and a roar, and it stopped working.

   _____

   _____

2. Steve and Charlie ask Goodman about the car starting. He says he doesn't know how it happened.

   _____

   _____

3. In this story, the people are frightened. Maybe there are aliens. Maybe the aliens are invading. They have a lot to think about.

   _____

   _____

4. Steve is surprised at everyone's behavior. Charlie is suspicious. Don is making accusations, but he keeps his head through it all.

   _____

   _____

5. The aliens discuss the plans for taking over earth. They appear to be very effective.

   _____

   _____

6. Fear was the tool the aliens used. "Love your neighbor" was not something these people practiced. It accomplished what the aliens wanted.

   _____

   _____

"The Monsters Are Due on Maple Street" by Rod Serling

Reading Strategy: Predicting

As you read or watch a story, you may be tempted to **predict**, or guess, what will happen next. How can you know what will happen? You can't be sure, but you may have an idea based on clues that are planted in the story. These clues might be things that characters say or do, or things that have already happened. As you continue to read, you will discover the actual outcome and see if your prediction was right or wrong. Later, you can make more predictions about the remainder of the story and then see how accurate those predictions are.

For example, at the beginning of "The Monsters Are Due on Maple Street," there is a loud roar and a flash of light in the sky. These clues might lead you to predict that a meteor is about to hit the town. Not until the end of the story do you discover that the light was really from an alien space craft.

DIRECTIONS: Use the following chart to record your predictions in "The Monsters Are Due on Maple Street." For each prediction, list the clues that influence your thinking. Later, record the outcome to see how accurate your prediction was. One example is provided.

Clue	Prediction	Outcome
There is a roar and a strange light in the sky.	A meteor will strike the town.	An alien space craft is hovering over the town.

"The Monsters Are Due on Maple Street" by Rod Serling

Literary Analysis: Plot in Drama

The **plot** is the sequence of events in the play. Most plots follow a similar pattern, beginning with the **exposition,** which introduces the characters and the basic situation. Next, the central **conflict** is presented. This is a struggle between opposing forces that drives the action of the story. The conflict increases during the **rising action** and comes to a peak at the **climax.** The story ends with the **falling action** and the **resolution,** in which the readers or audience members finally learn the outcome of the conflict.

In a play, the exposition is often presented to the audience by means of the list of characters and the stage directions or, for an audience, the visual clues of the setting. In "The Monsters Are Due on Maple Street," the narrator also contributes to the exposition. Soon, the characters and setting are established and the other elements of the plot begin to appear.

DIRECTIONS: Below is a figure commonly used to illustrate plot development. Some elements of the plot have been described. On the lines provided, describe the other plot elements.

Climax: Charlie shoots and kills Pete Van Horn.

Rising Action:

_____

_____

_____

_____

_____

_____

Falling Action: Panic takes control, behavior deteriorates, people turn against each other.

Climax

Rising Action

Falling Action

Exposition

Conflict Introduced

Resolution

Exposition: Characters: the men, women, and children living on Maple Street. Situation: the normal activities of a suburban neighborhood, until a roaring flash of light passes overhead.

Conflict: _____

_____

_____

_____

_____

_____

Resolution: _____

_____

_____

_____

_____

_____

Unit 8: Drama

"The Cremation of Sam McGee" by Robert Service
"Washed in Silver" by James Stephens
"Winter" by Nikki Giovanni

Build Vocabulary

Shades of Meaning

Sometimes two words can be synonyms but still have different shades of meaning. For example, the words *run* and *dash* both refer to the action of moving quickly. But *dash* is a more specific word, meaning to run very quickly, and usually for only a short amount of time. You would *dash* across the street, but you would not *dash* in a 26-mile marathon.

A. DIRECTIONS: Circle the word in parentheses whose shade of meaning is better for the sentence.

1. I (looked, peeked) through the door crack to see what was hidden in the room.

2. The terrified kids (shrieked, cried) on the roller-coaster.

3. We (carried, lugged) the heavy suitcases up the stairs to the attic.

Using the Word Bank

whimper	cremated	ghastly	stern
loathed	grisly	radiance	burrow

B. DIRECTIONS: Write the Word Bank word that best completes each sentence.

1. The driver _____ having to change the flat tire in the rain.

2. The injured dog began to _____ softly in the darkness.

3. The _____ look on her face made us think she'd seen a ghost.

4. The undertaker _____ the corpse and then boxed the ashes.

5. The _____ parent insisted that the child finish his homework.

6. Sixteen ambulances were needed after the _____ bus accident.

7. The _____ of the freshly fallen snow led me to put on my sunglasses.

8. A groundhog must _____ beneath the earth to make its cozy home.

Recognizing Synonyms

C. DIRECTIONS: Circle the letter of the word that is most *similar* to the meaning of the word in CAPITAL LETTERS.

1. STERN
   a. strict
   b. friendly
   c. forward
   d. backward

2. BURROW
   a. carry
   b. tunnel
   c. lend
   d. build

3. WHIMPER
   a. laugh
   b. explain
   c. wonder
   d. cry

"The Cremation of Sam McGee" by Robert Service
"Washed in Silver" by James Stephens
"Winter" by Nikki Giovanni

Build Spelling Skills: *hw* Sound Spelled *w* or *wh*

Spelling Strategy   The Word Bank word *whimper* can be pronounced two different ways. You can either stress the letters *wh* by making a *hw* sound, or you can pronounce the *wh* merely as *w*. Several other words follow the same rule.

Examples: which   whine   where

In most other words, the *w* sound is spelled with a *w*, not *wh*.

Examples: witch   wine   wear

A. Practice: Add either *w* or *wh* to spell each word below. (A clue to the word appears in parentheses). Write the entire word. Use a dictionary for help, if necessary.

1. _____eel (part of a car or bike)   _____

2. _____eat (grain used for flour)   _____

3. _____est (the opposite of east)   _____

4. _____at (often begins a question)   _____

5. _____eapon (instrument for fighting)   _____

6. _____edding (marriage ceremony)   _____

7. _____ack (to hit very hard)   _____

8. _____aist (body part near the hips)   _____

9. _____ip (strap used for beating)   _____

B. Practice: In each sentence, find a word that begins with either *w* or *wh* that is spelled incorrectly. Cross out the word and spell it correctly. The first one is done for you.

1. Sam McGee was not used to traveling places ~~were~~ it was so cold. *(where)*

2. Sam was the only traveler in the group to wimper about the cold conditions.

3. He managed to wine quite a bit about the bone-chilling cold.

4. The moon spilled its radiance wile we watched in wonder.

5. The speaker in "Winter" is thinking about wich books to gather.

6. The witeness of the scene overwhelmed us.

Challenge: The letters *wh* are not always pronounced *w* or *hw*. In some words, *wh* is pronounced *h*. One example is the word *whole*. Can you think of three more words in which the letters *wh* are pronounced *h*? Hint: They are often question words.

_____   _____   _____

"The Cremation of Sam McGee" by Robert Service
"Washed in Silver" by James Stephens
"Winter" by Nikki Giovanni

Build Grammar Skills: Degrees of Comparison of Modifiers

Most adjectives and adverbs have different forms to show degrees of comparison. The three **degrees of comparison** are *positive*, *comparative*, and *superlative*. Most one- and two-syllable modifiers are made comparative by adding *-er*, and superlative by adding *-est* to the end. However, if adding *-er* or *-est* makes a word sound awkward (*eagerer*, for example), then *more* and *most* are used (*more eager*). *More* and *most* are used for all modifiers with three or more syllables, and for adverbs that end in *-ly*.

Positive	Comparative	Superlative
strong	stronger	strongest
obvious	more obvious	most obvious
slowly	more slowly	most slowly

Also remember that some modifiers have irregular comparative and superlative forms.

Irregular modifiers: bad, worse, worst   good, better, best   much, more, most

The relation between the modifier and the word being modified should always be clear. No matter what the degree of comparison, an adverb should always be close to what it modifies.

A. Practice: Underline the modifier in each sentence, then identify it as positive, comparative, or superlative.

_____ 1. The narrator in the poem "The Cremation of Sam McGee" is a faithful friend.

_____ 2. At the end of the poem, Sam McGee was the warmest he'd been in days.

_____ 3. "Washed in Silver" creates the loveliest images.

_____ 4. Do you think the "little boys and girls" in "Winter" are sicklier than at other times of the year?

_____ 5. In "Winter," it appears that the writer has more enjoyable plans for winter than the frog has.

B. Writing Application: Imagine you were a member of the party traveling with Sam McGee. Write sentences about your experiences. Use the comparative or superlative form of each of the modifiers below in a sentence.

1. good _____

2. cold _____

3. beautiful _____

4. slowly _____

"The Cremation of Sam McGee" by Robert Service
"Washed in Silver" by James Stephens
"Winter" by Nikki Giovanni

Reading Strategy: Interpreting Figures of Speech

Poets choose their words very carefully in order to recreate memorably for the reader the images and ideas they want to convey. **Figures of speech**—words or phrases that are not meant to be taken literally—are used in most writing but are most common in poetry. The following chart lists and describes four major types of figures of speech. You have probably used one or more of these types of figures of speech in your own speaking or writing.

Type	Description	Example
Simile	Comparison between two unlike ideas using *like* or *as*	"it stabbed *like* a driven nail"
Metaphor	Comparison between two unlike things without using *like* or *as*	"A promise made is a debt unpaid"
Hyperbole	Deliberate exaggeration or overstatement	"I'm chilled clean through to the bone"
Personification	The giving of human characteristics to a nonhuman subject	"the stars o'erhead were dancing heel to toe"

DIRECTIONS: As you read poems in this group, look for the use of figures of speech. Cite one or more example from each poem, or write an example of your own figures of speech about the poems.

Poem	Figure of Speech From or About the Poem	Type of Figure of Speech
"The Cremation of Sam McGee"		
"Washed in Silver"		
"Winter"		

Unit 9: Poetry

Name _____ Date _____

"The Cremation of Sam McGee" by Robert Service
"Washed in Silver" by James Stephens
"Winter" by Nikki Giovanni

Literary Analysis: Types of Poetry

Poetry comes in a variety of styles because poets write for a variety of reasons. They may write to entertain, inform, share an experience or idea, persuade, or trigger an emotion. Different **types of poetry** enable poets to accomplish different purposes, create different effects, and bring out different responses or emotions in readers. This grouping of poems explores both **narrative poetry** and **lyric poetry.** While both types of poem may rely on common poetic devices such as rhythm and figures of speech, they differ in significant ways. Here are some of the main features of these two types of poems:

• **Narrative poetry** tells a story. Like most short stories, a narrative poem has a plot, characters, and a setting. Like many poems, a narrative poem includes rhythm, repetition, and rhyme. Narrative poets often use rhythm and repetition to create a musical effect and to highlight key details of the poem.

• **Lyric poetry** expresses a poet's personal thoughts and feelings. Once sung to the music of a stringed instrument called a *lyre,* lyric poetry employs lively, musical language. Vivid words that appeal to the senses help you share the poet's vision or experience. Lines and phrases from lyric poems can echo in your mind like the words of a song (the song's *lyrics*). Nature and love are common themes in lyric poetry.

DIRECTIONS: Use the Venn diagram to compare and contrast narrative poetry and lyric poetry. Include elements described in the definitions given above. Also include details you know about poetry in general. List similarities in (or right below, if you need more space) the overlapping region of the diagram. List differences in the appropriate outer regions.

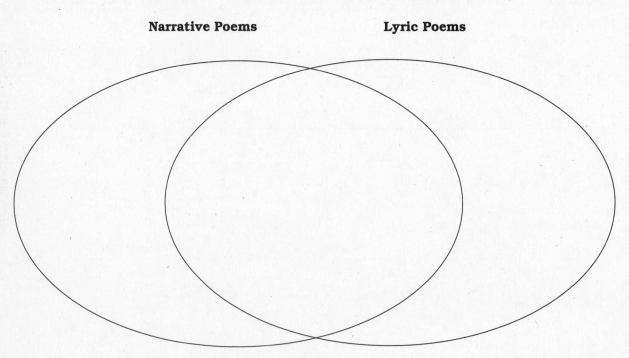

Narrative Poems   **Lyric Poems**

Both

"Seal" by William Jay Smith
"The Pasture" by Robert Frost
Three Haiku by Matsuo Bashō, translated by Daniel C. Buchanan

Build Vocabulary

Synonyms

Many words in the English language have **synonyms**—words with similar meanings. For example, the words *big, large, huge,* and *gigantic* are synonyms. Synonyms are helpful because they enable writers to avoid repeating the same word over and over. By using other words with a similar meaning, poets add variety and interest to their work.

A. DIRECTIONS: Circle the letter of the word that is a synonym for the underlined word in each sentence.

1. The inventor searched for a <u>solution</u>, and finally he found the _____.
   a. question   b. problem   c. answer   d. experiment

2. He was not only surprised by the <u>comment</u>, but also offended by the _____.
   a. speaker   b. remark   c. joke   d. compliment

3. She snapped the perfect <u>photograph</u> and later framed the _____.
   a. camera   b. illustration   c. artist   d. picture

4. The story <u>confused</u> most readers; only a few weren't _____ by it.
   a. puzzled   b. written   c. fascinated   d. entertained

Using the Word Box

pasture	totters	swerve	utter

B. DIRECTIONS: Write the Word Bank Word that best completes each sentence.

1. The driver managed to _____ and avoid the out-of-control truck.

2. If the gymnast _____ for even two seconds, she can lose points.

3. The cows went out to the _____ to enjoy the grass and sunshine.

4. Always think about what you are going to say before you _____ anything.

Analogies

C. DIRECTIONS: For each related pair of words in CAPITAL LETTERS, choose the pair that best expresses a *similar* relationship. Circle the letter of your choice.

1. COWS : PASTURE ::
   a. wolves : prairie
   b. forest : bears
   c. zoo : animals
   d. horses : riders

2. SWERVE : CURVE ::
   a. line : circle
   b. wait : go
   c. shape : triangle
   d. leap : jump

3. UTTER : MOUTH ::
   a. hands : fingers
   b. listen : ears
   c. nose : smell
   d. eyes : two

4. ROCKING CHAIR : TOTTERS ::
   a. seat : cushion
   b. television : channels
   c. worm : wiggles
   d. jumps : frogs

"Seal" by William Jay Smith
"The Pasture" by Robert Frost
Three Haiku by Matsuo Bashō, translated by Daniel C. Buchanan

Build Spelling Skills: *cher* Sound Spelled *ture*

Spelling Strategy   The Word Bank word *pasture* ends with the *cher* sound spelled *ture*. Many other words also contain the *cher* sound spelled *ture*, including *mature*, *denture*, and *legislature*.

A. Practice: At the right, write the word that matches each clue. The first three letters of each word are given in parentheses. Each word ends with *ture*.

1. a musical introduction (ove) __ __ __ __ __ __ __ __

2. an exciting experience (adv) __ __ __ __ __ __ __ __ __

3. the science of farming (agr) __ __ __ __ __ __ __ __ __ __ __

4. a motion with your hands (ges) __ __ __ __ __ __ __

5. a formal, prepared speech (lec) __ __ __ __ __ __ __

6. to make in a factory (man) __ __ __ __ __ __ __ __ __ __ __

7. things mixed together (mix) __ __ __ __ __ __ __

8. way of sitting or standing (pos) __ __ __ __ __ __ __

9. to make a hole in (pun) __ __ __ __ __ __ __

10. a photo or illustration (pic) __ __ __ __ __ __ __

B. Practice: In each sentence, find a word with the *cher* sound that is spelled wrong. Cross out the word and spell it correctly. The first one is done for you.

1. Have you ever been invited to join a friend in the ~~pascher~~? *pasture*

2. The speaker in "The Pasture" is going out to retrieve a young creachure in the field.

3. In "Seal," the speaker describes in vivid detail the many feachures of a seal.

4. A seal has the kind of poscher that can bend and swerve easily in the water.

5. In the first of "Three Haiku," try to picher the sun shining on a mountain path.

6. The speaker makes the wait for spring sound like an exciting advencher.

Challenge: Many English words rhyme with the word *utter*—*clutter* and *mutter*, for example. Make a list of five or six more words that rhyme with *utter*, and then write a two-line poem, using a different "utter" word at the end of each line.

_____   _____   _____

_____   _____   _____

_____

_____

"Seal" by William Jay Smith

"The Pasture" by Robert Frost

Three Haiku by Matsuo Bashō, translated by Daniel C. Buchanan

Build Grammar Skills: Placement of *only*

The position of the word *only* can affect the entire meaning of a sentence. Place *only* just before the word or phrase it modifies. Otherwise, the sentence may not make sense.

Incorrect: I only eat fresh food.

Meaning: The only thing I do with fresh food is eat it. (I don't harvest it, cook it, or store it.)

Correct: I eat only fresh food.

Meaning: There is just one kind of food I eat: fresh food.

A. Practice: Read each sentence. Decide if the placement of the word *only* makes sense. If it does not, cross out the word *only* and insert it where it belongs in the sentence. One example is given.

                              only
1. Spring arrives ‿after thin layers of mist ~~only~~ settle.

2. The seal is not the water animal that only hunts for fish.

3. The farmer only raked leaves in the fall.

4. The farmer only fetched the calf and not its mother.

5. The sun only rises in the east.

6. The seal only has two flippers.

B. Writing Application: Decide where the word *only* should go in each sentence to make the most sense. Write your sentence, including the word *only*.

1. Does a seal live in the water?

_____

2. I have seen seals at the zoo.

_____

3. The farmer grew corn.

_____

4. Come along if you have time.

_____

5. The sun rose a few minutes ago.

_____

6. Three customers may enter at one time.

_____

"Seal" by William Jay Smith
"The Pasture" by Robert Frost
Three Haiku by Matsuo Bashō, translated by Daniel C. Buchanan

Reading Strategy: Reading According to Punctuation

Poetry, like prose, contains punctuation marks to help guide readers. However, poetry punctuation often can be more important than prose punctuation in helping you understand the meaning of a passage. Since the words in a poem sometimes appear in short or even unstructured lines, the commas, semicolons, and periods you find are important guides for understanding where to pause and stop as you read. You must **read according to the punctuation.**

For example, in the second of Three Haiku, the question mark at the end of the first line indicates where the question ends. The second and third lines comprise a single sentence. No punctuation appears at the end of the second line. That signals that you shouldn't pause there; instead you should read straight through to the end of the third line, where a period appears.

DIRECTIONS: For each poem, record examples of punctuation that help you understand how the poem should be read. One example is provided.

Name of Poem	Example of Punctuation	What It Tells You About Reading
"Seal"		
"The Pasture"		
Three Haiku	question mark after the word *indeed*	Read the line as a question.

"Seal" by William Jay Smith

"The Pasture" by Robert Frost

Three Haiku by Matsuo Bashō, translated by Daniel C. Buchanan

Literary Analysis: Form in Poetry

Poems, like houses, come in different shapes and sizes, or **forms**.

- In a **traditional English poem,** lines often are grouped into **stanzas,** similar to how prose sentences are grouped into paragraphs. "The Pasture" is a traditional English poem.

- In a **concrete poem,** the lines are shaped to create a picture that suggests the poem's subject. "Seal" is a concrete poem.

- **Haiku** is a traditional form of Japanese poetry consisting of three lines. The first and last lines have five syllables each, and the middle line has seven syllables.

DIRECTIONS: Write your answers to the following questions.

1. If you were to rewrite "The Pasture" as a concrete poem, what shape do you think would best express the main idea of the poem? Why?

   _____

   _____

2. If you were to rewrite "The Pasture" as a haiku, what five- or seven-syllable line might you write and still retain the phrase "You come too"?

   _____

   _____

3. If you were to rewrite "Seal" as a traditional English poem, how many stanzas would you include? What would be the main idea in each stanza?

   _____

   _____

4. If you were to rewrite "Seal" as a haiku, what would one of your lines be?

   _____

   _____

5. If you were to rewrite Three Haiku as one traditional English poem, how many stanzas would you include? What would be the main idea in each stanza?

   _____

   _____

6. If you were to rewrite Three Haiku as one concrete poem, what shape do you think would best express the main idea in each of the three poems?

   _____

   _____

© Prentice-Hall, Inc.

"Martin Luther King" by Raymond Richard Patterson
"Annabel Lee" by Edgar Allan Poe

Build Vocabulary

Using the Root -found-

When you see the word *found*, you probably think of the past tense of *find*, as in *I found the lost cat*. But there is also a word root *-found-*, meaning "bottom," that is unrelated to the word *find*. The word root *-found-* appears, for example, in the word *foundation*—the bottom part of a structure.

A. DIRECTIONS: Use one of the following words with the root *-found-* to complete each sentence. Write the word in the blank.

foundation   profound   founder   founded

1. The college was _____ in 1976 by a group of wealthy investors.

2. The speaker made a _____ comment that had several layers of meaning.

3. The earthquake did serious damage to the building's _____.

4. Thomas Jefferson was a _____ of our government.

Using the Word Bank

beset	profound	coveted

B. DIRECTIONS: Write the Word Bank word that best completes each sentence. Note that one word is used twice.

1. The effects of the tragedy were so _____ that the whole town was affected.

2. The losing team _____ the grand prize that the winners took home.

3. The man was _____ by so many troubles that he didn't know what to do.

4. The emotions expressed in these two poems are _____ .

Recognizing Antonyms

C. DIRECTIONS: Circle the letter of the word or phrase that is most *opposite* in meaning to the word in CAPITAL LETTERS.

1. PROFOUND
   a. deep
   b. shallow
   c. pleasant
   d. rude

2. BESET
   a. free from
   b. watch
   c. listen
   d. felt by

3. COVETED
   a. valuable
   b. sorry
   c. planned
   d. unwanted

"**Martin Luther King**" by Raymond Richard Patterson
"**Annabel Lee**" by Edgar Allan Poe

Build Spelling Skills: *kwa* Sound Spelled *qua*

Spelling Strategy   Some words that contain the *kwa* sound spelled *qua* include *quarrel* and *squad*.

A. Practice: Fill in the missing *qua* in each word. Write the entire word. Then write its meaning. Look in a dictionary if you don't know the meaning of a word.

1. ___ ___ ___ drant   _____

Meaning: _____

2. ___ ___ ___ ntity   _____

Meaning: _____

3. s ___ ___ ___ lid   _____

Meaning: _____

4. s ___ ___ ___ dron   _____

Meaning: _____

5. ___ ___ ___ ndary   _____

Meaning: _____

B. Practice: Complete each word in the following list by adding the letters *qua*. Then complete each sentence by choosing the appropriate word from the list and writing it on the line. Use each word once.

___ ___ ___ lified   ___ ___ ___ rrel

s___ ___ ___ wk   ___ ___ ___ lities

1. In "Martin Luther King," the poet describes King's _____ of love and passion.

2. King taught the world that a _____ can be settled in a peaceful, nonviolent manner.

3. Poets might agree that some words are quiet whereas others _____ loudly.

4. Poe's sad loss was what _____ him to write the poem "Annabel Lee."

Challenge: Many of the words that contain <u>qu</u> have common roots. Using a dictionary, find out where the following roots came from and what they meant. Then give an example of a word using each root.

quad _____

quant _____

qual _____

"Martin Luther King" by Raymond Richard Patterson
"Annabel Lee" by Edgar Allan Poe

Build Grammar Skills: Capitalization

Most writers apply standard rules of **capitalization,** or the usage of upper-case letters, in their works. It is customary to capitalize
- the beginning of a sentence or quotation
- proper nouns—names of people, geographical places, and specific groups, events, and times
- the pronoun *I*
- the titles of people (Miss, Rabbi, Admiral) and titles of things (books, plays, poems, etc.)
- proper adjectives—adjectives derived from proper nouns

> **Examples:** The poem captures the essence of Dr. King.
> Dad said, "He died in Memphis in April of 1970."
> I will visit there next Saturday.

A. Practice: Each sentence that follows contains one or more capitalization errors. Circle the words that should be capitalized.

1. Like king, poet raymond richard patterson is of african descent.

2. dr. king made many important contributions to American life.

3. we remember his achievements each year in january.

4. People who saw king at the famous rally in washington in 1963 will never forget it.

5. Edgar allan poe has been given credit for inventing the modern mystery.

6. Although "annabel Lee" is not a mystery, it has a mysterious feeling to it.

7. Have you read another well-known poe poem, "the Raven"?

B. Writing Application: No rules of capitalization have been applied to the following sentences. Rewrite each sentence on the lines provided, supplying all needed capital letters.

1. poe was born in boston, but when his mother died, he went to live with the allans in richmond, virginia.

_____

_____

2. shortly after leaving the u.s. army, poe began publishing stories, and was soon editing a magazine: the *southern literary messenger*.

_____

_____

3. many famous people, such as hollywood actor charleton heston, joined with martin luther king, jr., in the efforts to end discrimination.

_____

_____

Name _____ Date _____

"Martin Luther King" by Raymond Richard Patterson
"Annabel Lee" by Edgar Allan Poe

Reading Strategy: Paraphrasing

It has been said that you can't really know how well you understand something until you have to explain it to someone else. This rule certainly applies to poetry. After you read a poem, can you tell a friend what it means in your own words? You can find out by **paraphrasing** each line or stanza; that is, restating it in your own words. As you paraphrase, be sure not to change the meaning of the passage; only express it in a different way.

For example, in "Martin Luther King," the author writes: "His love so deep, so wide, / He could not turn aside." You might paraphrase the passage like this: "King had too much love in him to ignore the problems of others."

DIRECTIONS: Select your favorite passages from the two poems you read. For each passage or stanza, paraphrase the main idea in your own words. One example is provided.

Stanza	Paraphrase
His love so deep, so wide, / He could not turn aside	He had too much love in him to ignore the problems of others.

"Martin Luther King" by Raymond Richard Patterson
"Annabel Lee" by Edgar Allan Poe

Literary Analysis: Rhythm and Rhyme

Many poems contain the special qualities of **rhythm** and **rhyme.** These are usually among the first things a person responds to in a poem. Rhythm and rhyme work together to make a poem memorable and help establish the reader's response.

• **Rhythm** is a poem's pattern of stressed (ˊ) and unstressed (ˇ) syllables. For example:

Hĭs lóve, sŏ déep, sŏ wíde,

Hĕ cóuld nŏt túrn ăsíde.

As you read a poem, the same rhythm may be repeated in each line or set of lines.

• **Rhyme** is the repetition of a sound in certain words, often at the ends of lines. In the lines above, for example, the words *wide* and *aside* rhyme. As a poem continues, a rhyme pattern often develops. For example, in "Martin Luther King," the pattern is *aabbccddee.* The first two lines have one rhyme, the next two lines have a different rhyme, and so on.

DIRECTIONS: Complete each item below.

1. Indicate the rhythm in the following sets of lines. Mark the stressed and unstressed syllables, as shown in the example above.

   a. His passion, so profound,

      He would not turn around.

   b. But our love it was stronger by far than the love

      Of those who were older than we—

2. List the rhyming words in each poem.

   a. "Martin Luther King"

      _____

      _____

   b. "Annabel Lee"

      _____

      _____

"Full Fathom Five" by William Shakespeare
"Onomatopoeia" by Eve Merriam
"Maestro" by Pat Mora

Build Vocabulary

Words Based on Onomatopoeia

Onomatopoeia refers to words that imitate the sounds they describe. Comic books often use onomatopoeic words such as *boom, pow, whack,* and *zap*. Other examples of onomatopoeia include *hiss* and *sizzle*.

A. Directions: Write an original sentence using each of these onomatopoeic words.

1. gurgle _____

2. buzz _____

3. hum _____

4. thud _____

5. whack _____

6. ping _____

Using the Word Bank

sputters	knell	maestro	snare

B. Directions: Write the Word Bank word that matches each clue.

1. It's someone with great musical talent. _____

2. It's how spiders catch flies. _____

3. It's what a broken-down car does on the highway. _____

4. It may be sounded at a funeral service. _____

Analogies

C. Directions: For each related pair of words in CAPITAL LETTERS, choose the lettered pair that best expresses a *similar* relationship. Circle the letter of your choice.

1. HUNTERS : SNARE ::
   a. pitchers : catcher   b. shoes : dance   c. farmers : harvest   d. authors : writers

2. SPUTTERS : SPITS ::
   a. pushes : shoves   b. works : plays   c. peanuts : butters   d. mouths : tongues

3. MAESTRO : ORCHESTRA ::
   a. leader : follower   b. student: teacher   c. star : show   d. hospital : doctor

4. KNELL : BELL :
   a. rain : lightning   b. clap : thunder   c. song : dance   d. drum : stick

"Full Fathom Five" by William Shakespeare
"Onomatopoeia" by Eve Merriam
"Maestro" by Pat Mora

Build Spelling Skills: *n* Sound Spelled *kn*

Spelling Strategy In the Word Bank word *knell*, the *k* is silent, so the word is pronounced "nell." Several other words in English also begin with a silent *k* followed by *n*, including the words *knowledge* and *knuckle*.

A. Practice: In the crossword puzzle, write the words starting with *kn* that match the clues.

1. information you have acquired

2. rap on a door

3. what you turn in order to open a door

4. a joint in your finger

5. make a sweater with yarn and two needles

6. work dough with hands to make bread

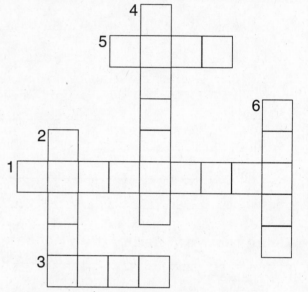

B. Practice: In each sentence, find a word that is supposed to start with *kn* that is spelled wrong. Cross out the word and spell it correctly. The first one is done for you.

1. "Full Fathom Five" describes how sea nymphs ring the father's ~~nell~~ ^knell^ hourly.

2. The speaker in the poem seems to have intimate nowledge of the sea.

3. In "Onomatopoeia," the rusty spigot makes a nocking sound before giving water.

4. The poet used many words that she new to describe the sounds of a rusty spigot.

5. In "Maestro," no one in the audience nows what the musician is thinking about.

6. The maestro has a musical nack that his parents helped cultivate when he was a child.

Challenge: Most words beginning with *kn* came into English from Old English, Dutch, and German. The words *knave* and *knight* still remind us of those ancient origins. Another old-fashioned "*kn*" word is *Knickerbocker*. Look up the word in a dictionary, and answer the following questions.

1. Who were the Knickerbockers? _____

2. Who are sometimes called Knickerbockers today? _____

3. When spelled with a lower-case *k*, what are *knickerbockers*? _____

BONUS: The name of which basketball team is an abbreviation for *Knickerbockers?*

"Full Fathom Five" by William Shakespeare
"Onomatopoeia" by Eve Merriam
"Maestro" by Pat Mora

Build Grammar Skills: Interjections

An **interjection** is an exclamation that expresses a feeling or emotion, such as surprise, pain, joy, disappointment, or uncertainty. Some common interjections are *ugh, hey, oh no, gee, goodness, whoops, um, alas, huh,* and *hooray.* An **exclamation point (!)** usually follows an interjection that expresses a strong emotion. A **comma (,)** sets off an interjection that expresses a mild emotion or interrupts a sentence.

Examples: <u>Say</u>, that's my jacket!
What is my, <u>er</u>, grade?
<u>Super!</u> I'll be right over.

A. Practice: Rewrite each sentence. Correct the punctuation when necessary. Underline the interjection in the corrected sentence you wrote.

1. Boy. The image of the bones turned to coral is kind of uh spooky.

_____

2. Wow. Shakespeare's description of drowning is unsettling.

_____

3. Well. I think the use of sound is delightful in Merriam's poem.

_____

4. Gosh, the poem "Maestro" is so inspiring.

_____

5. Say. Let's find out more about Pat Mora.

_____

B. Writing Application: Write a sentence to express each emotion indicated. Include an interjection in each sentence you write, and use the correct punctuation.

1. hesitation _____

_____

2. pain _____

_____

3. joy _____

_____

4. impatience _____

_____

5. amazement _____

_____

"Full Fathom Five" by William Shakespeare
"Onomatopoeia" by Eve Merriam
"Maestro" by Pat Mora

Reading Strategy: Clarifying Word Meanings

Poets select words that create effects, convey ideas, and help them share their thoughts, feelings, and experiences. To do this, they may use words that are unfamiliar to you, or they may use words in unexpected ways. In order for you to fully appreciate a writer's work and unlock a poem's message, you may need to **clarify word meanings.** The most reliable way to learn the definition of a word is checking a dictionary, footnote, or glossary. If a dictionary is not handy, you may be able to determine a word's meaning by using context clues, or by applying your knowledge of word roots. Checking a dictionary later can confirm your guess.

Of course, even if you use a dictionary, context is important in helping you determine precisely how the author is using the word, particularly when reading poetry. Reread the work carefully, to determine what the writer is really saying. Look for clues in other lines or in the title. Ask yourself questions about the images in the poem. Determine if an image is a figure of speech. Get information from another source, such as a note about the author.

DIRECTIONS: Follow the directions for each item, to clarify word meaning.

1. Use a dictionary to learn the meaning of the underlined word in this sentence, then write a short statement about what the writer is describing.

    The bright, <u>pellucid</u> waves permit my eyes to wander far beyond the shore.

    _____

2. The word *furrow* means a long, narrow groove or track cut in the earth by a plow. But that is not how the writer uses it here. Using context clues and the definition of the word, determine what image the writer is trying to create.

    The wind sings across the water, turning the silver surface
    Into moving furrows that grow before my eyes.

    _____

3. The word *fathom* is defined one way in a footnote to Shakespeare's poem, but it is not the only definition. Use context clues to determine the meaning as it is used here, and write your definition. Then, check a dictionary to see how close you got.

    I cannot fathom him at all. He is a puzzle, and I find
    His words don't help me figure out his motives or his mind.

    _____

4. What would you guess about the underlined word below if you noticed that the title of the poem in which the line appeared was titled "The Giant Clam"?

    This mighty <u>mollusk</u> anchored in the coral bed,
    The family's largest child,

    _____

5. In this passage, the words are familiar but are not used in the usual way. In this context, how do you think the writer is defining *meat* and *chew*?

    I need to write to live, it is my meat.
    I chew on words, and find the taste is sweet.

    _____

Name _____ Date _____

Literary Analysis: Sound Devices

Poets often use **sound devices**—techniques that enhance the poem's musical sound. Two of the most popular techniques are *onomatopoeia* and *alliteration*.

- **Onomatopoeia** is the use of a word that sounds like the noise it describes. *Buzz* and *splat* are examples of onomatopoeia.
- **Alliteration** is the repetition of the same sound at the beginnings of words or in stressed syllables. A tongue twister such as *Peter Piper picked a peck of pickled peppers* is an example of alliteration.

DIRECTIONS: As you read the three poems, record examples of onomatopoeia and alliteration that you find. One example is provided.

Name of Poem	Onomatopoeia	Alliteration
"Full Fathom Five"		Full fathom five thy father lies
"Onomatopoeia"		
"Maestro"		

"The Village Blacksmith" by Henry Wadsworth Longfellow
"Loo-Wit" by Wendy Rose
"Fog" by Carl Sandburg
"Life" by Naomi Long Madgett

Build Vocabulary

Using the Prefix *dis-*

The prefix *dis-* before a word can mean "away," "apart," "not," or "the opposite of." For example, the word *dismiss* means "to send away." *Disrespectful* means "not respectful." *Disconnect* means "to do the opposite of connect."

A. DIRECTIONS: Match each word on the left with its definition on the right. Write the letter of the definition on the line next to the word it defines.

____ 1. dislocate   a. to do the opposite of hide or cover

____ 2. disappear   b. lying; not honest

____ 3. discover   c. to pull away or out of place

____ 4. dishonest   d. do the opposite of appear

Using the Word Bank

| brawny | haunches | buttes | crouches | unravel | dislodge |

B. DIRECTIONS: Write the Word Bank word that can replace the italicized word or phrase in each sentence.

1. A kangaroo has powerful *legs* that help it jump high and far. _____

2. The hikers attempted to climb one of the steep *hills* on the plain. _____

3. Doctors managed to *pull* out the bullet from the victim's shoulder. _____

4. The old knitted sweater began to *become untangled and separated*. _____

5. The tiger *bends* low in the tall grass to hide from its prey. _____

6. The *muscular* arms of the rescuers were comforting. _____

Recognizing Antonyms

C. DIRECTIONS: Circle the letter of the word or phrase that is most *opposite* in meaning to the word in CAPITAL LETTERS.

1. CROUCHES
   a. hides
   b. straightens
   c. escapes
   d. sleeps

2. UNRAVEL
   a. polite
   b. argue
   c. climb
   d. tangle

3. DISLODGE
   a. leave
   b. rest
   c. insert
   d. sell

"The Village Blacksmith" by Henry Wadsworth Longfellow
"Loo-Wit" by Wendy Rose
"Fog" by Carl Sandburg
"Life" by Naomi Long Madgett

Build Spelling Skills: Adding Endings to Words Ending in Consonant-Vowel-Consonant

Spelling Strategy   If a word ends in consonant-vowel-consonant and the final syllable is not stressed, you usually do not double the final consonant before adding *-ed* or *-ing*.

   Example un*rav*el + ed = un*rav*eled   un*rav*el + ing = unraveling

   If, however, the final syllable is stressed, you double the final consonant.

   Example oc*cur* + ed = oc*curred*   oc*cur* + ing = occuring

A. Practice: Add *-ed* or *-ing* to each word, as indicated. Write the new word on the lines at the right. Hint: Say the word out loud or to yourself, and listen for the stressed syllable.

1. offer + ed = _____

2. label + ing = _____

3. commit + ed = _____

4. travel + ing = _____

5. rebel + ed = _____

6. refer + ing = _____

7. control + ed = _____

8. focus + ing = _____

B. Practice: Complete each sentence by adding *-ed* or *-ing* to each word in parentheses. Write the new word on the line.

1. The blacksmith spent many hours (sorrow) _____ for his lost wife.

2. As the children (scamper) _____ home, they would stop to watch the flaming forge.

3. The sides of the old volcano were (shudder) _____ .

4. Volcanic ash (blanket) _____ the countryside after the eruption.

Challenge: You know that *happy* and *unhappy* have opposite meanings, as do *appropriate* and *inappropriate*. However, can you assume the same thing about *ravel* and *unravel* and *flammable* and *inflammable*? Look up these words in a dictionary, and write down their definitions.

1. ravel / unravel _____

2. flammable / inflammable _____

What do you notice? _____

"The Village Blacksmith" by Henry Wadsworth Longfellow
"Loo-Wit" by Wendy Rose
"Fog" by Carl Sandburg
"Life" by Naomi Long Madgett

Build Grammar Skills: Semicolons

A **semicolon (;)** is a punctuation mark that looks like a period over a comma. The semicolon signals a pause. A semicolon signals a less final pause than a period but a stronger separation than a comma. Semicolons are used to join independent clauses (groups of words, with a subject and verb, that can stand on their own) that are not already joined by the conjunctions *and, but, for, not, or, so,* or *yet.* However, independent clauses should be joined by a semicolon only when there is a close relationship between the clauses.

Example: Blacksmithing is an ancient craft; some modern artisans hope to revive it.

You can also use semicolons to avoid confusion in sentences that already contain several commas.

Examples: His hair is crisp, black, and long; his face is tan; his brow is wet with honest sweat.

A. Practice In each of the following sentences, semicolons are either missing or in the wrong place. On the line below each sentence, write the semicolon with the words that should appear on either side of it.

Example: The blacksmith is a good man the poet highlights this in the last stanza.
Answer: man; the

1. Blacksmiths wear protective; clothing for example, they usually wear a leather apron.

   _____

2. The blacksmith in Longfellow's poem seems to have a positive attitude about life Madgett's view in "Life" is less positive.

   _____

3. The study of volcanoes can be dangerous scientific crews must learn safety techniques.

   _____

4. Some famous volcanoes include Mt. Vesuvius, which is in Italy Krakatoa in Indonesia, which destroyed an entire island and Mt. Fuji in Japan which hasn't erupted in many years.

   _____

5. Fog is low-hanging clouds of tiny water droplets, smog is actually polluted air.

   _____

B. Writing Application: Write four sentences, one about each poem in this group. In each sentence, include a semicolon used correctly.

1. _____

2. _____

3. _____

4. _____

"The Village Blacksmith" by Henry Wadsworth Longfellow
"Loo-Wit" by Wendy Rose
"Fog" by Carl Sandburg
"Life" by Naomi Long Madgett

Reading Strategy: Using Your Senses

Poetry often contains vivid images, or word pictures, because poets usually want to share more than one aspect of an experience with the reader. Reading poetry is more interesting and more involving if you **use your senses** to share the poet's experience. As you read a poem, focus on details that appeal to your senses. Does the poet describe the way something looks or feels? Is there a suggestion of a noise, a flavor, a fragrance? What words does the poet use to help you experience these things? Are comparisons made or word pictures painted? Look for words that describe or mimic sounds. Think about descriptions that suggest things you could see or touch, things you could smell or taste. Use the details supplied by the poet to connect with the poem based on your own experience.

For example, in "The Village Blacksmith," the poet writes, "His brow is wet with honest sweat." Close your eyes and imagine the experience. Even if you've never seen a blacksmith, you know what sweating from heat and hard work is like. Are you able to imagine what the blacksmith is feeling? Or what he looks like? If so, you are using your senses well.

DIRECTIONS: In the chart, record details from each of the four poems that invite you to engage your senses. One example is provided. Note that every poem does not necessarily appeal to all five senses.

	Sight	Hearing	Touch	Taste	Smell
"The Village Blacksmith"		heavy sledge . . . like a sexton ringing the village bell			
"Loo-Wit"					
"Fog"					
"Life"					

"The Village Blacksmith" by Henry Wadsworth Longfellow
"Loo-Wit" by Wendy Rose
"Fog" by Carl Sandburg
"Life" by Naomi Long Madgett

Literary Analysis: Figurative Language

Poets frequently employ **figurative language**—language not meant to be taken literally— in order to add vividness to their writing. Figurative language includes the following devices:

- A **simile** is a comparison between unlike items that uses the word *like* or *as.*

  "The moon is like a giant balloon."

- A **metaphor** is a direct comparison between two unlike items, describing one as if it were the other. A metaphor does not use the word *like* or *as.*

  "The moon is a giant balloon."

- **Personification** is language that gives human traits to something nonhuman.

  "The moon smiled down on Earth."

DIRECTIONS: As you read the four poems, record examples of similes, metaphors, and personification that you find.

Name of Poem	Passage	Type of Figurative Language
"The Village Blacksmith"		
"Loo-Wit"		
"Fog"		
"Life"		

"Popocatepetl and Ixtlaccihuatl" by Juliet Piggott

Build Vocabulary

Using the Prefix be-

The prefix be- means "make happen." For example, the word becalm means "to make calm." The word befriend means "to make a friend of."

A. Directions: In each sentence, replace the italicized phrase with one of the following words:

befogged   become   bedazzled   bejeweled

1. The selfish man would (come to be) _____ generous in his old age.

2. The audience was (made dazzled) _____ by the magician's tricks.

3. Never try to drive your car when your windshield is (made foggy) _____.

4. The designer fashioned a fancy (made with jewels) _____ belt.

Using the Word Bank

besieged	decreed	relished	brandishing
unanimous	refute	routed	edifice

B. Directions: Write the Word Bank word that best completes each sentence.

1. The new _____ took up an entire block in the downtown area.

2. The actors _____ the audience's thunderous applause.

3. The president was _____ with requests from lots of different people.

4. The better team _____ its opponent in the championship game.

5. The bank robber was caught on camera _____ his gun.

6. The king _____ that all males over twenty-one must join his army.

7. After the professor explained his theory, critics attempted to _____ it.

8. The bill passed by a _____ vote of 100 to 0.

Recognizing Antonyms

C. Directions: Circle the letter of the word most *opposite* in meaning to the word in CAPITAL LETTERS.

1. RELISHED: a. loved   b. hated   c. insulted   d. praised

2. REFUTE: a. accept   b. deny   c. loan   d. borrow

3. ROUTED: a. dug   b. found   c. corrected   d. lost

4. BRANDISHING: a. writing   b. appearing   c. hiding   d. apologizing

5. UNANIMOUS: a. divided   b. together   c. doubtful   d. nasty

"Popocatepetl and Ixtlaccihuatl" by Juliet Piggott

Build Spelling Skills: Long e Words With *ie*

Spelling Strategy   In most words having a long e sound spelled with *i* and *e*, the combination is *ie*, not *ei*. However, if the *i* and *e* follow a *c*, the combination is then *ei*.

   Examples: f<u>ie</u>ld   rec<u>ei</u>ve

There are some exceptions to the rule "*i* before *e* except after *c* ." When in doubt, consult a dictionary.

   Exceptions: leisure   neither   either   seize   protein   weird

A. Practice: Fill in the missing letters *i* and *e* in each word. Then write the entire word.

1. s __ __ ge   _____   6. n __ __ ther   _____

2. rec __ __ pt   _____   7. p __ __ ce   _____

3. n __ __ ce   _____   8. l __ __ sure   _____

4. th __ __ f   _____   9. y __ __ ld   _____

5. conc __ __ ted   _____   10. prot __ __ n   _____

B. Practice: In each sentence, find a word or words with the letters *i* and *e* together. If a word is misspelled, cross it out and write it correctly. If the word is spelled correctly, write *C* above it. The first one is done for you.

                                                                                    believed
1. "Popocatepetl and Ixtlaccihuatl" is a legend that people once ~~beleived~~ to be true.

2. The Emperor initially refused to yeild in his insistence that his daughter never marry.

3. Later, however, he changed his mind after his land was beseiged by the enemy.

4. He decreed that whoever defeated the enemy would receive Ixtla's hand in marriage.

5. Each of the concieted warriors wished to prove himself worthy of the beautiful Ixtla.

6. The Emperor's soldiers marched bravely onto the battlefeild and fought hard.

7. They raised their sheilds to protect themselves from enemy spears.

8. During the long and feindish battle, Popo proved himself the best warrior.

9. However, some jealous warriors decieved the Emperor by saying Popo had been killed.

10. Upon hearing the news, Ixtla was seized by an illness and quickly died.

Challenge: The Word Bank word *routed* becomes the word *roused* when you change a single letter. What other words can you make by changing a single letter in the word *routed*? Make a list. Then compare it with a classmate's.

"Popocatepetl and Ixtlaccihuatl" by Juliet Piggott

Build Grammar Skills: Parentheses and Brackets

Parentheses ( ) are punctuation marks used to set off material that is not essential to the understanding of the sentence—that is, you should be able to take out the information in parentheses and still have a sentence that makes sense. Parentheses can be used to add non-essential, supplementary information to the middle of a sentence, or if you want to add one or more sentences of such information. Parentheses are also used to set off supplementary numerical information, such as dates.

> **Examples:** A few of the warriors (those who were jealous of Popo) carried a false report to the Emperor.
> Popo went to Princess Ixtla's grave. (Ixtla had died at the report of Popo's death.) He spent the rest of his days there.
> José María Velasco (1840–1912) was a well-known Mexican landscape artist.

Brackets [ ] are another kind of punctuation. Brackets are used to enclose a word or phrase added by a writer to the words of another, generally to supply information not included in the quotation. In the following example, "he" is replaced with brackets and the pronoun's antecedent, so that a reader would know to whom "he" refers.

> **Example:** Piggott writes, "After a little while, [the Emperor] demanded to be told which of his warriors had been responsible for the victory."

A. Practice: Each of the following sentences contains material that should be enclosed in parentheses. Identify this material and insert the needed parentheses.

1. The English word *volcano* comes from Vulcan, the mythological Roman god of fire and metalworking they believed the volcano was Vulcan's furnace.

2. Piggott's story retells the Aztec legend of how Popocatepetl and Ixtlaccihuatl two volcanoes at the head of the valley where the Aztec's had their capital came into being.

3. The volcanoes of this story may have existed in the days when the new people were just learning to grow corn maize.

4. The Emperor's enemies were firmly entrenched around the royal city Tenochtitlan it is now called Mexico City.

5. The warriors grabbed their obsidian machetes razor-sharp knives made of volcanic glass and headed into battle.

6. With the arrival of Spanish warrior Hernando Cortéz 1485–1547, Aztec life changed forever.

B. Writing Application: Write three sentences about the story, using quotations from the story if necessary, correctly using parentheses or brackets, as indicated.

1. (parentheses) _____
   _____

2. (brackets)_____
   _____

3. (parentheses) _____
   _____

"Popocatepetl and Ixtlaccihuatl" by Juliet Piggott

Reading for Strategy: Rereading or Reading Ahead

Legends, folk tales, and myths contain clues within the text that reveal more about the culture represented. As you read actively, ask the usual questions: *Who? What? Where? When? Why?* To help you answer these questions, and to find deeper meaning in what you read, use these two techniques.

- **Read ahead.** Skim the story for the names of places and characters. Make notes to help you remember unfamiliar names, places, or events. Reading ahead may also supply explanations or additional information that can clarify an earlier passage.

- **Reread.** If you don't understand a certain passage, go back and read it again. Rereading can help you find or clarify connections among the words and sentences that you may have missed the first time through. This strategy can also help you set names, places, and unfamiliar words in your mind.

DIRECTIONS: Use the following chart to take notes on unfamiliar names, places, events, customs, or objects you may encounter as you read this legend. Indicate whether you found it more helpful to reread or to read ahead as you sought to clarify each idea you noted.

Point to Clarify	Clarified by
	____Rereading ____Reading ahead
	____Rereading ____Reading ahead
	____Rereading ____Reading ahead
	____Rereading ____Reading ahead
	____Rereading ____Reading ahead
	____Rereading ____Reading ahead
	____Rereading ____Reading ahead
	____Rereading ____Reading ahead

"Popocatepetl and Ixtlaccihuatl" by Juliet Piggott

Literary Analysis: Legend

A **legend** is a traditional story about the past that is believed to be based on real events or people. Legends have been passed down orally from one generation to another. The original details in a legend often become exaggerated over time and eventually describe characters doing amazing feats that would be unlikely to occur in real life.

In addition, the events in a legend often help us understand the values and attitudes of the culture that produced the legend. For example, in the myth, the Aztecs' respect for bravery is reflected in the way Popo leads the warriors to victory.

DIRECTIONS: In the chart below, record examples of story details and the Aztec values and attitudes that the details reflect. An example is provided. Finally list examples of exaggeration found in the story.

DETAILS FROM THE LEGEND	CULTURAL VALUES AND ATTITUDES
The people are devoted to the Emperor.	Shows Aztecs' respect for leadership.

EXAGGERATIONS

"The People Could Fly" by Virginia Hamilton
"All Stories Are Anansi's," retold by Harold Courlander
"The Lion and the Statue" and **"The Fox and the Crow"** by Aesop

Build Vocabulary

Using the Prefix *sur-*

A. DIRECTIONS: The prefix *sur-* means "above" or "over." Match each word on the left with its definition on the right. Write the letter of the definition on the line next to the word it defines.

____ 1. surplus

a. to rise above to a visible level

____ 2. surmount

b. an amount charged that is above the normal charge

____ 3. surface

c. an amount that is above what is needed

____ 4. surcharge

d. to climb above and get over

Write an original sentence using each word below with the prefix *sur-*.

5. surround _____

6. survive _____

7. surrender _____

Using the Word Bank

croon	shuffle	flatterers	glossy
acknowledge	surpass	yearned	gourd

B. DIRECTIONS: Write the Word Bank word that matches each clue.

1 It's how a person felt who longed for something deeply. _____

2. It's what many singers like to do. _____

3. It's a kind of fruit whose shell can be used as a cup. _____

4. It's how a tired or lazy person might walk. _____

5. It often describes photographs that shine. _____

6. They may not mean the nice things they say. _____

7. This is what you must do to break a record. _____

8. This means to recognize or admit. _____

C. DIRECTIONS: For each pair of words in CAPITAL LETTERS, choose the lettered pair that best expresses a *similar* relationship. Circle the letter of your choice.

1. SINGER : CROON ::
   a. painter : artist
   b. lawyer : legal
   c. dancer : tap
   d. speech : speaker

2. WALK : SHUFFLE ::
   a. talk : remember
   b. speak : mumble
   c. cards : play
   d. throw : catch

"The People Could Fly" by Virginia Hamilton
"All Stories Are Anansi's," retold by Harold Courlander
"The Lion and the Statue" and **"The Fox and the Crow"** by Aesop

Build Spelling Skills: The *aw* Sound Spelled *au*

Spelling Strategy In many words, the *aw* sound is spelled *au*. Learn these words as you come across them in your reading.

Examples: daunt   haul   fraud

A. Practice: Write a word with the *aw* sound spelled *au* to complete each sentence. The word's first letter is given as a clue.

1. The audience gave the speaker a warm round of a_____.

2. A comma tells you to p_____ for a moment before reading on.

3. The scientists got ready to l_____ the missile into space.

4. Many people like to eat spaghetti with a zesty tomato s_____.

5. The frightening movie continued to h_____ the woman for many years.

6. You should accept the blame if something is your f_____.

7. The electric company tried to find out the c_____ of the blackout.

B. Practice: In each of the sentences below, find a word in which the *aw* sound is supposed to be spelled *au*. If the word is misspelled, cross it out and write it correctly. The first one is done for you.

                                                        taunt
1. In "The People Could Fly," the Overseer would ~~tawnt~~ the slaves with insults.

2. The cruel Driver assawlted the slaves with his cracking whip.

3. In time, the slaves were able to lawnch themselves skyward to freedom.

4. Anansi could outwit the other animals becawse of his trickster powers.

5. If a spider like Anansi could applawd, how many pairs of hands would be clapping?

6. Lion was undawnted by the statue showing Hercules overcoming another lion.

7. Crow planned to hawl a large piece of cheese off to her tree until Fox came along.

Challenge: The Word Bank word *shuffle* can mean either to walk slowly dragging the feet or to rearrange things or mix things up. What different meanings do you know for the word *sage*? Write sentences that show the different meanings of sage. Use a dictionary for help if necessary.

_____

_____

"The People Could Fly" by Virginia Hamilton
"All Stories Are Anansi's," retold by Harold Courlander
"The Lion and the Statue" and **"The Fox and the Crow"** by Aesop

Build Grammar Skills: Quotation Marks

You use **quotation marks** to set off a speaker's actual words in a sentence. Notice where a comma is used to separate the quotation from the rest of the sentence.

> **Examples:**   The doctor asked, "How do you feel?"
> "Not very well," said the patient.

Notice in the second example that the comma appears before the end quotation mark, not after it.

> **Incorrect:**   "Take this medicine", said the doctor.
> **Correct:**   "Take this medicine," said the doctor.

A. Practice: Rewrite each of the following sentences, inserting quotation marks to set off a speaker's exact words. Also use commas correctly to separate the quote from the rest of the sentence.

1. The Lion said I think lions are stronger than men.

   _____

2. No, men are definitely stronger the man replied.

   _____

3. The man argued Look how Hercules tears the lion's mouth!

   _____

4. That is still no proof replied the Lion.

   _____

5. The fox said I'd really love to hear you sing!

   _____

6. I'm very happy to hear that answered the crow.

   _____

7. Then the crow cried Now I've lost my cheese!

   _____

B. Writing Application: Complete the sentences that have been started below. Use quotations marks and a comma in each sentence.

1. The man said _____

2. Your argument doesn't work _____

3. The crow said _____

4. I'll sing for you _____

5. I've taught you a lesson _____

"The People Could Fly" by Virginia Hamilton
"All Stories Are Anansi's," retold by Harold Courlander
"The Lion and the Statue" and **"The Fox and the Crow"** by Aesop

Reading Strategy: Recognizing Cultural Context

One good way to appreciate a folk tale is to **recognize** its **cultural context;** that is, pay close attention to details about the time and place of the story and the customs and beliefs of its characters. Sometimes, background notes supply details that help you understand cultural context. For example, you may better appreciate "All the Stories Are Anansi's" after learning that the Ashanti of western Africa have passed down trickster tales for generations. Often, however, you can discover clues within the stories that help you determine time, place, customs, and beliefs. For example, even without a background note, the animals named in "Anansi" are a clue that the story takes place in Africa.

DIRECTIONS: Use the following chart to record details about the cultural contexts of each of the selections. Include information about the time and place of the story and the customs and beliefs of the characters.

FOLK TALE: Time and Place:	
Customs	**Beliefs**

FOLK TALE: Time and Place:	
Customs	**Beliefs**

FOLK TALE: Time and Place:	
Customs	**Beliefs**

FOLK TALE: Time and Place:	
Customs	**Beliefs**

FOLK TALE: Time and Place:	
Customs	**Beliefs**

"The People Could Fly" by Virginia Hamilton
"All Stories Are Anansi's," retold by Harold Courlander
"The Lion and the Statue" and **"The Fox and the Crow"** by Aesop

Literary Analysis: Folk Tales and Fables

A **folk tale** is a story that originally was composed orally and then passed from generation to generation by word of mouth. There are many types of folk tales, including **fables,** legends, myths, and tall tales. Today, writers who retell folk tales try to capture the spirit of the original tales, so that the stories convey the same important values and ideas.

Most folk tales have a recurring character or popular hero or heroine. One reason the folk tale remains popular is that people enjoy telling their children and grandchildren about characters who reinforce or illustrate their cultural ideals.

DIRECTIONS: In the chart below, record details about a major character in each folk tale or fable. Supply adjectives that best describe the character. Then give an example from the story that illustrates the descriptive adjectives. An example is provided.

Tale	Character	Adjectives	Examples
"The People Could Fly"	Toby	caring, longing	He helps Sarah escape the overseer

"Phaëthon, Son of Apollo" by Olivia E. Coolidge
"Demeter and Persephone" by Anne Terry White
"Icarus and Daedalus" by Josephine Preston Peabody

Build Vocabulary

Using the Word Part *-domin-*

The word root *-domin-* means "master" or "ruler." It is found in the Word Bank word *domin-ion*, meaning "region or area that someone rules."

A. DIRECTIONS: Choose one of the following words to match each definition below. Write your word at the right, one letter per blank.

    domination   dominate   dominant   domineering

1. ruling with a heavy hand   _ _ _ _ _ _ _ _ _ _ _

2. to rule over   _ _ _ _ _ _ _ _

3. the act of ruling over   _ _ _ _ _ _ _ _ _ _

4. ruling; main   _ _ _ _ _ _ _ _

Using the Word Bank

mortal	dominions	vacancy
sustained	dissuade	

B. DIRECTIONS: Write the Word Bank word that best completes each sentence.

1. The judge _____ the lawyer's objection.

2. The counselor managed to _____ the student from dropping out of school.

3. The king enjoyed seeing the extent of his _____.

4. I wonder what it would be like if a _____ could instead live forever.

5. The hotel has only one _____.

Recognizing Antonyms

C. DIRECTIONS: Circle the letter of the word most *opposite* in meaning to the word in CAPITAL LETTERS.

1. SUSTAINED
    a. undermined
    b. assisted
    c. carried
    d. helped

2. DISSUADE
    a. condemn
    b. resolve
    c. encourage
    d. clean

"Phaëthon, Son of Apollo" by Olivia E. Coolidge
"Demeter and Persephone" by Anne Terry White
"Icarus and Daedalus" by Josephine Preston Peabody

Build Spelling Skills: The *sw* Sound Spelled *su*

Spelling Strategy In many words, such as the Word Bank word *dissuade*, the sw sound is spelled *su*. You should learn these words as you come across them in your reading.

Examples: dissuade   persuade   suede   suite   suave

A. Practice: Use the example words above to complete the crossword puzzle.

1. to convince
2. soft, fuzzy type of leather
3. two or more connected rooms
4. advise someone against an action
5. gracious or polite in a smooth way

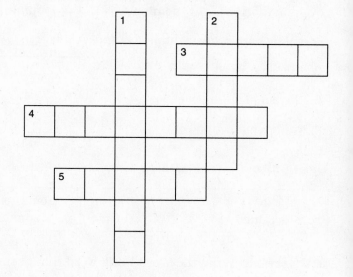

B. Practice: Complete each sentence below with one of the following words:

dissuade   persuade   suede   suave

1. Clymene seeks to _____ Phaëthon that he is Apollo's son.

2. Apollo tries to _____ his son from riding the chariot.

3. Persephone is the very charming and _____ daughter of Demeter.

4. If Daedalus had needed a harness for the wings, he might have made it of something strong, such as leather, but soft, such as _____ .

Challenge: The Word Bank word *amber* names a color. In recent years it has also become a popular name for a girl. How many other colors can you think of that serve as a person's or a pet's name or nickname? Make a list. Then compare your list with a classmate's.

_____

_____

_____

"Phaëthon, Son of Apollo" by Olivia E. Coolidge
"Demeter and Persephone" by Anne Terry White
"Icarus and Daedalus" by Josephine Preston Peabody

Build Grammar Skills: Using Commas in a Series With Dependent Clauses

Commas are used to separate items whenever there are three or more similar items listed together in a **series.**

> **Examples:** The palace of Apollo gleamed with bronze, silver, gold, and ivory.
> The horses climbed high, dropped swiftly, and flung themselves from side to side.

In addition, a **dependent clause**, also called a subordinate clause, is usually set off by one or two commas. A comma is always used following an introductory dependent clause.

> **Example:** *When his mother spoke,* Eros leaped lightly to his feet.

It is also used to set off any dependent clause that is parenthetical or nonessential.

> **Examples:** The wings, *which were made of feathers and wax,* would carry Daedalus and his son away from Crete.
> Daedalus gave his son a warning, *which Icarus quickly forgot.*

A. Practice: In each of the following sentences, insert one or more comas as necessary to separate introductory words or phrases, or to separate items in a series.

1. Greek myths have been borrowed adapted retold and performed in many ways over the generations.

2. Phaëthon was stronger swifter bolder and more honorable than most others.

3. Because Epaphos challenged him Phaëthon went to find his father.

4. The long pole was decorated with jewels: topaz diamond emerald and ruby.

5. When Phaëthon's chariot fell to earth the resulting blaze scorched the land.

6. Phaëthon clung to the inside of the chariot which was completely out of control.

7. Demeter who was mournful over her daughter's disappearance punished the Earth.

8. The cattle died seeds withered crops dried up and men and oxen toiled in vain.

9. After he built the Labyrinth Daedalus was imprisoned on Crete.

10. Though the air became warmer Icarus continued to fly higher.

B. Writing Application: Write sentences about the events in the myths. Include at least one series, separated by commas and at least one dependent clause set off by one or two commas.

1. _____

2. _____

3. _____

"Phaëthon, Son of Apollo" by Olivia E. Coolidge
"Demeter and Persephone" by Anne Terry White
"Icarus and Daedalus" by Josephine Preston Peabody

Reading Strategy: Making Predictions

As you read a myth, you may be able to **predict** future events by paying close attention to details. Your predictions should be based on what you know about the characters so far and what you know about events that have already occurred in the story.

For example, in "Icarus and Daedalus," Daedalus is described as the most cunning person of his time. You learn that he once built a labyrinth so clever that a person inside could not escape from it without a magic clue. That information might help you predict that Daedalus will figure out a way to escape from the island of Crete. Later, after you finish the story, you can check to see if your prediction was correct.

DIRECTIONS: Use the details in each myth to make predictions about what will happen to characters in the story. Record your clues, or details, and your predictions in the chart below. One example is provided.

Title	Clue	Prediction
"Icarus and Daedalus"	No one is more cunning than Daedalus.	He will find a way to escape from Crete.

"Phaëthon, Son of Apollo" by Olivia E. Coolidge
"Demeter and Persephone" by Anne Terry White
"Icarus and Daedalus" by Josephine Preston Peabody

Literary Analysis: Myth

Long ago, ancient peoples created **myths**—stories about gods or heroes in order to explain natural events or express their beliefs about right and wrong. Today, of course, scientists would dispute the reasons suggested by myths for events that we observe in our natural world. For example, modern scientists would reject the notion that the occurrence of spring is actually Persephone's annual visit to earth, as suggested in "Demeter and Persephone." Nevertheless, myths remain popular today because they reflect imagination and a sincere sensitivity to the natural world.

DIRECTIONS: Complete the chart with details from each myth that explain natural events or reflect beliefs about right and wrong. One example is provided.

Myth	Explanation of Natural Event	Belief About Right or Wrong
"Demeter and Persephone"	Spring occurs because of Persephone's annual visit to earth.	

Unit 10: Myths, Legends, and Folk Tales

ANSWERS
Unit 1: Independence and Identity

"The Cat Who Thought She Was a Dog and the Dog Who Thought He Was a Cat" by Isaac Bashevis Singer

Build Vocabulary (p. 1)

A. Sample Sentences:

1. The bridge construction team is progressing.
2. The prognosis for a full recovery is good.
3. Liquid fuel will propel the rocket.
4. We must proceed with the plan to expand the library.

B. 1. vanity 2. protruded
   3. afflicted 4. enthralled
   5. anguish 6. console

C. 1. c 2. b

Build Spelling Skills: The *gw* sound spelled -*gu* (p. 2)

A. 1. languish
   2. linguist
   3. LaGuardia
   4. linguine
   5. guacamole
   6. Uruguay
   7. guava

B. 2. trilingual
   3. distinguished
   4. iguana
   5. languished
   6. extinguished

Build Grammar Skills: Nouns (p. 3)

A. 2. dog (animal), rabbits (animal), cat (animal), mice (animal)

   3. sack (thing), peddler (person), beads (thing), pearls (thing), earrings, (thing), brooches (thing), rings (thing), kerchiefs (thing), trinkets (thing)

   4. mirror (thing), frame (thing), women (person), house (thing)

   5. peasant (person), Jan Skiba (person), name (thing)

   6. daughter (person), nose (thing),

   7. women (person), vanity (idea), girls (person), city (place)

B. 1–4: Student sentences should illustrate an understanding of the use of nouns.

Reading Strategy: Clarifying Word Meanings (p. 4)

Unfamiliar Word

The cat lurked after mice.
. . . bedazzled by all the pretty doodads.
. . . he said a half gulden
. . . that they would find suitors . . .
. . . she became terribly perplexed.
When the peddler came for his monthly installment . . .
. . . bought kerchiefs and slippers for the women.

Restatement or Explanation

Dog chased rabbits, cat lurked
The peddler laid out all his wares, including false beads, fake pearls, tin earrings, etc.
. . . a half gulden, which was a lot of money for poor peasants
were pretty enough and that they would find suitors
she became terribly perplexed. She had never before seen such a creature.
When the peddler came for his monthly installment, Jan Skiba gave him back the mirror . . .
. . . and in its stead bought kerchiefs and slippers for the women.

Clarification

Lurking is a hunting action
Doodads are small objects or ornaments of little value
A gulden is a kind of money
Suitors are boyfriends.
Perplexed means "confused."
The installment is the partial payment Mrs. Skiba agreed to make to the peddler.
Slippers are practical garments, as are kerchiefs.

Literary Analysis: The Moral of a Story (p. 5)

A. "The Manager and His Assistant": Treat others as you would have them treat you.

   "The Two Horses": Don't judge worth solely by appearance.

   "The Dogs and the Bone": There is no honor among thieves.

"The Cat Who Thought She Was a Dog and the Dog Who Thought He Was a Cat" by Isaac Bashevis Singer *(continued)*

B. The moral should express the idea that helping others is often the best way to help oneself.

"Two Kinds" by Amy Tan

Build Vocabulary (p. 6)

A. Sample responses:

2. Jing-mei's mother put behind her the *sadness* of what happened in China.

3. Surely, Jing-mei had enough *cleverness* to be a prodigy.

4. After Jing-mei's failed performance, her mother seemed filled with *hopelessness*.

5. The gift of the piano symbolized the *kindness* of Jing-mei's mother.

6. *Frankness* is a quality that Jing-mei's mother had in abundance.

B. 1. c 2. f 3. a 4. g 5. b 6. d 7. h 8. e

C. 1. b 2. c

Build Spelling Skills: Adding Suffixes to Words Ending in y (p. 7)

A. 1. laziness 2. prying 3. merciful
4. steadying 5. annoyance 6. supplying
7. soggiest 8. handiest 9. partied
10. employable

B. The mother <u>tried</u> to force her daughter to be a prodigy in various fields, from the <u>pettiness</u> of memorizing state capitals to the <u>loftiness</u> of <u>playing</u> the piano. After being <u>notified</u> that she would be <u>studying</u> piano, the young daughter met her piano teacher. The elderly instructor wasn't the <u>spriest</u> of individuals. He was deaf, and the <u>daughter's</u> <u>testiness</u> over having to submit to piano lessons led her to play carelessly and with <u>sloppiness</u>, making errors her teacher couldn't hear.

Challenge Words used in student paragraphs should demonstrate ability to add suffixes to words ending in *y* correctly.

Build Grammar Skills: Common and Proper Nouns (p. 8)

A. 2. common noun: teacher; proper noun: Mr. Chong

3. common noun: friend; proper noun: Lindo Jong

4. common noun: magazines; proper nouns: *Ripley's Believe It or Not, Good Housekeeping, Reader's Digest*

5. common noun: piece; proper noun: Pleading Child

6. common noun: piece; proper noun: Perfectly Contented

B. Accept original sentences or sentences based on the story.

Sample responses:

1. Sharon lived in Chicago.

2. Mr. Williams told Pauline to practice.

3. Uncle Bill and Aunt Mildred enjoyed listening to Vivian perform.

Reading Strategy: Applying Word Identification Strategies (p. 9)

2. impatient; patient; im-; not patient; annoyed by delay

3. ungrateful; grateful; un-; -ful; not grateful or thankful

4. invisible; visible; in-; not visible; not able to be seen

5. unreachable; reach; un-, -able; not reachable; not able to be touched

6. disproved; prove; dis-; -ed; proven wrong

7. review; view; re-; look at again

8. nervousness; nervous; -ness; the quality or condition of being nervous or agitated

9. humorous; humor; -ous; having humor; being amusing or funny

10. forgiveness; forgive; -ness; a forgiving; pardon

Literary Analysis: Characters' Motives (p. 10)

1. Jing-mei; 2

2. Jing-mei's mother; 6

3. Jing-mei; 5

4. Jing-mei; 1

5. Jing-mei's mother; 3

6. Jing-mei's mother; 4

from *Song of Myself* by Walt Whitman
"I'm Nobody" by Emily Dickinson
"Me" by Walter de la Mare

Build Vocabulary (p. 11)

A. 1. equality
2. equally
3. equalize

B. 1. c 2. e 3. f 4. a 5. g 6. d 7. b

C. 1. d 2. b 3. c

Build Spelling Skills: The *kw* Sound Spelled *qu* (p. 12)

A. 1. quiver
2. quartet
3. queasy
4. quack
5. quart
6. earthquake

B. 1. quoted
2. qualities
3. quarter
4. quizzes
5. quarrel

Challenge

Sample sentences:

1. If I work four hours instead of one, I will quadruple my pay.
2. The quadriceps muscle in the thigh aids walking and running.
3. A horse is a quadruped that can use its four feet to run fast.

Build Grammar Skills: General and Specific Nouns (p. 13)

A. 2. general: feelings; specific: love
3. general: qualities; specific: beauty
4. general: events; specific: battles
5. general: writers; specific: poets

B. Writing Application Sample Sentences:

1. Poets create images with words as painters create landscapes with brushes.
2. During the Civil War, Walt Whitman nursed wounded soldiers, including his brother.

Reading Strategy: Identifying Analogies, Similes, and Metaphors (p. 14)

1. Analogy: Being a "Somebody" is compared to being a Frog. A "Somebody" wants to be known for his or her accomplishments and talks about them, just as a frog croaks all day.
2. Simile: The poet's Self is compared to a tree. The poet sees his own personality as being unique, as no two trees are alike.
3. Metaphor: The poet compares himself to the world. The poet considers himself to be a world.

Literary Analysis: The Speaker in Poetry (p.15)

A. Sample responses:

"Song of Myself"—Likes: self, learning, loafing, taking it easy; Dislikes: Perhaps those who worry too much about other's opinions of them. Mood(s): celebratory; content, cheerful

"I'm Nobody"—Likes; being a nobody (unknown, unrecognized); Dislikes: Somebodies (important or famous persons), being public; Mood(s): The use of exclamation points indicates an enthusiastic and emphatic mood

"Me"—Likes: trees, flowers, the sun, dewdrops; Dislikes: Perhaps being alone like the "cypress forlorn"; Mood(s): decisive

B. Sample responses:

1. Probably A, B, C
2. Probably C, D; Possibly A, B
3. Probably C; Possibly A, B

"My Furthest-Back Person" by Alex Haley

Build Vocabulary (p. 16)

A. 1. unwritten
2. Haley was astonished because the results of his research had been unexpected.
3. Working uninterrupted for long periods of time, the writer made much progress on his book.

B. 1. eminent 2. intrigue 3. uncanny
4. cherished 5. queried 6. destination

C. 1. b 2. c

Build Spelling Skills: Adding Prefixes (p. 17)

A. 1. rearrange
2. misspell
3. uninterested
4. reeducate
5. teammate
6. unbelievable
7. rebuild
8. unnecessary

B. 1. unfortunate
2. unable
3. unkind
4. rename
5. recaptured
6. retraced

Challenge

Sample responses:

1. The students in French class were asked to <u>recite</u> new vocabulary words.

2. In our town, most people <u>recycle</u> newspapers.

3. After the thunderstorm, we were unable to <u>rekindle</u> the campfire.

4. Dissatisfied with the painting, the artist began to <u>resketch</u>.

5. Would you please <u>resubmit</u> your torn and smudged report?

Build Grammar Skills: Collective Nouns (p. 18)

A. 1. class / students

2. tribe / ancestors

3. number / scholars

4. couple / scholars

5. clan / ancestors

6. group / officials

7. trio / interpreters

8. herd / goats

9. clan / relatives

10. throng / villagers

B. Writing Application sample sentences:

1. The <u>team</u> of scientists has spent many years searching for a cure for cancer.

2. A <u>bunch</u> of grapes is a healthful snack.

3. A <u>flock</u> of Canada geese glided overhead.

4. Most of the <u>crew</u> of sailors on the aircraft carrier was on deck as the ship sailed into the harbor.

Reading Strategy: Breaking Down Long Sentences (p. 19)

A. 2. Subject: I
What subject did: kept wishing Grandma could hear how her stories had led me to the "*Kamby Bolong*"

3. Subject: Kunta Kinte
What subject did: was down in some ship sailing
Where: from the Gambia River to Annapolis
When: later that summer

B. 1. Now flat broke, I went to some editors I knew, describing the Gambian miracle, and my desire to pursue the research.

2. Doubleday contracted to publish, and *Reader's Digest* to condense the projected book.

3. Then I had advances to travel further.

Literary Analysis: Personal Essay (p. 20)

The following excerpts relate personal experiences typical of a personal essay:

1, 2, 8, 9, 11, 12, 13

"The Third Level" by Jack Finney

Build Vocabulary (p. 21)

A. 1. cartoonist

2. guitarist

3. ecologist

4. columnist

5. soloist

6. conversationalist

B. Anecdotes should use all of the words in the Word Bank and have logical plots.

C. 1. b 2. d

Build Spelling Skills: Adding the Suffix *-ist* to Words (p. 22)

A. 1. cyclist

2. dental hygienist

3. machinist

4. geologist

5. conservationist

6. separatist

B. Charley was ordinary. He was not an <u>extremist</u> of any kind. Sam was a <u>therapist</u> who specialized in treating mental <u>illness</u>. When Charley told Sam about the third level, Sam thought Charley was an <u>escapist</u>. Sam was a <u>realist</u> at first, but he changed as he listened to Charley. Like Charley, Sam had a preference for the past. When he did travel into the past, he needed to change his profession. A <u>psychiatrist</u> would not have had much business in the Galesburg of 1894.

Challenge

1. psychologist

2. podiatrist

3. optometrist

4. cardiologist

5. orthopedist

Build Grammar Skills: Concrete and Abstract Nouns (p. 23)

A. 1. Concrete: Charley, tunnel Abstract: fantasy
2. Concrete: doorway Abstract: past
3. Concrete: ticket, town Abstract: values, peace
4. Concrete: clerk, bills, currency Abstract: future
5. Concrete: customer Abstract: dishonesty
6. Concrete: Charley Abstract: attitude
7. Concrete: savings, bank Abstract: plan
8. Concrete: money Abstract: value, exchange

B. Writing Application

Sample responses:
1. mind
2. journey
3. efforts
4. surprise

Reading Strategy: Using Context to Unlock Meaning (p. 24)

1. Clues to Meaning: I was in; began angling left and slanting downward
   Meaning From Context: A passage that changes direction
   Dictionary Meaning: A long passageway or hall
   Numbers of Types of Context Clues: 5
2. Clues to Meaning: Clerk figured; I had enough for two coach tickets; I counted out the money
   Meaning From Context: An amount of money needed to buy coach tickets
   Dictionary Meaning: Money paid for transportation in a train, plane, etc.
   Numbers of Types of Context Clues: 4, 6
3. Clues to Meaning: Bought old-style; You can buy old money at almost any coin dealer's
   Meaning From Context: Money
   Dictionary Meaning: Money in circulation
   Numbers of Types of Context Clues: 1, 2
4. Clues to Meaning: A new stamp is issued; stamp collectors buy some; use them to mail envelopes to themselves; first day of sale; postmark proves the date; envelope is called a first-day cover; they're never opened

Meaning From Context: An envelope on which is a postage stamp postmarked on the first day the stamp is issued
Dictionary Meaning: An envelope with a stamp and postmark of philatelic significance
Numbers of Types of Context Clues: 1, 2, 4, 5

Literary Analysis: Time in a Setting (p. 25)

Events of 1894 in Order: 10, 8, 5, 13, 1

Events of the Present in Order: 6, 12, 4, 3, 14, 2, 7, 11, 9

"A Day's Wait" by Ernerst Hemingway

Build Vocabulary (p. 26)

A. 1. b 2. d 3. a 4. c

Sample answers:
5. A radio is like a television without the <u>video</u>.
6. We rented a <u>videotape</u> to watch on Saturday night.
7. It was <u>evident</u> from the look on his face that he was worried.
8. The lawyer entered the gun as <u>evidence</u> during the trial.

B. 1. evidently
2. epidemic

C. 1. b 2. d

Build Spelling Skills: Changing the Adjective Ending -ent to the Noun Ending -ence (p. 27)

A. 1. competence
2. diligence
3. excellence
4. existence
5. difference
6. persistence
7. permanence

B. 1. coherence
2. silence
3. insistence
4. intelligence

C: Either the first or the third syllable may be stressed.

Build Grammar Skills: Pronouns (p. 28)

A. 1. it, him
2. he, they

3. them

4. His, himself

5. we, ourselves

B. Sample answers:

1. I don't want my father in the room because he will become upset to see me die.

2. I have tried reading books, but I can't concentrate on any of them.

3. My temperature is so high that I know it will cause my death.

4. I wish I could share my fear with other people, but they wouldn't understand.

5. After my father explained things to me, we were both able to relax a little.

Reading Strategy: Identifying Word Roots
(p. 29)

bound
 build
 set of steps to follow
independent
 empty
 kept away from, prevented
bound
 different
 differing from one another
independent
 base or place
 not solidly
bound
 place
 location, site
independent
 measure
 measures of long distance
bound
 heat
 instrument to measure heat
bound
 carry
 significance

Literary Analysis: Internal Conflict (p. 30)

Sample answers:

1. He is unable to follow the story because he is too worried about dying.

2. He says he'd rather stay awake because he is too nervous or scared to sleep.

3. He thinks he has a deadly disease that anyone who comes near him will catch.

4. He is too afraid.

5. He doesn't understand that his temperature, on the Fahrenheit scale, is not life-threatening.

6. He felt hopeless since he was certain he was going to die.

"Was Tarzan a Three-Bandage Man?" by Bill Cosby
"Oranges" by Gary Soto

Build Vocabulary (p. 31)

A. 1. gently

2. kiddingly

3. loudly

4. beautifully

Sample answers:

5. I took the threat seriously.

6. Simply tell the truth and all will be fine.

7. Some clothing is worn loosely in the summer.

8. I frequently read books in my spare time.

B. 1. hissing

2. tiered

3. dejectedly

4. incorporate

5. tourniquets

6. rouge

C. 1. b 2. a

Build Spelling Skills: *k* Sound Spelled *qu*
(p. 32)

A. 1. racquetball: a game similar to tennis

2. unique: one of a kind

3. croquet: an outdoor game in which balls are hit through hoops

4. quiche: a pie-like food made with eggs

B. 1. tourniquets

2. unique

3. techniques

4. racquet

C. Sample answers:

1. The actor's grand performance was a tour de force.

2. One tourist got lost after leaving the travel group.

3. The winner of the tournament will receive a trophy.

Build Grammar Skills: Personal Pronouns (p. 33)

A. 1. we, first, plural; it, third, singular

2. my, first, singular; you, second, plural

3. me, first, singular; their, third, plural

B. Sample answers:

1. They now incorporate themselves with the help of their agents.

2. He speaks of childhood years and jokes about them.

3. The comedian writes about them in his article.

Reading Strategy: Context Clues (p. 34)

Sample answers:

• Unfamiliar Word: bowlegged; Context Clues: bow, change the shape of your legs; Predicted Meaning: having legs curved like a bow.

• Unfamiliar Word: acne; Context Clues: bad skin; Predicted Meaning: a skin disease.

• Unfamiliar Word: dejectedly; Context Clues: My mother says I gotta stop . . . ; Predicted Meaning: sadly.

Literary Analysis: Anecdote (p. 35)

1. Cosby; entertains and/or teaches a lesson; humorous tone

2. Cosby; entertains and/or makes a point; serious and funny

3. Soto; entertains; poignant or gentle tone

4. Cosby; makes a point; serious

5. Soto; makes a point; poignant or serious

Unit 2:   Common Threads

from *In Search of Our Mothers' Gardens* by Alice Walker

Build Vocabulary (p. 36)

A. 1. acronym

2. homonym

3. synonymous

4. anonymity

B. 1. b 2. d 3. g 4. a 5. e 6. f 7. c

C. 1. b 2. d

Build Spelling Skills: The Root *-nym-* (p. 37)

A. 1. acronym

2. synonym

3. patronymic

B. 1. patronymic

2. pseudonym

3. synonym

4. homonym

5. antonym

Challenge:

1. c 2. b 3. a

Sample answers:

4. The fans honored the luminaries of the NBA.

5. The luminous moon brightened the night sky.

6. The lantern provided enough luminosity to help us find our way back to camp.

Build Grammar Skills: Subject and Object Pronouns (p. 38)

A. 1. she; subject complement,

2. she; subject pronoun; subject of the sentence

3. them; object pronoun; direct object of the sentence

4. It; subject pronoun; subject of the sentence

5. us; object pronoun; direct object

B. Sample Answers:

1. She and I would talk late into the night.

2. We wrote her into our journals.

3. My mother's legacy enriches me and them as well.

Reading Strategy: Recognizing Word Roots (p. 39)

name / pseudonym, synonym

kind / type, prototype

work / laborious, elaborate

confusion / turbulent, turbine

break / corrupt, rupture

breathe / spirit, conspiracy

roll / revolve, evolve

pull / attract, tractor

mindful of / remember, memorial

Literary Analysis: Tribute (p. 40)

A sample answer is given on the worksheet.

"Seventh Grade" by Gary Soto
"Melting Pot" by Anna Quindlen

Build Vocabulary (p. 41)

A. 1. to act on each other 2. able to be changed one for the other 3. connected one with another 4. a place where two roads cross each other

B. Sample answers:

1. speaking in syllables that sounded something like French

2. scowled some more

3. he didn't want Mr. Bueller to reveal that Victor didn't know how to speak French

4. scowling

5. a student can choose which elective to take

6. the old-timers felt that they were intruding on the old neighborhood

7. called people of other ethnic groups by degrading names

8. he thought it looked cool.

C. 1. a 2. c

Build Spelling Skills: Using *c* for the *k* Sound (p. 42)

A. country, coins, canary, kitchen, turkey, monkey

1. country

2. turkey

3. monkey

4. coins

5. canary

6. kitchen

B. 1. confide

2. cultivate

3. keel

4. kilometer

5. casserole

6. concurrent

Challenge: Sample answers:

1. The mellifluous sounds of the clarinet filled the air.

2. Because they invest their money wisely, the Sanchez family is growing more affluent every year.

3. The effluent from the industrial plant was polluting the river.

4. The remarks of the second speaker were superfluous, since everything had already been said by the first.

5. We pitched our tent near the confluence of the two streams.

Build Grammar Skills: Introduction to Verbs (p. 43)

A. 1. were, linking verb

2. ate, action verb

3. seemed, action verb

4. stare, action verb

5. watched, action verb

6. moved, action verb

B. Sample answers:

1. Victor waited on line for a packet of papers. (waited, action)

2. Teresa was a girl in Victor's French class. (was, linking)

3. The models in the magazine scowled at the camera. (scowled, action)

4. Mr. Bueller seemed to be a very sensitive person. (seemed, linking)

5. Victor answered Mr. Bueller's question in nonsense syllables. (answered, action)

6. Victor and Michael were good friends. (were, linking)

Reading Strategy: Interpreting Idioms (p. 44)

Literal Meaning

pressed down hard on

mind was in a different location

to toss small bits of brightly colored paper

arrived at a good blend

live in an appliance that cooks food with a great build-up of steam in a closed metal pot

Figurative Language

had romantic feelings toward

was thinking about other things

celebrate

arrived at a compromise

routinely experience stress

Literary Analysis: Tone (p. 45)

Sample answer: "I ain't making a face, *ese*. This *is* my face." The informality of the language and the use of slang contribute to the informal, friendly tone of the story.

"Fable" by Ralph Waldo Emerson
"Thumbprint" by Eve Merriam
"If—" by Rudyard Kipling

Build Vocabulary (p. 46)

A. 1. unicorn

2. univalve

3. uniform

4. unicycle

B. Sample answers:

1. it could move around

2. it makes it possible to determine if a particular person has touched something

3. kindness because I do not want to be around someone who is cruel

4. fakes

5. broken-down cottage.

C. 1. b 2. c

Build Spelling Skills: *k* Sound Spelled *qu* (p. 47)

A. mystique, technique, oblique, statuesque, picturesque

B. statuesque, oblique, picturesque, technique, mystique

1. picturesque

2. technique

3. oblique

4. mystique

5. statuesque

Challenge: Sample answers:

1. With great aplomb, the speaker walked to the front of the stage.

2. If I go into that ice cream store, I will succumb to temptation.

3. The plumb showed that the water in the pool was eight feet deep.

4. Judging by those dark clouds, it is doubtful that we will have a sunny day tomorrow.

5. The soldiers waited in the redoubt for the attack to begin.

Build Grammar Skills: Verb Tenses (p. 48)

A. 1. wrote, past

2. entered, past

3. will be, future

4. enjoys, present

5. succeed, infinitive; was, past

6. demonstrates, present

B. Sample answers:

1. Emerson's poem "Fable" points out that everything in the world has its own role.

2. Emerson wrote poems and essays.

3. I will enjoy reading other poems by Emerson.

4. Merriam describes her own thumb in "Thumbprint."

5. The poem "Thumbprint" was fun to read.

6. I will think of this poem next time I see a fingerprint.

7. Kipling's poem "If—" is one long sentence.

8. Kipling won the Nobel Prize for Literature in 1907.

9. Tomorrow I will rent the movie *The Man Who Would Be King*, which is based on a Kipling short story.

Reading Strategy: Paraphrasing Figurative Language (p. 49)

Sample responses:

1. **"Fable":** "If I cannot carry forests on my back / Neither can you crack a nut." Even though you have abilities that I lack, you also lack abilities that I possess.

2. **"Thumbprint":** "My signature / thumbing the pages of my time." I am a unique individual who is making her mark on the world.

3. **"If—":** "If you can keep your head when all about you / Are losing theirs and blaming it on you . . ." If you can remain calm when things get bad . . .

"Fable" by Ralph Waldo Emerson
"Thumbprint" by Eve Merriam
"If—" by Rudyard Kipling *(continued)*

Literary Analysis: Rhyme (p. 50)

"Fable": squirrel/quarrel (half rhyme);
  Prig/big; weather–together; year–sphere;
  disgrace–place; I–spry; track–back;
  put–nut (half rhyme)

"Thumbprint": alone/own; key/university;
  brain/rain; sum/become

"If—": The first four lines and every other line
  for the rest of the poem form exact
  rhymes.

"Mother to Son" by Langston Hughes
"The Courage That My Mother Had" by Edna St. Vincent Millay
"The Hummingbird That Lived Through Winter" by William Saroyan

Build Vocabulary (p. 51)

A. 1. transports
  2. transatlantic
  3. transparent
  4. transplant

B. 1. brooch
  2. transformation
  3. quarried
  4. pathetic

C. 1. d 2. a 3. c 4. c

Build Spelling Skills: Making the Plural of Words Ending in *ch* (p. 52)

A. 1. matches
  2. ranches
  3. lunches
  4. itches
  5. hunches
  6. inches
  7. crutches
  8. churches

B. 1. punches
  2. arches
  3. riches
  4. searches
  5. branches
  6. touches

Challenge: It may be pronounced with a long
  u or a long *o* sound.

Build Grammar Skills: Principal Parts of Irregular Verbs (p. 53)

A. 2. took
  3. C
  4. left
  5. taken
  6. did
  7. C

B. Sample answers:
  1. The mother on the stairs had gone on
    even when life was unbearably hard.
  2. The daughter with the brooch had not
    taken up her mother's courage.
  3. The small hummingbird left in the
    spring.

Reading Strategy: Using Word Parts (p. 54)

Familiar Part
winter, time
up
hold
suspend
heart; break
table, spoon
weak
guard

Possible Meaning
during winter
going up
take in
hanging
painfully sad
full amount that fits a large spoon
getting weak
someone who guards

Related Word
Wintry
backward, uphill
beholden
suspension
heartbroken
teaspoonful
weakness
guarding

Literary Analysis: Symbol (p. 55)

Sample answers:
Selection: "Mother to Son"
Symbol: splinters

Idea That It Represents: The mother's hardships

Selection: "The Courage That My Mother Had"

Symbol: rock

Idea That It Represents: the mother's courage

Selection: "The Hummingbird That Lived Through Winter"

Symbol: the bird

Idea That It Represents: the spirit of life and living

Unit 3:   What Matters

"The Third Wish" *by Joan Aiken*

Build Vocabulary (p. 56)

A. 1. mischievous
2. disastrous
3. wondrous
4. famous
5. hazardous
6. nervous

B. 1. remote
2. malicious
3. extricate
4. presumptuous
5. composure
6. rash

C. 1. a 2. d 3. b

Build Spelling Skills: Adding the Suffix *-ous* (p. 57)

A. 1. spacious
2. industrious
3. adventurous
4. melodious
5. harmonious
6. glorious
7. envious
8. courageous
9. furious
10. adding ous

B. 1. mysterious
2. desirous
3. rapturous
4. various
5. luxurious

Challenge: Sample answer: When adding the suffix *-ous* to *presume*, first drop the final *e* and add *ptu* before finally adding *ous*.

Build Grammar Skills: Adjectives (p. 58)

A. 1. straight, empty
2. strange, distant
3. great, white, little
4. grateful, several
5. gorgeous, pretty, blue-green
6. obedient, unhappy
7. kind, second
8. withered, white

B. Sample answers:

1. Joan Aiken possesses a creative imagination.
2. Mr. Peters led a lonely and quiet existence in the forest.
3. Leita was a swan who became an attractive woman.
4. The dark and remote forest is a perfect setting for the story.
5. I think the story has an interesting ending.

Reading Strategy: Clarifying Word Meanings (p. 59)

Sample Answer:

Detail to Clarify
Entangled
Verge

Meaning of Detail
caught up or stuck in
edge

Strategy Used
Question; reread
pause

Literary Analysis: Modern Fairy Tale (p. 60)

Sample answers:

Mysterious and Fantastic Events: Swans turn into human beings; Mr. Peters is found dead with a leaf and white feather.

"The Third Wish" *by Joan Aiken* (*continued*)

Magic and Wishes: Mr. Peters is granted three wishes; Mr. Peters has each of his wishes come true.

Unusual Animals: One swan is transformed into a little man; another swan is transformed into a beautiful woman.

Details About Contemporary Life: Mr. Peters drives a car; he finds beautiful music on the radio for Leita to listen to.

"A Boy and a Man"
by James Ramsey Ullman
from *Into Thin Air* by Jon Krakauer

Build Vocabulary (p.61)

A. 1. d 2. a 3. e 4. c 5. b

B. 1. reconnoiter
2. taut
3. denigrate
4. prone
5. malevolent
6. pummeled

C. 1. b 2. d 3. a 4. d

Build Spelling Skills: Hyphenating Words With Double Consonants (p. 62)

A. 1. com-mute
2. bal-lot
3. rab-bit
4. rid-dle
5. shuf-fle
6. sup-pose
7. hor-rid
8. scis-sors
9. dag-ger
10. bat-tle

B. 2. slip-pery
3. embar-rassed
4. sup-porting
5. ter-rifying
6. sum-mit

Challenge: 1. reconnoiter, from Old French <u>reconoistre</u>, meaning "know"— The pilot will reconnoiter the area to locate enemy troops. 2. reconnaissance, from Old French <u>reconoistre</u>, meaning "know" or "recognize"—

After making his reconnaissance, the pilot will report what he knows about the location of enemy troops. 3. connoisseur, from Old French <u>connoisseor</u>, meaning "know"—He is a connoisseur of good food and always knows the best restaurants.

Build Grammar Skills: Placement of Adjectives (p. 63)

A. 1. *calm* modifies *Rudi*; *entire* modifies *operation*
2. *helpless* modifies *climber*
3. *both* and *numb* modify *hands*; *difficult* modifies *climb*
4. *good* modifies *advice*; *young* modifies *boy*
5. *exhausted* and *terrified* modify *Jon Krakauer*
6. *expert* modifies *climber*; *great* modifies *beauty*
7. *important* modifies *safety*; *risky* modifies *adventure*
8. *grateful* modifies *Krakauer*; *highest* modifies *peak*

B. Sample answers:
1. Mountains can be dangerous places to climb.
2. My footing was steady during the climb.
3. I had a strong grip on the rock.
4. The day turned too windy to continue climbing.
5. The entire climb was beautiful and unforgettable.

Reading Strategy: Predicting (p. 64)

Sample answers:

Detail or Hint: Rudi removes his clothing.

My Prediction: He will get frostbite.

Actual Outcome: He survives the bitter cold.

Detail or Hint: Rudi knows the mountains well.

My Prediction: He will advise Captain Winter.

Actual Outcome: He does advise Captain Winter.

Detail or Hint: Krakauer is balanced on an unsteady ladder.

My Prediction: The ladder will fall.

Actual Outcome: The ladder holds.

Literary Analysis: Conflict with Nature (p. 65)

Sample answers:

1. Rudi can't see the man in the crevasse. It's exciting because he has little time to act and doesn't know what to do.

2. Rudi faces the possibility of freezing to death, especially since he doesn't realize how cold it actually is. His race against time creates suspense.

3. Rudi struggles to find the strength to hold on. There is suspense in not knowing if he'll succeed or lose the man.

4. The ladder is unsteady, leading to the possibility that it will fall or tilt. Suspense is created in not knowing if the quivering ice will hold or give way.

5. The serac comes unbolted from the glacier and crashes down. There is excitement in waiting to see if the serac will hit the climber or push him off the glacier.

6. The ladders can be crushed inside the crevasse. There is suspense in waiting to see if that will happen to Krakauer.

"The Charge of the Light Brigade"
by Alfred, Lord Tennyson
from *Henry V*
by William Shakespeare
"The Enemy" by Alice Walker

Build Vocabulary (p. 66)

A. 1. maid
2. soared
3. flour
4. I made the bed and fluffed the pillows.
5. The knight raised his sword.
6. My favorite flower is the rose.

B. 1. blundered
2. sundered
3. dismayed
4. reeled
5. volleyed

C. 1. a 2. d 3. b

Build Spelling Skills: Adding *-ed* to a Verb (p. 67)

A. 1. preferred
2. enjoyed
3. programed
4. traveled
5. permitted
6. allowed
7. rebelled
8. focused
9. unwrapped
10. offered

B. 1. traveled
2. conferred
3. shattered
4. occurred
5. controlled
6. unsnapped

Build Grammar Skills: Possessive Adjectives (p. 68)

A. 1. its
2. their
3. our
4. his
5. my
6. her
7. our

B. 1. their
2. his
3. its

Reading Strategy: Using Word Parts (p. 69)

Familiar Part
on
may
house
man
snap
hurry

Prefix or Suffix
-ward
dis-; -ed
-hold
-hoods
un-; -ed
-ly

Overall Meaning
go ahead
upset
common to your home
manliness
opened up
in a hasty way

"The Charge of the Light Brigade"
by Alfred, Lord Tennyson
from *Henry V* by William Shakespeare
"The Enemy" by Alice Walker *(continued)*

Literary Analysis: Repetition (p. 70)

Sample answers:

1. Repeating the phrase *half a league* gives the feeling of the soldiers marching steadily forward.

2. The parallel phrases "jaws of Death" and "mouth of hell" emphasize the feeling of horror.

3. Repetition of the word *flashed* helps readers imagine flashing sabers.

4. Repetition of the word *honor* emphasizes the speaker's admiration for the brave soldiers.

5. The rhymes *shell, fell, well,* and *hell,* as well as the steady rhythm of the lines, help convey a feeling that the battle is terrible and unstoppable.

6. Repetition of the pronoun *we* helps emphasize Henry's feelings that the soldiers are all one family.

"The Californian's Tale"
by Mark Twain
"Valediction" by Seamus Heaney

Build Vocabulary (p. 71)

A. 1. c 2. d 3. a 4. e 5. b

B. 1. humiliation
2. desolation
3. furtive
4. balmy
5. apprehensions
6. abundant
7. gravity
8. predecessors

C. 1. b 2. c 3. a 4. d 5. b

Build Spelling Skills: Words With Silent *l*
(p. 72)

A. 1. calm
2. palm
3. walk
4. talk
5. half
6. calf

7. chalk
8. psalm

B. 1. balmy
2. walked
3. talked
4. calm
5. calf
6. half

Challenge: Definition: "a capturing" or "an arrest"—The burglar was taken to jail after his apprehension. Definition: "the ability to apprehend or understand"—My apprehension of the problem is that the lockers are too small.

Build Grammar Skills: Adverbs (p. 73)

A. 1. *frequently* modifies *roams*
2. *admiringly* modifies *looks*
3. *eagerly* modifies *invites*
4. *lovingly* modifies *speaks*
5. *later* modifies *come*
6. *soon* modifies *will arrive*
7. *eventually* modifies *learns*
8. *terribly* modifies *misses*

B. Sample answers:

1. Henry quickly revealed the letter from his wife.

2. I never did learn the wife's name.

3. Henry's friends treated him gently.

4. Henry always thought his wife was alive.

5. I finally left the house the next day.

Reading Strategy: Summarizing (p. 74)

Sample answers:

Main Events: The traveler tours Henry's home; Henry talks about his wife; Henry reads the letter; Henry's friends visit; Henry's friends get him drunk and sleepy.

Important Details: The house has a pretty garden, nice carpeting, wallpaper, and pictures; the bedroom is daintily decorated; the photograph shows a beautiful young girl; Henry says his wife is visiting her family and will return Saturday night; Henry's friends ask about the wife; Henry's friends give him drink after drink on Saturday night.

"Valediction" summary: The speaker mourns the loss of the woman who is no longer with him.

Literary Analysis: Local Color (p. 75)

Sample notes:

lonesome land, peaceful expanses of grass and woods, drowsy hum of insects; white counterpane, dressing-table with mirror and pin-cushion, real wash-stand with real china-ware bowl; little walnut bracket, daguerreotype-case; "Oh, she's away now. She's gone to see her people"; "Presently he was back with his picture-case in his hand."

"Stopping by Woods on a Snowy Evening" by Robert Frost
"Miracles" by Walt Whitman
"Four Skinny Trees" by Sandra Cisneros

Build Vocabulary (p. 76)

A. 1. ferociously
2. ferociousness
3. ferocious
4. ferocity

Sample answers:

5. The shark is not as ferocious as some people think.
6. The lion's ferocity kept other animals away from it.
7. The tornado ferociously tore up the town.
8. The ferociousness of the mad dog posed a real threat.

B. 1. distinct
2. downy
3. exquisite
4. ferocious

C. 1. d 2. a

Build Spelling Skills: *z* Sound Spelled *s* (p. 77)

A. 1. cheese
2. laser
3. loser
4. rise
5. reason
6. busy
7. use
8. raisins
9. surprise
10. noisy

B. 1. knows
2. chooses
3. resembles
4. reason
5. observes
6. busy

Challenge: exQUIsite; EXquisite.

Build Grammar Skills: Adverbs Modifying Adjectives and Adverbs (p. 78)

A. 1. *most* modifies *impressed*
2. *quite* modifies *some*
3. *very* modifies *responsible*
4. *rather* modifies *skinny*
5. *so* modifies *many*
6. *more* modifies *inspiring*
7. *almost* modifies *always*
8. *usually* modifies *ignored*

B. Sample answers:
1. The horse is very confused about the delay.
2. The girl very carefully studies the four skinny trees.
3. The man thinks each event is most miraculous.
4. The girl is quite obviously impressed by the trees.

Reading Strategy: Interpreting Figures of Speech (p. 79)

Sample answers:

"Stopping by Woods . . ."

Passage: "But I have promises to keep . . ."

Personal Response: I cannot go away this weekend because I promised to help a friend study.

"Four Skinny Trees"

Passage: "I am the only one who understands them."

Personal Response: No one else in my family really understands the problems I have.

"Miracles"

Passage: "Or sit at table at dinner with the rest . . ."

Personal Response: I love the family conversations and jokes we trade at dinner.

Literary Analysis: Levels of Meaning (p. 80)

Sample answers:

"Stopping by Woods . . ."

Literal meaning: The traveler stops momentarily in the woods.

"Stopping by Woods on a Snowy Evening"
by Robert Frost
"Four Skinny Trees" by Sandra Cisneros
"Miracles" by Walt Whitman (continued)

What the events mean to the character(s): The traveler appreciates the woods' beauty.

How the events relate to life: We should all take the time to acknowledge the beauty and wonders of the natural world.

"Four Skinny Trees"

Literal meaning: The trees are skinny.

What the events mean to the character(s): Like the trees, the narrator struggles to survive in the world.

How the events relate to life: We need to cling tightly to things we believe in, even when others around us do not.

Unit 4:   Resolving Conflicts

"The Night the Bed Fell"
by James Thurber

Build Vocabulary (p. 81)

A. 1. exhausted
2. excavate
3. exiled
4. extend
5. exceptional

B. 1. deluge
2. culprit
3. allay
4. perilous
5. pungent
6. extricate
7. ominous
8. fortitude

C. 1. d 2. c 3. a 4. b 5. d 6. b

Build Spelling Skills: *j* Sound Spelled *g* (p. 82)

A. 1. college
2. village
3. biology
4. oxygen
5. garbage
6. cage
7. stage
8. luggage
9. huge
10. engine

B. 1. advantage
2. dangerous
3. logical
4. damage

5. bandage

Challenge: 1. deluxe; 2. alley (Students may also suggest alloy or Allah.)

Build Grammar Skills: Prepositions (p. 83)

A. 1. above
2. near
3. after
4. to
5. toward
6. inside
7. concerning
Message: an attic

B. Sample answers:
1. I lost my hat during a storm.
2. The hat had been on my head.
3. I didn't know it was gone until noon.
4. I looked for it after the storm.
5. I lost it because of the storm.

Reading Strategy: Picturing Events (p. 84)

1. Event: Briggs Beall comes to visit.

Sensory Details: wanted to set an alarm clock to ring every hour of the night; held his breath to test the speaker; put a glass of the spirits of camphor next to his bed

Senses Used: sound, smell

2. Person: Aunt Sarah Shoaf

Sensory Details: feared that a burglar would blow chloroform under her door through a tube; piled her money, silverware, and other valuables outside her door before going to bed; left a note for potential burglars

Senses Used: smell, physical sensation, sight

Literary Analysis: Humorous Essay (p. 85)

Sample answers:

What really happened: James's cot overturned.

What Grandfather thought: He had disappeared earlier, thinking the Civil War was still on.

What Briggs thought: He thought he had stopped breathing and was suffocating.

What the narrator thought: He didn't think anything since he went to sleep after falling.

What Mother thought: She thought Father had fallen and was caught under the bed.

What Father thought: He thought that the house was on fire.

What Roy thought: He thought Father was in trouble in the attic.

What Herman thought: He thought that Mother had become hysterical for no reason.

"All Summer in a Day"
by Ray Bradbury

Build Vocabulary (p. 86)

A. 1. vital statistics
   2. vitality
   3. revitalize
   4. vitamin

B. 1. c 2. b 3. d 4. a 5. d 6. a 7. b

Build Spelling Skills: Words in Which the *choo* Sound Is Spelled *tu* (p. 87)

A. 1. actually
   2. spiritual
   3. eventually
   4. situation
   5. tumultuous
   6. saturate

B. 2. ritual
   3. natural
   4. statue
   5. immature
   6. mutually
   7. unfortunately
   8. punctual
   9. congratulated
   10. situation

Challenge: Sample answer: Unfortunately for the children, staying inside was a natural situation.

Build Grammar Skills: Prepositional Phrases (p. 88)

A. 2. (after seven years)
   3. (with excitement) (for the appearance) (of the sun)
   4. (from the room) (into the jungle)
   5. (inside the closet) (during the event)
   6. (about Margot) (throughout her ordeal)

B. Sample answers:
1. On Earth, Margot didn't have to live without the sun.
2. She had lived on Venus since she was two years old.
3. The children ran through the tunnels of the underground city.
4. It would rain for seven years.

Reading Strategy: Comparing and Contrasting Characters (p. 89)

Sample responses:

Margot: remembers the warmth and light of the sun; spent half of her life on Earth; quiet; frail

Margot's Classmates: couldn't remember a time when there was no rain; spent all their lives on Venus; aggressive

Both: looked forward to seeing the sun

Literary Analysis: Setting (p. 90)

Sample details: Indoors: echoing tunnels; great thick windows. Outdoors: sweet crystal fall of showers, the sun showed its face to the stunned world, clear bead necklaces on the roof.

"The Highwayman" by Alfred Noyes
"The Real Story of a Cowboy's Life"
by Geoffrey C. Ward

Build Vocabulary (p. 91)

A. 1. seashell
   2. bookstore
   3. airplane
   4. mountainside

B. 1. landlord
   2. torrent
   3. tawny
   4. bound
   5. brandished
   6. cascade

"The Highwayman" by Alfred Noyes
"The Real Story of a Cowboy's Life"
by Geoffrey C. Ward (*continued*)

7. strive

C. 1. c 2. a 3. b

Build Spelling Skills: Use a Hyphen in Compound Adjectives (p. 92)

A. Sample answers:

1. quick-footed — The quick-footed athlete managed to win the race.

2. six-legged — An insect is a six-legged creature.

3. thin-skinned — A thin-skinned person cannot tolerate much teasing.

4. empty-handed — Try not to return empty-handed from your food search.

B. 1. thick-skinned
2. red-lipped
3. kind-hearted
4. mean-spirited
5. well-traveled

Challenge: Sample answers: landfall, landfill, landform, land grant, landholder, land-locked, landlubber, landmark, land mine, landowner, landscape, landslide.

Build Grammar Skills: Mechanics: Dashes and Hyphens (p. 93)

A. Practice

1. The letter arrived exactly on time—an amazing fact since it was mailed in rural Mexico!

2. It took herds—this may be hard to imagine—about fifty days to get from Texas to Nebraska.

3. Two railway centers—Omaha and St. Louis—were the main destinations of cattle drives.

B. Practice

1. nearly forty-five inches across
2. won by a three-fifths majority
3. an all-American scene
4. is an ex-rancher

C. Writing Application

Sample responses:

1. Cattle drives were less glamorous than some people think—cowboys often died during the journey.

2. A cowboy's saddle—you may not have known this—was his most prized possession, since it served as his chair, his workbench, and his pillow at night.

3. Charles Goodnight, an ex-cowboy, enforced strict rules during cattle drives.

4. The half-mile line of cattle basking in the sun must have been a magnificent sight.

Reading Strategy: Identify Cause and Effect (p. 94)

Sample answers:

"The Highwayman"

Tim loves Bess—Tim warns the British about the highwayman's arrival—Bess shoots herself to warn the highwayman—The highwayman escapes

"The Real Story of a Cowboy's Life"

Cowboys drive the cattle long distances—The cattle get hungry—They eat settlers' crops—The settlers become angry

Literary Analysis: Suspense (p. 95)

Sample answers:

"The Highwayman"

Details that arouse your interest: Tim overhears the highwayman; Bess is tied up; the highwayman is on his way back.

What you want the end to reveal: Will the highwayman avoid the ambush? Will the highwayman and Bess be together again?

"The Real Story of a Cowboy's Life"

Details that arouse your interest: Cattle start to rumble; the cattle train comes to a river; the cowboys anger the settlers.

What you want the end to reveal: Will any cattle escape? Will everyone cross the river safely? Will the settlers and cowboys fight?

"Justin Lebo" by Phillip Hoose
"The Rider" by Naomi Shihab Nye
"Amigo Brothers" by Piri Thomas
"The Walk" by Thomas Hardy

Build Vocabulary (p. 96)

A. 1. reread
2. reseal
3. reset
4. redial

B. 1. coalition
2. yield
3. superimposed
4. perpetual
5. devastating
6. realign
7. evading
8. dispelled

C. 1. a 2. d 3. b

Build Spelling Skills: Use No Hyphen After the Prefix *re-* (p. 97)

A. Sample answers:

1. reexamine   The doctor had to reexamine the patient after losing his medical chart.
2. reread   I didn't hear the last sentence, so please reread it aloud to me.
3. resharpen   Please resharpen the pencil because the point is dull.
4. resubscribe   After one year, you may resubscribe to the magazine.
5. re-sent   I re-sent the package after it was returned for insufficient postage.

B. 1. recycle
2. reconsiders
3. rethinks
4. replan
5. restrengthen
6. replaying

Challenge:

1. remove, re-move.
2. resolve, re-solve.

Build Grammar Skills: Coordinating Conjunctions (p. 98)

A. 1. Mr. Lebo (and) Justin worked on the boy's two racing bikes after every race.

2. Justin made some bicycles, (but) more people wanted them.
3. Justin needed help, (so) a neighbor wrote a letter to the newspaper.
4. Justin got great results, (for) many people saw the letter.
5. When you bicycle, you don't feel loneliness (or) pain.
6. Antonio (and) Felix were close friends who didn't talk much about the fight.
7. Each boy boxed hard (and) exercised daily to prepare for the bout.
8. The friends fought each other (and) left the ring together.
9. They stayed friends, (for) they knew what was really important.
10. The man did not walk (or) speak with his friend on his way to the tree.

B. Sample answers:

1. Rollerskates and bicycles both offer great exercise.
2. Never quit or cry while preparing for a fight.
3. I've built several bikes, but they're not enough.
4. I can build them before school or after school.
5. I don't have my friend anymore, yet I remember him well.

Reading Strategy: Make Inferences (p. 99)

Sample answers:

"Justin Lebo"

Detail: Justin makes about 200 bikes for people.

Inference: Justin has a lot of energy.

"The Rider"

Detail: The rider wonders if bicycling might be a cure for loneliness.

Inference: The rider sometimes feels lonely.

"Amigo Brothers"

Detail: The two boys leave the ring before the winner is announced.

Inference: The boys don't care who won the bout.

"The Walk"

Detail: The speaker describes his walk to his friend.

Inference: The speaker misses his friend.

"**Justin Lebo**" by Phillip Hoose
"**The Rider**" by Naomi Shihab Nye
"**Amigo Brothers**" by Piri Thomas
"**The Walk**" by Thomas Hardy
(*continued*)

Literary Analysis: Third-Person Point of View (p. 100)

Sample answers:

"Justin Lebo": When Justin was silent on the way home, his mother assumed he was lost in a feeling of satisfaction, but he was actu-

ally thinking about what would happen once everyone saw the bikes.

"Amigo Brothers": Antonio and Felix were so close that each felt himself to be a brother of the other. Both boys prayed for victory before the fight.

"The Rider": A third-person narrator might tell what causes both boys to grow lonely.

"The Walk": A third-person narrator might tell the thoughts and feelings of the weak, lame friend as well as those of the walker.

Unit 5:   Just For Fun

"Our Finest Hour"
by Charles Osgood

Build Vocabulary (p. 101)

A. 1. punishment
2. shipment
3. amazement
4. equipment
5. enjoyment

Sample answers:

6. I made an appointment with the doctor for 2:00.
7. Our local park could use some improvement.
8. There was no movement among the troops all day.

B. 1. correspondent
2. bewilderment

C. 1. c 2. a

Build Spelling Skills: Words with a Double *r* (p. 102)

A. 1. terrible
2. borrow
3. earring
4. horror
5. marriage

B. 1. terrible
2. correspondent
3. starred
4. errors
5. occurrences
6. horrible
7. interrupting

8. correct
9. embarrassed
10. sorrow

Challenge: or, respond, pond, on, dent

Build Grammar Skills: Subjects and Predicates (p. 103)

A. 2. The first report of the night appeared on the monitor.
3. It was the wrong story by a different reporter.
4. A second mistake occurred right after the first.
5. Charles Osgood felt bad about all the technical errors.
6. The confused president of the network visited Osgood at his desk.

B. Sample answers:

1. The evening news broadcast began in a normal way.
2. One reporter announced an unscheduled story.
3. The inexperienced crew worked to repair the problems.
4. One embarrassing story described death in Paris.
5. Some foreign visitors watched the unfortunate broadcast.

Reading Strategy: Recognizing Author's Purpose (p. 104)

Possible answers:

1. inform, amuse
2. reflect, inform

3. inform, amuse

4. amuse

5. Answer should reflect the purpose of the passage chosen by the student.

6. Answer should reflect the purpose of the passage chosen by the student.

Literary Analysis: Humor (p. 105)

Sample answers:

1. Example of Humor: Osgood looks at a monitor but sees only himself.

   Why It Is Funny: He expects to see a news report on the monitor.

2. The wrong report appears on the screen.

   Why It Is Funny: Osgood expects the report that he just introduced.

3. A report doesn't appear on the screen at all.

   Why It Is Funny: You expect the report to appear, since Osgood just introduced it.

4. A report about dead people appears on the screen.

   Why It Is Funny: It is a report that wasn't scheduled to air.

"Cat on the Go" by James Herriot

Build Vocabulary (p. 106)

A. 1. ineffective

2. inappropriate

3. inadmissible

4. inconvenient

B. 1. distraught

2. emaciated

3. intrigued

4. grotesquely

5. surreptitiously

6. inevitable

7. despondent

8. sauntered

C. 1. c 2. a 3. d 4. b 5. a

Build Spelling Skills: Silent gh (p. 107)

A. 1. right

2. eight

3. bought

4. caught

5. taught

6. straight

7. weight

8. high

9. light

10. night

B. 2. fight

3. sigh

4. thought

5. through

6. bright

7. straight

8. delight

Challenge: Sample answers: in, it, tab, a, able

Build Grammar Skills: Compound Subjects and Predicates (p. 108)

A. 1. A neighborhood <u>girl</u> and a stray <u>cat</u> appeared at the doctor's door.

2. The veterinarian <u>washed</u> the cat and <u>stitched</u> its torn body.

3. <u>James</u> and <u>Helen</u> kept the cat as a pet in their own home.

4. The cat <u>left</u> the house at night and <u>visited</u> other places in town.

5. <u>Friends</u> and <u>neighbors</u> told the Herriots about the cat.

6. The Herriots <u>laughed</u> at the stories and <u>enjoyed</u> their new pet.

7. A stranger <u>arrived</u> after a while and <u>reclaimed</u> his lost cat.

8. The <u>doctor</u> and his <u>wife</u> <u>missed</u> the cat and <u>visited</u> it later.

B. Sample answers:

1. The men and women in this town are friendly to me.

2. I sat and listened during an interesting meeting.

3. I ate cake and drank milk that was nearby.

4. Several adults and children came over to play with me.

5. I snooped around the hall and then crept back home.

Reading Strategy: Interpreting Idioms (p. 109)

Sample responses:

1. You will put the cat to sleep (euthanize him) to end his suffering.

2. Some people seemed to think it acceptable to subject cats to all sorts of cruelty.

3. He is extremely skinny and bony.

"Cat on the Go" by James Herriot (*continued*)

4. He felt great affection toward cats.
5. I wanted to avoid thinking about unpleasant things.
6. He was quite attractive.
7. Idioms and interpretations will vary.

Literary Analysis: Character Traits (p. 110)

Sample answers:

James Herriot: loving, dedicated, concerned, courageous

Helen Herriot: compassionate, playful, thoughtful, sentimental

Oscar: curious, daring, independent, strong

"The Luckiest Time of All"
by Lucille Clifton
"Father William" by Lewis Carroll
"The Microscope" by Maxine Kumin
"in Just-" by E. E. Cummings
"Sarah Cynthia Sylvia Stout Would Not Take the Garbage Out"
by Shel Silverstein

Build Vocabulary (p. 111)

A. 1. b 2. a

Sample answers:

3. You can read about current events in a newspaper.
4. Try to be patient until it's your turn.

B. 1. sage
2. curdled
3. incessantly
4. rancid
5. withered
6. supple

C. 1. b 2. d 3. a

Build Spelling Skills: Words with -cess- (p. 112)

A. 1. procession: people moving forward
2. cessation: a stopping
3. secession: the act of withdrawing from a group
4. necessity: something needed

B. 1. success
2. process
3. excess

4. recess
5. access

Challenge: Sample answers: supper, supplement, support, suppose, suppress

Build Grammar Skills: Complete and Incomplete Sentences (p. 113)

A. 1. incomplete
2. complete: <u>Grandmama</u> <u>met her husband-to-be</u>.
3. complete: <u>Father William</u> <u>laughed</u>.
4. incomplete
5. incomplete
6. complete: <u>His work</u> <u>paid off</u>.
7. complete: <u>The balloonman</u> <u>whistles</u>.
8. incomplete
9. incomplete
10. <u>The garbage</u> <u>piled up</u>.

B. Sample answers:
1. As a young girl, Grandmama threw a stone at the dog.
2. The rude son asked his father many annoying questions.
3. The dedicated inventor looked through the lens of his microscope.
4. The lame balloonman whistled in the park.
5. The pile of garbage stank up the whole neighborhood.

Reading Strategy: Clarify Word Meanings (p. 114)

Sample responses:
1. plaited: braided
2. twine: a strong string or rope
3. ointment: a substance applied to the skin for healing or cosmetic purposes
4. pincushions: small cushions in which pins and needles are stuck to keep them handy
5. scour: scrub vigorously
6. gristly: tough and stringy
7. Students should choose unfamiliar words and use the strategies to provide accurate definitions.

Literary Analysis: Hyperbole (p. 115)

Sample answers:
1. "The Luckiest Time of All": "Cutest one thing in the world next to you . . ."
2. "Father William": "And yet you incessantly stand on your head—"

3. "The Microscope": "This Anton's crazy in the head."

4. "in Just-": ". . . the world is mud- / luscious . . ."

5. "Sarah Cynthia Sylvia Stout . . .": "At last the garbage reached so high / That finally it touched the sky."

"Zoo" by Edward Hoch
"The Hippopotamus" by Ogden Nash
"How the Snake Got Poison"
by Zora Neale Hurston

Build Vocabulary (p. 116)

A. 1. e 2. d 3. a 4. c 5. b

B. 1. immensity
2. interplanetary
3. awe
4. wonderment

C. 1. d 2. b 3. a

Build Spelling Skills: Add *-ity* to Nouns Ending in *e* (p. 117)

A. 1. university
2. insanity
3. purity
4. intensity
5. sensibility
6. cavity

B. 1. creativity
2. sensibility
3. immensity
4. gravity

Challenge: Sample answers: ace, age, ape, are, ate, axe, ego, ewe, ice, one, ore, use

Build Grammar Skills: Direct and Indirect Objects (p. 118)

A. 1. DO: animals
2. IO: parents; DO: story
3. IO: hippopotamus; DO looks
4. DO: hippopotamus
5. DO: snake
6. DO: ladder
7. DO: poison
8. IO: snake; DO: rattle

B. Sample answers:
1. Children in Chicago visit the zoo.
2. The speaker gives the hippopotamus some consideration.
3. The snake uses poison to protect itself from its enemies.
4. The other animals fear the snake.

Reading Strategy: Evaluate an Author's Message (p. 119)

1. "Zoo": Author's Message: Strangeness depends on what is already considered normal. Supporting Details: The people and animals view each other as an oddity. Agree.

2. "The Hippopotamus": Author's Message: Beauty is in the eye of the beholder. Supporting Details: Hippopotami delight each other, though looking laughable to us. Agree.

3. "How the Snake Got Poison": Author's Message: Creatures have special ways of protecting themselves. Supporting Details: The snake has a poison to keep others away. The rattle warns other creatures to stay away. Agree.

Literary Analysis: Character's Point of View (p. 120)

Sample answers:

Point of view of: the horse-spider creatures; Understanding of Events: They think the people on Earth are the oddities being observed; Actions: They tell their families to join them next time to see the Zoo.

Point of view of: the hippopotamus; Understanding of Events: It sees people as being as strange as people see it; Actions: It concentrates on attracting its own kind.

Point of view of the snake: Understanding of Events: He is in danger since he crawls on the ground; Actions: He tells God that he needs his poison to keep from getting trampled.

Unit 6: Short Stories

"After Twenty Years" by O. Henry

Build Vocabulary (p. 121)

A. 1. b 2. e 3. a 4. c 5. d

B. 1. spectators
2. dismally
3. intricate
4. simultaneously
5. absurdity
6. destiny

C. 1. d 2. b 3. c

Build Spelling Skills: *-er* and *-or* (p. 122)

A. 1. writer
2. operator
3. actor
4. manager
5. instructor

B. 1. teller
2. embezzler
3. traveler
4. prisoner
5. contributor
6. reader and editor or readers and editors

Challenge:

1. from the Arabic word *qismah*, meaning "portion, lot, or fate"
2. from a Sanskrit word, *karma*, meaning "action, effect, or fate"

Build Grammar Skills: Clauses (p. 123)

A. 1. Independent clause: Haven't you heard from your friend. Subordinate clause: (since) you left. Subjects: *you* and *you*. Verbs: *have heard* and *left*.
2. Independent clause: Jimmy will meet me here. Subordinate clause: (if) he's alive. Subjects: *Jimmy* and *he*. Verbs: *will meet* and *is* (shortened to '*s*).
3. Independent clause: It was exactly ten o'clock. Subordinate clause: (when) we parted at the restaurant door. Subjects: *it* and *we*. Verbs: *was* and *parted*.
4. Independent clause: each turned to gaze at the other's face. Subordinate clause: (When) they came into the glare. Subjects: *each* and *they*. Verbs: *turned* and *came*.

B. Sample answers:

1. The policeman twirled his club as he walked down the street.
2. Jimmy and I made an agreement that we would meet here in twenty years.
3. If Jimmy is still alive, he'll be here.
4. After hearing that Bob was in the area, the police in Chicago sent a message.

Reading Strategy: Breaking Down Sentences (p. 124)

Break Down Sentences

Sample Responses:

Sentence: The few foot passengers astir in that quarter hurried dismally and silently along with coat collars turned high and pocketed hands.

Subject: foot passengers

Verb: hurried

Meaningful words about subject and verb: few, astir in that quarter, silently, coat collars turned high, pocketed hands

Sentence: And in the door of the hardware store the man who had come a thousand miles to fill an appointment, uncertain almost to absurdity, with the friend of his youth, smoked his cigar and waited.

Subject: man

Verb: smoked, waited

Meaningful words about subject and verb: had come a thousand miles, to fill an appointment, in the door of the hardware store

Literary Analysis: Surprise Ending (p. 125)

Sample answer is given on worksheet.

"Rikki-tikki-tavi" by Rudyard Kipling

Build Vocabulary (p. 126)

A. 1. survive
2. vivacious
3. vivarium
4. vivid

B. 1. c 2. d 3. f 4. b 5. a 6. e

C. 1. c 2. c 3. d

Build Spelling Skills: Homophones (p. 127)

A. Sample answers:

1. The mongoose was real, not a stuffed toy.
2. The boy needed a new reel to go with his old fishing rod.
3. The mongoose's tail was like that of a cat.
4. What a tale the boy would have to tell his friends!
5. The mongoose put his nose into the ink.
6. Everyone knows that the mongoose and the cobra are enemies.
7. The family gave the mongoose a piece of meat.
8. Because of Rikki-tikki, the garden animals could finally enjoy some peace.

B. 1. one
2. right
3. meat
4. write
5. meet
6. feet
7. won
8. feat

Challenge: Sample answers:

1. buzz
2. quack
3. pop
4. crackle
5. hiss
6. bam
7. sizzle
8. splash

Build Grammar Skills: Simple and Compound Sentences (p. 128)

A. 1. S 2. C 3. C 4. S 5. S 6. C

B. Sample answers:

1. Rikki-tikki was a mongoose. Rikki-tikki fought the cobras in the yard, and he won.
2. Teddy found Rikki-tikki on a garden path. Teddy and Rikki-tikki became good friends, but Teddy's mother was nervous at first.
3. Nag was a big black cobra. Nag was five feet long from tongue to tail, but he found it easy to hide in the yard.

Reading Strategy: Predict (p. 129)

A sample answer is given on the worksheet.

Literary Analysis: Plot (p. 130)

Sample answers: Exposition: Rikki-tikki gets flooded out of his parents' burrow and is saved by Teddy and his parents. Rising Action: Rikki-tikki learns about the cobras that are terrorizing the animals in the yard. He has some confrontations with them. He kills Karait, another snake in the yard. He is instrumental in killing Nag, the male cobra. Climax: Rikki-tikki kills Nagaina, the female cobra, who had been threatening Teddy. Falling action: All the garden animals celebrate the death of the cobras. Resolution: Teddy and his parents are grateful, and Rikki-tikki keeps the garden safe from then on.

"Papa's Parrot" by Cynthia Rylant

Build Vocabulary (p. 131)

A. Practice

1. contentment
2. enjoyment
3. pavement
4. resentment
5. enchantment
6. befuddlement
7. engagement

B. Writing Application

7. stroll
8. merely
9. cling

Build Spelling Skills: Unusual Spellings (p. 132)

1. l; 2. c; 3. l; 4. c; 5. w; 6. b; 7. k; 8. h; 9. t; 10. c

1. hymn, m; 2. foreign, g; 3. condemn, n;
4. doubted, b; 5. exhibit, h; 6. knowledge, k;
7. watching, t; 8. receipt, p

Sample answers:

1. Most people like music.
2. The police rushed to the scene of the accident.
3. The plumber needed a wrench to loosen the pipe.

Build Grammar Skills: Complex Sentences (p. 133)

A. 1. I 2. S 3. C 4. C 5. I 6. S

"Papa's Parrot" by Cynthia Rylant (*continued*)

B. Sample answers:

2. Mr. Tillian spoke to the parrot so that he wouldn't feel so lonely.

3. Because they had more money for other things, the children stopped coming in to the candy store.

4. Although he loved his father, Harry didn't spend much time with him.

5. Mr. Tillian had to order more candy if his supplies started to run low.

6. While Mr. Tillian was in the hospital, Harry went to the candy store to sort candy and feed Rocky.

Reading Strategy: Identify with a Character (p. 134)

Sample answer: Event—Mr. Tillian buys a parrot. Character's Reaction: Harry tells his father he thinks it is the strangest thing his father has ever done. How I Would React: I would say it was a good idea because the parrot might draw customers.

Literary Analysis: Characterization (p. 135)

Sample answers are given on the worksheet.

"Suzy and Leah" by Jane Yolen

Build Vocabulary (p. 136)

A. 1. one who is paid
2. one who stands
3. one who is absent
4. one who escapes
5. one who is appointed

B. Using New Words

1. porridge
2. portholes
3. permanent
4. rickety
5. steel
6. refugee

Build Spelling Skills: Adding -ee (p. 137)

A. 1. selectee
2. grantee
3. examinee
4. refugee

B. devotee, employee, honoree, attendee

1. devotee
2. attendee
3. employee
4. honoree

Challenge:

1. a garment that is worn over everything else
2. a shirt whose neck goes right up to the chin, giving the wearer the look of a turtle sticking its head out of its shell
3. rubber-soled shoes, so quiet that one can sneak around in them

Build Grammar Skills: Adverb Clauses (p. 138)

A. 1. when I looked back; modifies *was gone*
2. if she had only asked; modifies *wouldn't have minded*
3. At least; modifies *writes*
4. If I write all this down, modifies *will not forget*
5. Thought that would have been true; modifies *didn't answer*

B. Sample answers:

1. when: When Suzy looked back, the girl with dark braids and bangs was gone.
2. where: Where one little boy grabbed Suzy's hand, Suzy felt itchy.
3. how: Suzy could get to know Leah better if she invited her over for dinner.
4. why: Suzy thinks Leah is a grouch because she never smiles.
5. to what extent: The stories were so awful that Suzy could hardly believe them.
6. when: Avi stopped speaking when he was hidden away in a cupboard by his grandmother.
7. where: Leah does not like the school where boys and girls study together.
8. how: Leah is afraid that the Americans will turn on the Jews as the Germans did.
9. why: Leah does not tell anyone about her pain because she is afraid.
10. to what extent: Leah stared at the girl until she was forced to look down.

Reading Strategy: Drawing Inferences (p. 139)

Sample answer: Detail: Suzy laughs because the refugees don't know that oranges must be peeled. Inference: Suzy doesn't understand that they have never seen an orange.

Literary Analysis: Setting (p. 140)

1. August to October 1944
2. a city in the United States
3. all of it
4. none
5. extremely

"Ribbons" by Laurence Yep
"The Treasure of Lemon Brown" by Walter Dean Myers

Build Vocabulary (p. 141)

A. 1. desensitize
    2. extrasensory
    3. insensitivity
    4. sensational

B. 1. d 2. g 3. h 4. e 5. b 6. c 7. a 8. f

C. 1. b 2. a 3. d

Build Spelling Skills: Adding the Suffix -ious (p. 142)

A. 1. laborious
    2. envious
    3. gracious

B. 1. spacious
    2. furious
    3. glorious
    4. victorious

Challenge:

1. to grind together
2. a rock having light-colored layers of quartz alternating with darker minerals
3. an elf or dwarflike creature from folklore
4. a tiny insect

Build Grammar Skills: Adjective Clauses (p. 143)

A. 1. that had kept me going—modifies *hope*
    2. that held my satin toe shoes—modifies *box*
    3. which were callused from three years of daily lessons—modifies *feet*
    4. that I had never seen before—modifies *hate and disgust*
    5. that someone had stretched out and twisted—modifies *taffy*
    6. that feet were not meant to—modifies *way*

7. which was my old collection of fairy tales by Hans Christian Andersen—modifies *story*

B. Sample answers:

1. The dark sky, which was full of gray clouds, reflected Greg Ridley's mood. (modifies *sky*)
2. Greg's father, who wanted his son to succeed, said ball-playing would depend on Greg's report card. (modifies *father*)
3. Down the block was an old tenement building that should have been condemned. (modifies *building*)
4. From the couch, Greg could see the blinking neon sign that was missing one letter. (modifies *sign*)

Reading Strategy: Ask Questions (p. 144)

Sample answers are given on the worksheet.

Literary Analysis: Theme (p. 145)

Sample answer: Theme for "The Treasure of Lemon Brown": Old people have a lot they can teach younger people. Detail: Lemon Brown knew how to play harmonica well enough to support a family.

"Stolen Day" by Sherwood Anderson

Build Vocabulary (p. 146)

Using the Latin Root -flam-

A. 1. It can burst quickly into flames.
    2. Its color resembles a flame.
    3. It is resistant to flames.

B. Using the Word Bank

Sample Answers:

1. limped to show that his joints were sore
2. feel hot; burn
3. hardly ever smiled

C. Practice

1. c 2. d

Build Spelling Skills: The Spelling mn (p. 147)

A. autumn, column, condemn, hymn, solemn, limn

1. column
2. hymn
3. limn
4. solemn

5. autumn

6. condemn

B. Across:

3. column

5. limn

6. solemn

Down:

1. hymn

2. autumn

3. condemn

Challenge:

1. minnow

2. salmon

3. tuna

4. trout

5. goldfish

6. flounder

Build Grammar Skills: Subject and Verb Agreement (p. 148)

A. Practice

1. She comes right over to me.

2. I am getting more and more hungry.

3. The band meets after school on Tuesdays.

4. They arrive home for supper.

5. The class plays outside at recess.

6. Everyone has always been saying we ought to have a party.

B. Sample answers:

1. I am assigning more math homework.

2. They read more accurately now.

3. We are studying math today.

4. He doesn't feel well today.

5. You must finish your essay by Friday.

6. You seem to need more practice with fractions.

Reading Strategy: Understanding Author's Purpose (p. 149)

Sample answers:

1. to amuse; to make the reader think

2. to amuse; to explore a character's behavior

3. to prompt the reader's sympathy; to explore a character's behavior

4. to amuse; to explore a character's behavior; to prompt the reader's sympathy

5. to inform; to capture a special time or place

6. to explore a character's behavior; to prompt the reader's sympathy; to make the reader think

7. to amuse; to capture a special time or place; to explore a character's behavior

8. to capture a special time or place

Literary Analysis: Point of View (p. 150)

1. The narrator is a young boy who takes a day off from school.

2. The narrator uses the pronoun "I" and takes a direct part in the action of the story.

3. The first-person narrator, by definition, only knows what his character can personally observe. All observations are filtered through that narrator's perspective.

4. You might know more about why Walter acts as he does, how the narrator's mother felt when she discovered the drowned child, what the teacher thought about the narrator's complaints, and how the other family members felt when they heard the details of what really happened on the "stolen day."

5. The author wanted to tell the story with the thoughts and feelings of the boy who experienced it, without the outside authority of an external voice making judgments or influencing the reader's response to the story.

"How to Enjoy Poetry"
by James Dickey

Build Vocabulary (p. 151)

A. 1. intermission

2. interfere

3. interstate

4. intergalactic

Sample answers:

5. Do not <u>interrupt</u> when someone is speaking.

6. Most American public schools are now <u>interracial</u>.

7. The cars stopped at the <u>intersection</u>.

8. You <u>intertwine</u> hair to make a braid.

B. 1. prose

2. inevitability

3. vital

4. interacts

C. 1. d   2. b   3. a   4. c

Build Spelling Skills: Change the Adjective Ending *-able* to the Noun Ending *-ility* (p. 152)

A. 1. believability

2. liability

3. lovability

4. flammability

5. washability

6. detectability

7. bendability

8. workability

9. traceability

10. wearability

B. 1. durability

2. capability

3. unforgettability

4. predictability

5. readability

6. ability

Challenge: *Inept* means "not suitable or fit." *Incessant* means "not ceasing." *Indelible* means "not erasable." There is no such word as *ept, cessant,* or *delible.*

Build Grammar Skills: The Four Functions of Sentences (p. 153)

A. 1. interrogative

2. imperative

3. declarative

4. declarative

5. imperative

6. exclamatory

7. interrogative

8. declarative

9. interrogative

10. exclamatory

Message: Read poetry!

B. Sample answers:

1. What will happen if you give to a poem?

2. Concentrate when you read that poem.

3. I think about meaning when I read a poem.

4. How beautiful the poem's language is!

Reading Strategy: Identifying Main Ideas (pp. 154)

Suggested responses:

Where Poetry is Coming From

Hint in Passage: . . . people have known that words and things/actions/feelings . . . can go together in thousands of different ways . . .

Author's Main Idea: Poetry is a diverse form of writing.

Your Connection With Other Imaginations

Hint in Passage: . . . something from within you must come to it and meet it and complete it.

Author's Main Idea: Poetry demands interaction with the reader.

Which Sun? Whose Stars?

Hint in Passage: Poetry makes possible the deepest kind of personal possession of the world.

Author's Main Idea: Poetry speaks to each reader in a unique way.

Where to Start

Hint in Passage: . . . open yourself as wide as you can and as deep as you can to the moment . . .

Author's Main Idea: Readers of poetry should find their own way.

"How to Enjoy Poetry" by James Dickey
(*continued*)

The Poem's Way of Going

Hint in Passage: Part of the spell of poetry is in the rhythm of language . . .

Author's Main Idea: Poets make their work memorable with the rhythms and rhymes they use.

Some Things You'll Find Out

Hint in Passage: . . . so deliciously memorable that nothing else is like it . . .

Author's Main Idea: Writing poems has many possibilities.

How It Goes With You

Hint in Passage: Connections between things will exist for you in ways that they never did before.

Author's Main Idea: Your encounters with poetry can change you forever.

Literary Analysis: Expository Essay (p. 155)

Sample answers:

1. Instruction: Find your own way to open yourself to the moment of your own existence.

Important Details: Concentrate on one thing, such as a handful of gravel or an ice cube;

let it call up an image from your own life; think and feel.

2. Instruction: Focus on the rhythm and rhyme of a poem.

Important Details: Make up limericks; be inventive with your language.

3. Instruction: Deepen your encounter with poetry.

Important Details: The more your encounter deepens, the more your own life experience will deepen; you will see things by means of words.

"No Gumption" by Russell Baker
"The Chase" by Annie Dillard

Build Vocabulary (p. 156)

A. 1. expelled
   2. propelled
   3. dispelled
   4. repelled

B. 1. e 2. c 3. f 4. a 5. g 6. d 7. b
C. 1. b 2. a 3. d 4. c

Build Spelling Skills: Double the Final Consonant Before Adding -ed or -ing (p. 157)

A. 1. controlled
   2. expelling
   3. preferred
   4. committing
   5. permitted
B. 1. admitted
   2. upsetting
   3. preferred
   4. beginning
   5. impelled

Challenge Sample answers: perfect, perfection, perforate, perforation, perform, performance, perfume

Build Grammar Skills: Participles and Participial Phrases (p. 158)

A. 2. Mrs. Baker was a <u>concerned</u> (mother) who worried about her son.
   3. Russell eventually found that to be a writer was a more <u>enchanting</u> (profession).
   4. In "The Chase," Anne was a <u>valued</u> (player) on the boys' football team.
   5. <u>Throwing snowballs</u> at <u>passing cars</u>, (Anne) angered one driver.
   6. The <u>fuming</u> (driver) got out of his car and chased the girl for many blocks.

B. Sample answers:
   1. Not excited about selling magazines, Russell longed for another career.
   2. Getting hit by a snowball was an upsetting experience for the driver.
   3. Looking for a way out of hard work, Russell chose to become a writer.
   4. The relieved girl was glad when the long chase finally ended.
   5. Thinking about it later, Anne realized how much fun she had had.

Reading Strategy: Understand the Author's Purpose (p. 159)

Sample answers:

"No Gumption"

Passage: "You've got no more gumption than a bump on a log," she said.

Purpose: to entertain

Passage: ". . . the best she could hope for was a career as a nurse or a schoolteacher, the only work that capable females were considered up to in those days."

Purpose: to inform

"The Chase"

Passage: "This was fine sport. You thought up a new strategy for every play and whispered it to the others."

Purpose: to persuade

Passage: "In winter, in the snow, there was neither baseball nor football, so the boys and I threw snowballs at passing cars."

Purpose: to inform

Literary Analysis: Autobiography (p. 160)

Sample answers:

Character: Russell

Impression: He has no gumption.

Examples: He doesn't like selling magazines. He enjoys writing because it requires no gumption.

Character: Annie

Impression: She is as tough as the boys.

Examples: She plays football and baseball with them. She has good aim with a snowball. She endures a long chase in the streets.

"Nolan Ryan, Texas Treasure"
by William W. Lace

Build Vocabulary (p. 161)

A. 1. b 2. d 3. a 4. c 5. g 6. h 7. e 8. f

B. Using New Words

1. franchise
2. keenly
3. excel
4. wholesome
5. memento
6. reserved

Build Spelling Skills: Add Suffixes to Words Ending with *e* (p. 162)

A. 1. homeless: without a home
2. serenity: calmness and peacefulness
3. servile: like that of slaves

B. 1. encouragement
2. combination
3. broken
4. exciting
5. wholesome

Challenge: arts, rats, tars

Build Grammar Skills: Appositives and Appositive Phrases (p. 163)

A. 1. Appositive or phrase: a no-hitter; Word described: game
2. Appositive or phrase: bacon, sausage, and cream soups; Word described: foods
3. Appositive or phrase: America's greatest pitcher; Word described: title
4. Appositive or phrase: a Texan at heart; Word described: Ryan
5. Appositive or phrase: the player people came to see; Word described: Ryan

B. Sample answers:
1. Ryan wants to be remembered as a "gamer"—a player who tries very hard in every game.
2. He is possibly the best-known ball player in his home state, Texas.
3. Ryan's records include two very impressive ones—most strikeouts and most no-hitters.

Reading Strategy: Distinguishing Fact and Opinion (p. 164)

Possible responses:

Facts:

His fellow players are sometimes just as eager as fans to get his autograph.

Ryan has always taken good care of his body.

He doesn't eat fried foods and doesn't often eat large meals.

He has many other business interests and spends much time on charity work.

In the three seasons with Nolan Ryan, the team had 15 [sell-out crowds], mostly on nights Ryan pitched.

He earns an estimated $1 million to $2 million a year from . . . endorsements.

Ryan holds almost 50 major league records.

"Nolan Ryan, Texas Treasure"
by William W. Lace
(*continued*)

Opinions:

Mental fitness probably has been just as important.

The talented pitcher has not allowed fame and fortune to change his personality, as many star athletes have.

I still represent small-town Texas, and that's fine with me.

If you saw him in a shopping mall or talked to him in the grocery store, you'd think he was just another middle-aged guy.

Ryan is possibly the best-known person in the state of Texas.

You may be in on something truly spectacular, like a no-hitter.

And Ryan's accomplishments are even more enjoyable because of the kind of person he is as well as the kind of pitcher.

Literary Analysis: Biography (p. 165)

Sample answers:

Subject: Nolan Ryan

Author's View: Ryan is a unique ballplayer.

Examples: He holds almost fifty records. He is a modest, family-centered man despite his great accomplishments. He gives himself completely to every game.

from *Barrio Boy* by Ernesto Galarza
"I Am a Native of North America"
by Chief Dan George
"Rattlesnake Hunt"
by Marjorie Kinnan Rawlings
"All Together Now" by Barbara Jordan

Build Vocabulary (p. 166)

A. 1. mortuary
   2. immortal
   3. mortician
   4. immortalize

B. 1. mortality
   2. communal
   3. desolate

4. formidable
5. tolerant

C. 1. c 2. d 3. a 4. b

Build Spelling Skills: *it* Sound Spelled *ate* (p. 167)

A. 1. delicate Sample answer: The doctor performed a delicate operation.
   2. intricate Sample answer: The intricate problem was difficult to solve.
   3. separate Sample answer: The children slept in separate bedrooms.

B. 1. adequate
   2. separate
   3. delicate

Challenge: Sample answers: commune, communicate, communication, communion, communism, community, commute, commuter

Build Grammar Skills: Infinitives (p. 168)

A. Practice

1. to pick
2. NO INFINITIVE
3. to strike.
4. to attend; to speak
5. to match
6. to know; to tell
7. to live; to serve
8. to accept
9. to work
10. to be

B. Writing Application

Possible responses:

1. "Barrio Boy"

Learning to speak English is more difficult than I imagined.

2. "I Am a Native of North America"

Chief Dan George learned to respect the earth and other people while he was growing up.

3. "Rattlesnake Hunt"

I enjoyed learning about how to hunt snakes.

4. "All Together Now"

It is possible to overcome intolerance if everyone works together.

Reading Strategy: Determining Main Points
(p. 169)

Sample answers:

1. from *Barrio Boy*

Passage: "At Lincoln, making us into Americans did not mean scrubbing away what made us originally foreign."

Hint in Passage: Scrubbing away at something makes it disappear.

Author's Main Point: He could be a proud American without being ashamed of being a Mexican.

2. "Rattlesnake Hunt"

Passage: ". . . I think I should have lain down and died on top of the rattlesnake, with no need of being struck and poisoned."

Hint in Passage: A person would not really die from a snake without being poisoned by it.

Author's Main Point: She was extremely terrified of snakes.

3. "All Together Now"

Passage: "Today the nation seems to be suffering from compassion fatigue . . ."

Hint in Passage: Fatigue is a physical condition of the human body.

Author's Main Point: Americans must work together as one body to energize themselves and overcome their lack of human compassion.

Literary Analysis: Essay (p. 170)

Sample answers:

1. From *Barrio Boy* is a personal essay because the author gives an informal account of his enrollment and entry into an American school.

2. "Rattlesnake Hunt" is a descriptive essay because it details the experience of a rattlesnake hunt and the people who participate in it.

3. "I Am a Native of North America" is a reflective essay because the author presents his thoughts about his childhood and his ideas on how Americans of different cultures can survive.

4. "All Together Now" is a persuasive essay because the author presents arguments for the necessity of racial tolerance and suggests ways of achieving it.

Unit 8: Drama

A Christmas Carol: Scrooge and Marley, Act I by Charles Dickens dramatized by Israel Horovitz

Build Vocabulary (p. 171)

A. 1. b 2. d 3. a 4. c

B. 1. ponderous
   2. morose
   3. misanthrope
   4. void
   5. benevolence
   6. implored
   7. destitute

C. 1. b 2. d 3. a 4. c 5. b 6. c

Build Spelling Skills: Add *-stitute* (p. 172)

A. 1. substitute
   2. institute
   3. destitute
   4. constitute

B. 1. destitute
   2. constitute
   3. institute
   4. substitute

Challenge: Sample answers: me, is, a, an, rope

Build Grammar Skills: Active Voice (p. 173)

A. Practice

   1. meets; A
   2. is visited; P
   3. appears; A
   4. was; A
   5. rings; A
   6. is made; P
   7. died; A
   8. has been dragged; P

A Christmas Carol: Scrooge and Marley, Act I by Charles Dickens dramatized by Israel Horovitz (*continued*)

B. Writing Application

1. The angry ghost of Jacob Marley warned Scrooge.
2. Three Spirits will haunt you.
3. His ferret eyes searched the darkness.
4. Marley speaks to the audience.
5. The reader must pay careful attention to Scrooge's pain.

Reading Strategy: Envision (p. 174)

Sample answers:

Setting: A single spotlight on Jacob Marley. Bob Cratchit sits in a dismal tank of a cubicle. There are various pictures on the walls; all of them now show likenesses of Marley.

Scrooge: Scrooge seizes his ruler and whacks at the image of the boy outside. He is the misanthrope, the malcontent, the miser. Seeing nothing but screws and nuts, Scrooge refuses the memory. Scrooge freezes, staring at the field beyond.

Marley: He is ancient, awful, dead-eyed. Cackle-voiced. He is horrible to look at: pigtail, vest, suit as usual, but he drags an enormous chain now, to which is fastened cash-boxes, keys, padlocks, ledgers, deeds, and heavy purses fashioned of steel. He is transparent.

Cratchit: Cratchit rubs his hands together, puts on a white comforter and tries to heat his hands around his candle. They move to the door. Cratchit hops up to open it for them.

Literary Analysis: Elements of Drama (p. 175)

Sample answers:

1. Scrooge's refusal even to look at the calling card shows how callous and uncaring he is toward other people.
2. Scrooge's remark indicates that he is cold-hearted and has no pity for people in need.
3. Scrooge's temporary vision of Marley's face foreshadows the fact that a visit from Marley is going to take place soon.
4. Young Scrooge's comment reveals that, at an earlier time in his life, Scrooge was actually kindhearted and somewhat of an idealist. It helps us understand how much he has changed from youth to old age.

5. Scrooge's exclamations indicate that he is bothered by the past and its reminder of how empty and loveless his life has become.
6. This stage direction helps us understand the magical element of the drama, with its ghostly entrances and exits.

A Christmas Carol: Scrooge and Marley, Act II by Charles Dickens dramatized by Israel Horovitz

Build Vocabulary (p. 176)

A. 1. audit
   2. audition
   3. auditorium
   4. audiocassette
B. 1. compulsion
   2. audible
   3. astonish
   4. gnarled
   5. threadbare
   6. dispelled
   7. meager
   8. severe
C. 1. c 2. b 3. a 4. d

Build Spelling Skills: Words Starting With *gn* (p. 177)

A. 1. gnu
   2. gnome
   3. gnat
   4. gnaw
   5. gnarl
   6. gnash
B. 1. gnomes
   2. gnat
   3. gnashes
   4. gnaw
Challenge: Sample answers: align, assign, benign, design, ensign, malign, resign

Build Grammar Skills: Pronoun and Antecedent (p. 178)

A. Practice

1. him
2. they
3. their
4. them
5. she

6. his

7. his or her

8. they

B. Writing Application

Possible answers:

1. I liked <u>Marley</u>. **His** voice had such power when **he** tried to warn Scrooge.

2. <u>Mrs. Cratchit</u> is sad to see **her** husband so abused. **She** would like to tell Scrooge what she thinks.

3. The <u>cast</u> was wonderful. **They** did a great job of bringing the story alive.

4. My <u>friend</u> <u>and</u> <u>I</u> enjoyed **our** day at the theater.

Reading Strategy: Question (p. 179)

Sample answers:

Question: Why does Scrooge need to visit the present when he is already living in it?

Answer: It enables him to learn what the Cratchits say about him in their home, which he otherwise couldn't do.

Question: Why does the uncaring Scrooge ask that Tiny Tim's life be spared?

Answer: Scrooge has begun to change from an uncaring to a caring individual.

Question: Does Scrooge realize that the dead man being robbed of his possessions is really he himself?

Answer: No, since he tells the ghost, "This unhappy man—this stripped-bare corpse . . . could very well be my own."

Literary Analysis: Characterization and Theme in Drama (p. 180)

Sample answers:

Character's Quote: BOB: I'll give you Mr. Scrooge, the Founder of the Feast!

What It Reveals: Cratchit respects all people, even those who are mean.

Character's Quote: MRS. CRATCHIT: It should be Christmas Day, I am sure, on which one drinks the health of such an odious, stingy, unfeeling man as Mr. Scrooge.

What It Reveals: Mrs. Cratchit is not as forgiving nor tolerant as her husband.

Theme: Holidays can be valuable times for reflection on one's accomplishments in life.

Theme: Even the worst type of person has the potential for change and self-improvement.

"The Monsters are Due on Maple Street" by Rod Serling

Build Vocabulary (p. 181)

A. 1. d 2. a 3. b 4. c

B. 1. metamorphosis

2. scapegoat

3. sluggishly

4. defiant

5. assent

6. flustered

7. persistently

C. 1. b 2. c 3. a 4. d

Build Spelling Skills: f Sound Spelled ph (p. 182)

A. 1. graphics

2. sophomore

3. telephone

4. photograph

5. phrase

6. biography

7. catastrophe

8. trophy

9. geography

10. gopher

B. 1. phobia

2. phenomenon

3. phantom

4. phony

5. graphic

6. philosophy

Challenge: Sample answers: Elm, Oak, Chestnut, Cherry, Peach, Beech, Sycamore, Cedar, Pine, Spruce, Myrtle, Magnolia

Build Grammar Skills: Pronoun References (p. 183)

Practice and Writing Application

Possible Answers:

1. There's something wrong with the stove. There was a flash of light when that meteor struck, and a roar, and the stove stopped working.

"The Monsters are Due on Maple Street" by Rod Serling (*continued*)

2. Steve and Charlie ask Goodman about the car starting. Goodman says he doesn't know how it happened.

3. In this story, the people are frightened. Maybe there are aliens. Maybe the aliens are invading. The people have a lot to think about.

4. Steve is surprised at everyone's behavior. Charlie is suspicious. Don is making accusations. But Steve keeps his head through it all.

5. The aliens discuss the plans for taking over earth. The plans appear to be very effective.

6. Fear was the tool the aliens used. "Love your neighbor" was not something these people practiced. Fear accomplished what the aliens wanted.

Reading Strategy: Predict (p. 184)

Sample answers:

1. Clue: Maple Street loses its electrical power.

   Prediction: The people will stay inside their homes.

   Outcome: People go outside and talk.

2. Clue: Tommy warns that aliens are causing the trouble.

   Prediction: People will laugh at Tommy.

   Outcome: Some people take Tommy seriously.

3. Clue: Les Goodman has been seen looking at the sky.

   Prediction: He will turn out to be an alien.

   Outcome: He is not an alien.

Literary Analysis: Plot in Drama (p. 185)

Sample answers:

Conflict: The fear of alien invasion. The mistrust of individuals for the people around them. The conflict between the desire to be reasonable and the desire to be safe.

Rising Action: People start accusing each other of being aliens in disguise. People are spooked by everything that happens. Lights go on and cars start without explanation, causing additional panic.

Resolution: The aliens get what they want. Their plan works. People destroy each other.

Unit 9: Poetry

"The Cremation of Sam McGee"
by Robert Service
"Washed in Silver"
by James Stephens
"Winter" by Nikki Giovanni

Build Vocabulary (p. 186)

A. 1. peeked
   2. shrieked
   3. lugged
B. 1. loathed
   2. whimper
   3. whine
   4. cremated
   5. stern
   6. grisly

7. radiance
8. burrow

C. 1. a 2. b 3. d

Build Spelling Skills: *hw* Sound Spelled *w* or *wh* (p. 187)

A. 1. wheel
   2. wheat
   3. west
   4. what
   5. weapon
   6. wedding
   7. whack
   8. waist
   9. whip
B. 2. whimper
   3. whine

4. while

5. which

6. whiteness

Challenge: Sample answers: who, whom, whose, wholesome

Build Grammar Skills: Degrees of Comparison of Modifiers (p. 188)

A. 1. <u>faithful</u>, positive

2. <u>warmest</u>, superlative

3. <u>loveliest</u>, superlative

4. <u>sicklier</u>, comparative

5. <u>more enjoyable</u>, comparative

B. Sample answers:

1. That was the **best** trip I've ever taken.

2. It was **colder** than I had expected.

3. The scenery was the **most beautiful** I'd ever seen.

4. The cold made us move **more slowly**.

Reading Strategy: Interpreting Figures of Speech (p. 189)

Sample answer:

"The Cremation . . ." — "The Northern Lights have seen queer sights" (personification)

"he wore a smile you could see a mile"; (hyperbole)

"Washed in Silver" — "the moon drives royally" (personification)

"Winter" — "The speaker is as busy as an autumn squirrel." (simile)

Literary Analysis: Types of Poetry (p. 190)

Sample answer:

Similarities: Both types of poems can use vivid language, rhythm, rhyme, and figures of speech.

Differences: Narrative poems tell a story. They have a plot, character, and setting. They often use repetition to highlight key ideas.

Lyric poems are personal and expressive. They are often written about the themes of nature and love.

"Seal" by William Jay Smith
"The Pasture" by Robert Frost
"Three Haiku" by Matsuo Bashō, translated by Daniel C. Buchanan

Build Vocabulary (p. 191)

A. 1. c 2. b 3. d 4. a

B. 1. swerve

2. totters

3. pasture

4. utter

C. 1. a 2. d 3. b 4. c

Build Spelling Skills: *cher* Sound Spelled *ture* (p. 192)

A. 1. overture

2. adventure

3. agriculture

4. gesture

5. lecture

6. manufacture

7. mixture

8. posture

9. puncture

10. picture

B. 2. creature

3. features

4. posture

5. picture

6. adventure

Challenge: Sample answers: butter, cutter, flutter, gutter, putter, stutter, shutter, sputter

My model plane began to sputter,

And then it landed in the gutter.

Build Grammar Skills: Placement of *only* (p. 193)

A. 2. The seal is not the only water animal that hunts for fish.

3. The farmer raked leaves only in the fall.

4. The farmer fetched only the calf and not its mother.

5. The sun rises only in the east.

6. The seal has only two flippers.

B. Sample answers:

1. Does a seal live only in the water?

2. I have seen seals only at the zoo.

"Seal" by William Jay Smith
"The Pasture" by Robert Frost
"Three Haiku" by Matsuo Bashō, translated
by Daniel C. Buchanan (*continued*)

3. The farmer grew only corn.

4. Come along only if you have time.

5. The sun rose only a few minutes ago.

6. Only three customers may enter at one time.

Reading Strategy: Reading According to Punctuation (p. 194)

Sample answers:

a. Poem: "Seal"; Example of Punctuation: Exclamation point in the second line; What It Tells: Read the line with emphasis.

b. Poem: "The Pasture"; Example of Punctuation: Hyphen in the fourth line; What It Tells: Pause before reading "You come too."

c. Poem: Three Haiku; Example of Punctuation: In the first poem, no period until the end of the second line; What It Tells: Do not stop until the end of the second line.

Literary Analysis: Form in Poetry (p. 195)

Sample answers:

1. The shape of a leaf or calf would suggest the topic.

2. I'll go.—You come too. I am going.—You come too.

3. Stanza 1: How he dives and darts.
Stanza 2: How he swims and plunges;
Stanza 3: How he comes up with fish.

4. The seal dives from rocks.

5. Stanza 1: The sun rises on plum blossoms and a mountain path.
Stanza 2: Spring arrives with mist on a mountain.
Stanza 3: It is a quiet evening with fragrant blossoms.

6. Poem 1: a sun
Poem 2: a mountain
Poem 3: a bell

"Martin Luther King" by Raymond Richard Patterson
"Annabel Lee" by Edgar Allan Poe

Build Vocabulary (p. 196)

A. 1. founded

2. profound

3. foundation

4. founder

B. 1. profound

2. coveted

3. beset

4. profound

C. 1. b 2. a 3. d

Build Spelling Skills: *kwa* Sound Spelled *qua* (p. 197)

A. 1. quadrant: a quarter section of a circle

2. quantity: amount

3. squalid: dirty, filthy

4. squadron: a group of warships or aircraft

5. quandary: a problem about what to do

B. 1. qualities

2. quarrel

3. squawk

4. qualified

Challenge: Sample answers:

quad: from Latin *quadr-*, meaning *four*; quadrangle

quant: from Latin *quantus*, meaning *how much*; quantify

qual: from Latin *qualis*, meaning *of what sort*; qualification

Build Grammar Skills: Capitalization (p. 198)

A. 1. King, Raymond Richard Patterson, African

2. Dr. King

3. We, January

4. King, Washington

5. Edgar Allan Poe

6. "Annabel Lee"

7. Poe, "The Raven"

B. 1. Poe was born in Boston, but when his mother died, he went to live with the Allans in Richmond, Virginia.

2. Shortly after leaving the U. S. Army, Poe began publishing stories, and was soon editing a magazine: the *Southern Literary Messenger*.

3. Many famous people, such as Hollywood actor Charleton Heston, joined with Martin Luther King, Jr., in the efforts to end discrimination.

Reading Strategy: Paraphrasing (p. 199)

Sample answers:

a. Stanza: His passion, so profound, / He would not turn around.

Paraphrase: His passion was so great that he refused to give up his fight.

b. Stanza: So that her highborn kinsmen came / And bore her away from me.

Paraphrase: Her rich relatives came and took her away from me.

c. Stanza: The stars never rise but I see the bright eyes / Of the beautiful Annabel Lee.

Paraphrase: Every time the stars come out, they remind me of Annabel Lee's beautiful eyes.

d. Stanza: Some words are sad: / "I never had . . ."

Paraphrase: Some words in English help us to express regret.

Literary Analysis: Rhythm and Rhyme (p. 200)

1. a. His pássion, só prŏfouńd,
      He wóuld nŏt túrn ărouńd.
   b. Bŭt oúr lŏve ĭt wăs stronğer bў fár thăn thĕ lŏve
      Ŏf thóse whŏ wĕre ólder thăn wé—

2. a. age, rage; wide, aside; profound, around; Earth, worth; be, free.
   b. sea, Lee, me, we; ago, know; beams, dreams; rise, eyes; nighttide, side, bride.

"Full Fathom Five"
by William Shakespeare
"Onomatopoeia" by Eve Merriam
"Maestro" by Pat Mora

Build Vocabulary (p. 201)

A. Sample answers:

1. I could hear the water gurgle as the bathtub drained.

2. The buzz of the mosquito kept me awake.

3. She likes to hum the melody of her favorite song.

4. The box fell with a thud.

5. Never whack anyone with a stick.

6. The car went ping after hitting a pothole.

B. 1. maestro
      2. snare
      3. sputters
      4. knell

C. 1. c 2. a 3. c 4. b

Build Spelling Skills: *n* Sound Spelled *kn* (p. 202)

A. 1. knowledge
      2. knock
      3. knob
      4. knuckle
      5. knit
      6. knead

B. 2. knowledge
      3. knocking
      4. knew
      5. knows
      6. knack

Challenge: Answers:

1. descendants of Dutch settlers in New York

2. New Yorkers

3. loose-fitting trousers or breeches that are banded just below the knee

BONUS: the New York Knicks

Build Grammar Skills: Interjections (p. 203)

A. 1. Boy! The image of the bones turned to coral is kind of, uh, spooky.

2. Wow! Shakespeare's description of drowning is unsettling.

3. Well, I think the use of sound is delightful in Merriam's poem.

4. Gosh! The poem "Maestro" is so inspiring.

5. Say, let's find out more about Pat Mora.

B. Sample answers:

1. Er, is this the way?

2. Ouch! I stubbed my toe.

3. Great! I'll get my skates.

4. Come on! Can't you hurry?

5. Wow! What a mess!

Reading Strategy: Clarifying Word Meanings (p. 204)

Sample answers:

1. The writer can see for a long distance through the clear water.
2. The wind is making waves, which look like the furrows a plow makes.
3. fathom: to understand fully
4. Sample answer: A giant clam is a type of mollusk.
5. Sample answer: meat: something that nourishes you; chew: taking in, digesting

Literary Analysis: Sound Devices (p. 205)

Sample answers:

a. Poem: "Full Fathom Five"; Onomatopoeia: ding-dong.
b. Poem: "Onomatopoeia"; Alliteration: spigot sputters spatters.
c. Poem: "Maestro"; Alliteration: bit by bit; note to note.

"The Village Blacksmith"
by Henry Wadsworth Longfellow
"Loo-Wit" by Wendy Rose
"Fog" by Carl Sandburg
"Life" by Naomi Long Madgett

Build Vocabulary (p. 206)

A. 1. c 2. d 3. a 4. b
B. 1. haunches
   2. buttes
   3. dislodge
   4. unravel
   5. crouches
   6. brawny
C. 1. b 2. d 3. c

Build Spelling Skills: Adding Endings to Words Ending in Consonant-Vowel-Consonant (p. 207)

A. 1. offered
   2. labeling
   3. committed
   4. traveling
   5. rebelled

6. referring
7. controlled
8. focusing

B. 1. sorrowing
   2. scampered
   3. shuddering
   4. blanketed

Challenge:

1. <u>Ravel</u> and <u>unravel</u> mean "to separate" or "come apart."
2. <u>Flammable</u> and <u>inflammable</u> mean "capable of burning rapidly." Instead of having opposite meanings, they mean the same thing.

Build Grammar Skills: Semicolons (p. 208)

A. 1. clothing; for
   2. life; Madgett's
   3. dangerous; scientific
   4. Italy; Krakatoa, island; and
   5. droplets; smog
   6. as if
B. Sample answers:
1. "The Village Blacksmith" tells a story; it also inspires readers with life lessons.
2. In : "Loo-Wit," the author describes a volcano erupting; she compares it to an old woman waking up and picking up her weapons.
3. Sandburg compares fog to a cat; I think this means that it is soft and quiet.
4. Life is like a ticking watch; it runs for a while but eventually stops.

Reading Strategy: Using Your Senses (p. 209)

Sample answers:

"The Village Blacksmith": under a spreading chestnut tree, flaming forge (sight); bellows roar, he hears his daughter's voice (hearing); hard, rough hand (touch)

"Loo-Wit": old woman, sprinkles ashes on the snow (sight); bumpy bed, ropes lay prickly on her neck (touch), machinery growls, creaking floor (hearing); spits black tobacco (smell and/or taste)

"Fog": the fog comes in on little cat feet (touch, sight, hearing); harbor and city (smell, hearing, sight, taste)

"Life": toy, bright gold chain (sight); swings (touch); ticking (hearing)

Literary Analysis: Figurative Language
(p. 210)

Sample answers:

a. Poem: "The Village Blacksmith"; Passage: as strong as iron bands; Type of Figurative Language: simile.

b. Poem: "Fog"; Passage: The fog comes on little cat feet; Type of Figurative Language: metaphor.

c. Poem: "Life"; Passage: Life is but a toy that swings on a bright gold chain; Type of Figurative Language: metaphor.

d. Poem: "Loo-Wit"; Passage: But spits her black tobacco any which way; Type of Figurative Language: personification.

Unit 10:   Myths, Legends, and Folk Tales

"Popocatepetl and Ixtlaccihuatl"
by Juliet Piggott

Build Vocabulary (p. 211)

A. 1. become
2. bedazzled
3. befogged
4. bejeweled

B. 1. edifice
2. relished
3. besieged
4. routed
5. brandishing
6. decreed
7. refute
8. unanimous

C. 1. b 2. a 3. d 4. c 5. a

Build Spelling Skills: Long e Words with ie
(p. 212)

A. 1. siege
2. receipt
3. niece
4. thief
5. conceited
6. neither
7. piece
8. leisure
9. yield
10. protein

B. 2. yield
3. besieged
4. C
5. conceited
6. battlefield

7. shields
8. fiendish
9. deceived
10. C

Challenge: Sample answers: pouted, touted, rooted, rotted, rouged.

Build Grammar Skills: Parentheses and Brackets (p. 213)

A. 1. The English word *volcano* comes from Vulcan, the mythological Roman god of fire and metalworking (they believed the volcano was Vulcan's furnace).

2. Piggott's story retells the Aztec legend of how Popocatepetl and Ixtlaccihuatl (two volcanoes at the head of the valley where the Aztec's had their capital) came into being.

3. The volcanoes of this story may have existed in the days when the new people were just learning to grow corn (maize).

4. The Emperor's enemies were firmly entrenched around the royal city, Tenochtitlan (it is now called Mexico City).

5. The warriors grabbed their obsidian machetes (razor-sharp knives made of volcanic glass) and headed into battle.

6. With the arrival of Spanish warrior Hernando Cortéz (1485–1547), Aztec life changed forever.

B. Sample answers:

1. At the beginning of the story we learn that it was the Spaniards who conquered the Aztec capital of Tenochtitlan (1521).

2. The story tells us that Popo "gently lifted [Ixtlaccihuatl's] body and carried it out of the palace."

"Popocatepetl and Ixtlaccihuatl"
by Juliet Piggott (*continued*)

3. The mountain called Popocatepetl (supposedly named for an Aztec warrior) still sometimes emits smoke.

Reading for Success: Rereading or Reading Ahead (p. 214)

Students should identify unfamiliar items and note whether rereading or reading ahead was more helpful.

Literary Analysis: Legend (p. 215)

Sample answers:

Details Reflecting Cultural Values and Attitudes:

Ixtla obeys her father despite his harsh decrees—Reflects the importance of family

Popo is portrayed as a brave warrior—Shows Aztec respect for bravery.

Popo remains loyal to Ixtla even after her death—Reflects attitude toward love and loyalty.

Exaggerations: Popo kills each warrior in single combat with his obsidian-studded club; Popo carries Ixtla's body for several miles; Popo holds Ixtla's body while the pyramid is built; the pyramids are as large as mountains.

"The People Could Fly"
by Virginia Hamilton
"All Stories Are Anansi's"
retold by Harold Courtlander
"The Lion and the Statue" by Aesop
"The Fox and the Crow" by Aesop

Build Vocabulary (p. 216)

A. 1. d 2. d 3. a 4. c

Sample answers:

5. Waters surround an island.
6. People cannot survive without food.
7. The general finally agreed to surrender.

B. 1. yearned
2. croon
3. gourd
4. shuffle
5. glossy
6. flatterers

7. surpass
8. acknowledge

C. 1. c 2. b 3. a 4. d

Build Spelling Skills: The *aw* Sound Spelled *au* (p. 217)

A. 1. applause
2. pause
3. launch
4. sauce
5. haunt
6. fault
7. cause

B. 2. assaulted
3. launch
4. because
5. applaud
6. undaunted
7. haul

Challenge: Sample answers: *Sage* can mean "wise" or "a wise person." The experienced teacher gave sage advice. *Sage* can also refer to an herb used in cooking. The cook added sage and other herbs to the soup.

Build Grammar Skills: Quotation Marks (p. 218)

A. 1. The lion said, "I think lions are stronger than men."
2. "No, men are definitely stronger," the man replied.
3. The man argued, "Look how Hercules tears the lion's mouth!"
4. "That is still no proof," replied the lion.
5. The fox said, "I'd really love to hear you sing!"
6. "I'm very happy to hear that," answered the crow.
7. Then the crow cried, "Now I've lost my cheese!"

B. Sample answers:

1. The man said, "I disagree with your argument."
2. "Your argument doesn't work," the lion replied.
3. The crow said, "I think I have a nice voice."
4. "I'll sing for you," offered the crow.
5. "I've taught you a lesson," the fox announced.

Reading Strategy: Recognizing Cultural Context (p. 219)

Sample answers:

1. "The People Could Fly": Time: probably between 1600 and 1850. Place: an unnamed plantation, probably in the South. Customs: Slaves worked in the fields from sunup to sundown. Beliefs: Slaves were property and had no rights or freedom.

2. "All Stories Are Anansi's": Time: "in the beginning" (before the existence of humans). Place: Western Africa; Customs: Bargaining. Beliefs: Storytelling was a highly prized skill.

3. "The Lion and the Statue": Time: around 600 B.C. Place: ancient Greece. Customs: Reasoned debate, public facilities for all to enjoy, heroic art. Beliefs: Perspective is everything.

4. "The Fox and the Crow": Time: around 600 B.C. Place: ancient Greece. Customs: Bargaining, fair exchange. Beliefs: Watch for flatterers.

Literary Analysis: Folk Tales (p. 220)

Sample answers:

1. "The People Could Fly": Character: Toby. Adjectives: magical, happy. Examples: He laughs at the Overseer as he magically flies away from him.

2. "All Stories Are Anansi's": Character: Anansi. Adjectives: sly, clever, smart; Example: Anansi uses his wits to trick the three animals to seal his bargain with Nyame.

3. "The Lion and the Statue": Character: Lion. Adjectives: logical, calm. Example: He remains unaffected by the statue, logically reasoning that it does not reflect a lion's perspective, but a human's perspective.

4. "The Fox and the Crow": Character: Fox. Adjectives: cunning, flattering, quick-thinking, selfish. Example: He acts quickly to flatter the Crow to trick her to give up the cheese he longs for.

"Phaëthon, Son of Apollo"
by Olivia E. Coolidge
"Demeter and Persephone"
by Anne Terry White
"Icarus and Daedalus"
by Josephine Preston Peabody

Build Vocabulary (p. 221)

A. 1. domineering
2. dominate
3. domination
4. dominant

B. 1. sustained
2. dissuade
3. dominions
4. mortal
5. vacancy

C. 1. a 2. c

Build Spelling Skills: The *sw* Sound Spelled *su* (p. 222)

A. 1. persuade
2. suede
3. suite
4. dissuade
5. suave

B. 1. persuade
2. dissuade
3. suave
4. suede

Challenge: Sample answers: Rose, Violet, Crystal, Sienna, Red, Whitey, Pinky, Brownie, Blackie, Goldie, Olive, Ginger, Ebony, Blondie, Ruby.

Build Grammar Skills: Using Commas in a Series With Dependent Clauses (p. 223)

A. 1. Greek myths have been borrowed, adapted, retold, and performed in many ways over the generations.

2. Phaëthon was stronger, swifter, bolder, and more honorable than most others.

3. Because Epaphos challenged him, Phaëthon went to find his father.

4. The long pole was decorated with jewels: topaz, diamond, emerald, and ruby.

5. When Phaëthon's chariot fell to earth, the resulting blaze scorched the land.

"Phaëthon, Son of Apollo"
by Olivia E. Coolidge
"Demeter and Persephone"
by Anne Terry White
"Icarus and Daedalus"
by Josephine Preston Peabody (*continued*)

6. Phaëthon clung to the inside of the chariot, which was completely out of control.

7. Demeter, who was mournful over her daughter's disappearance, punished the earth.

8. The cattle died, seed withered, crops dried up, and men and oxen toiled in vain.

9. After he built the Labyrinth, Daedalus was imprisoned on Crete.

10. Though the air became warmer, Icarus continued to fly higher.

B. Sample answers:

1. Because he was proud and stubborn, Phaíthon insisted that he could drive the chariot.

2. The gods and goddesses in the story of Persephone include Pluto, Aphrodite, Eros, Demeter, Zeus, and Hermes.

3. After his son had drowned, Daedalus hung up his wings at the temple of Apollo.

Reading Strategy: Making Predictions
(p. 224)

Sample answers:

1. "Phaëthon, Son of Apollo": Clue: Apollo's horses require a strong hand on the rein, and the climb is steep. Prediction: Phaëthon will have an accident in the chariot.

2. "Demeter and Persephone": Clue: Pluto is struck with Eros' love arrow. Prediction: Pluto will fall in love.

3. "Icarus and Daedalus": Clue: Icarus ignores his father's warnings about flying. Prediction: He will experience a flying accident.

Literary Analysis: Myth (p.225)

Sample answers:

1. Myth: "Phaëthon, Son of Apollo." Explanation of Natural Event: The sun rises in the east because that is where Eos, goddess of the dawn, lives. Belief About Right or Wrong: It is wrong to disregard a parent's advice.

2. Myth: "Demeter and Persephone." Explanation of Natural Event: Spring occurs because of Persephone's annual visit to earth. Belief About Right or Wrong: It is wrong for people not to love; therefore, even Pluto should love.

3. Myth: "Icarus and Daedalus." Explanation of Natural Event: People don't fly because Daedalus decided never to fly again. Belief About Right or Wrong: It is wrong to disregard a parent's warning.